D0872312

Finding
My
Way

Finding My Way

*A Memoir of
Family, Identity,
and Political
Ambition*

———

Robin F. Schepper

GIRL FRIDAY BOOKS

Copyright © 2023 by Robin F. Schepper
All rights reserved.

No part of this book may be reproduced, or stored in a retrieval system, or transmitted in any form or by any means, electronic, mechanical, photocopying, recording, or otherwise, without express written permission of the publisher.

This is a memoir, and the events and experiences detailed in it have been presented as the author currently remembers them, to the best of her ability.

 GIRL FRIDAY BOOKS

Published by Girl Friday Books™, Seattle

Produced by Girl Friday Productions

Design: Paul Barrett
Production editorial: Abi Pollokoff
Project management: Kristin Duran

All photos courtesy Trudy Schepper Lofas unless otherwise noted.

ISBN (hardcover): 978-1-954854-96-3
ISBN (ebook): 978-1-954854-97-0

Library of Congress Control Number: 2022917368

*To my sons, Marat and Shokhan, who expanded my heart
and healed my wounds. Love you . . . more.*

CONTENTS

PART 6: FINDING PEACE

PROLOGUE

2019

Whenever I open one of the fabric-covered photo albums my mom saved, I find myself tracing the scalloped edges of each picture, captioned with the narrow cursive of my mom's writing. *1957—Hoffman's Farm, 1960—Queen Mary.* Though I've looked through this album, and the others she kept, countless times, I am continually hoping that somehow the pictures will reveal something new. *Perhaps today they will unlock the many secrets of my past and give me the answers I crave.*

Of course, I now have my own photo albums, ones featuring the life I've created around me: my husband, Eric, and the lights of my life, my adopted sons, Shokhan and Marat. These albums also depict my earlier years as well as highlights from my career: the international advance work I did for President Clinton (coordinating with foreign governments, US embassies, and the Secret Service to produce events and every detail of the president's travels), the four years I spent working for the Athens Olympic Games in Greece, and my first day on the job working for First Lady Michelle Obama, me striding confidently across the White House lawn.

They also reveal one thing for certain: I've come a long way.

But there are some truths they will never erase, unlock, or divulge. I grew up in the 1960s and 1970s in New York, and according to the Catholic Church, I was a bastard child because my mom never married my biological father. In fact, I never met him or even knew his identity until very recently. On top of that, my grandmother ran a "massage business" out of an upscale apartment building on Seventy-Ninth

Street, where she often asked me to help with mundane tasks, like erasing all the messages on her answering machine.

I grew up surrounded by other family secrets too, and over the years, the shame of the truth, and the work of keeping all these secrets hidden from the outer world, eroded my sense of self-worth, like a cancer eating away at healthy tissue. Living with secrets also meant living in a family that never behaved how I thought a family should. I periodically demanded the truth from both my mom and grandmother, but they ducked or avoided or placated or outright lied. Eventually, I realized I had no choice about the life I would need to build for myself. I would create my own worth and show everyone that a bastard child could succeed. I would seek out the truth and, in so doing, I would shape my own identity. And most importantly, I would create a family where honesty and love would bind us together instead of DNA.

Note: This story is based on memory. The dialogue is what I remember, not necessarily everything that was said verbatim. There may be minor mistakes in years and details, but the feeling and its effect are real and accurate. Some names have been changed and some characters have been combined for ease of storytelling.

PART 1

KEEPING SECRETS

FAMILY FRACTURE

1967

When people talk about New York, they always remark that it's so big, yet the city is only 13.4 miles long and 2.3 miles wide. I think they think it's so big because of the hopes and dreams that start there, which was certainly the case for my family.

My grandmother landed on Ellis Island in 1927, hoping to escape her parents in Germany and start a new life where she could go to school, learn to be a nurse, and live independently. My grandfather had come over from Austria in 1921 because, as a younger son, he wouldn't inherit the family farm and needed a way to support himself. Although my mom, once she'd grown up, moved to California to be a stewardess for Pan Am, she came back to New York after I was born with the hope that she could rely on family and not be judged for being an unmarried mother of a bastard daughter.

Initially, my mom and I lived in a squat, five-story brownstone on Eighty-Fifth Street between Second and Third Avenues. Ours was a modest "railroad-style" apartment in which every room ran into the next one. Our kitchen table was really a plank of wood cut to fit over the bathtub in the middle of the kitchen, and Mom placed a red-and-white gingham cloth over the plank to hide the bathtub's claw-foot legs.

I loved our Yorkville neighborhood, where everyone seemed to look like my grandmother, my mom, or me. Some had Germanic fair skin, light hair, and blue eyes like Nana and me, while others resembled my mom, with darker hair and dark eyes that favored Austrian and Hungarian bloodlines. I didn't learn English until I started school, and it seemed like everyone spoke German on my block, judging by the *Guten Morgen* and *Guten Abend* my mom offered to our neighbors as we walked along. The smell of garlic and the fragrance of sweet treats permeated the air. We often shopped for Hungarian salami at a local butcher's store, and the proprietor would always give me a few thin slices to eat right there on the spot. We also frequented a local German bakery to buy Linzer cookies or, on special occasions, *Schwarzwälder Kirschtorte*, German Black Forest cake.

My grandmother lived near us in a tall, beautiful building with a doorman. To this day, whenever I smell white vinegar, I always think of her. It was her cure for everything: it could remove stains in your carpet, bring down a fever, or heal a sprained ankle. She relied on vinegar compresses for just about any ailment, and when vinegar didn't do the trick, she used garlic. In fact, her mother, Oma, was convinced that garlic was what helped her live a long life. Because of these home remedies, I probably smelled like an Austrian potato salad much of the time.

Although my mom was never able to buy a home because we were barely scraping by on her meager salary working at the ticket counter for Air France, she always seemed to find decent apartments in good neighborhoods. My mom had also always dreamed of being an interior designer, and she practiced her creativity in our apartments, mingling Scandinavian-style white furniture with the Asian treasures she had accumulated during her time as a stewardess. She transformed her queen-sized wooden platform bed in the living room into a couch, with throw pillows covered in blue and brown batik patterns. She made the most of my tiny room, buying unfinished wooden bunk beds and painting them bright yellow to try to make the room cheerful. Every night, I would lie in my bed and listen to her read stories in German, usually from *Grimm's Fairy Tales*, and she would then tuck me in with a kiss on my forehead.

One night, this idyllic nightly ritual was rudely interrupted.

"Open up, it's the police!"

Mom secured the chain before unbolting the top and bottom locks and then cracking open the door.

"Yes, can I help you?" she answered through the sliver.

The voices outside the door explained that they were there to speak to me, and my mother let them in. Two officers—a man and a woman—crossed the threshold into our apartment. We all stood in our tiny dining area between my bedroom and the entryway. My mom straightened up and offered her hand.

"Good evening. My name is Trudy Schepper, and this is my daughter, Robin. She is a little shy."

I slowly stepped out from behind my mom and offered to shake one of the officer's hands as I had been taught to do.

"Good evening, Robin. How old are you?" He introduced himself, and I looked at my mom for reassurance before responding.

"I am four and a half."

"Why do you need to ask my daughter questions?" my mom asked. "She is very young, and she is just learning English."

"Ma'am, the call we got said that a child was being abused, so I need to ask both of you some questions."

My mom's eyes widened, and the muscles in her jaw stiffened.

"Excuse me," she said. "Are you accusing *me* of abusing my child? I love my daughter, and she is fine. Look at her, does she look unwell and abused? Who made the call?"

"We don't identify callers, but someone in the neighborhood said they heard screams, and it's our duty to look into cases of alleged child abuse."

"Officer," she said, inhaling deeply before continuing. "Feel free to ask my daughter questions. I may need to translate. But I already know it is my mom who made the call. She is crazy and imagines things that are not true. She should be in a mental hospital, not calling the police."

The female officer now spoke up. "Ma'am, we don't get involved in the details. We just want to make sure Robin is OK."

My mom had been pacing, but now she stopped and crouched down. She took hold of both my hands and looked at me reassuringly.

"Engelein, zieg deine Arme und Beine," she said. Then she stood up to face the officers. "I just asked my daughter to show you her arms and legs."

I was in my flannel nightgown with scalloped fringes and tiny flowers on it, hugging my favorite stuffed animal, a puppy. I kept my gaze lowered, looking at the police officers' large, polished black shoes as I lifted the nightgown. I pulled back my sleeves and showed them my arms. I felt so ashamed and hoped this would end quickly.

The officers peered down the back of my nightgown to inspect my back too, and I looked up to see my mom's eyes filling with tears. The next question startled me.

"Robin, does your mommy hurt you?" the male officer asked.

He motioned a swatting sign with his hand. My mom winced. I remember being confused, because my mom never spanked me or slapped me or did anything physical to me. If she was mad, I just got the silent treatment. Too scared to speak, I shook my head no and then ran to her. She hugged me tightly.

Both officers stood very straight. "Sorry for the interruption," the male officer continued. "But we have to check."

"It's not your fault," my mom said. "But what do I do if my mom keeps doing this? I don't want my daughter subjected to these encounters."

"I will file my report. I cannot confirm it was your mom who made the call. You can call the police station and try to explain the situation, but we have to respond to reports; we can't just take your word for it."

After they left, she shut the door, latched the two bolt locks, and put the chain back on. Then she took me by the hand, led me back to my bed, and kneeled in front of me. "Schatzi, I am so sorry for that," she said in German. "It won't happen again. Mommy is going to figure out a way so the bad people who said bad things about us can't find us."

"Mom, I heard you say it was Nana who called. Why does she think you are hurting me?"

"You understand more English than I thought. Nana is a little crazy; she imagines things. I don't know why. But don't worry, Schatzi. Now it is time to read a story before bed. Do you want to read *Froschkönig*?"

"OK, Mom," I replied. She climbed into my bottom bunk with me and started reading about the frog who became a king. When she finished the story, she planted a kiss on my forehead and pulled the covers up tightly around my neck.

"Gute Nacht, Schatzi."

"Good night, Mom," I replied as she turned on my night-light. She blew me a kiss from the doorway and then disappeared into the living room.

Less than a week later, we were on a plane to Florida. I thought we were just going on a vacation. Little did I know this was the first stop of our yearlong effort to hide from my Nana.

RUNNING AWAY

1967

My mom's many years working for Capital Airlines, Pan Am, and Air France had their perks. If we wanted to get on a plane and leave on a whim, we could. We arrived in Miami Beach that winter without a word about running away from Nana. We just spent time at the pool and ate dinner with some people from Austria who had been friends with my grandfather.

One day, we were at the pool when a tall man with blue eyes walked out of the building. He was slick with suntan oil from head to foot, and he had a stray lock of blond hair trailing down his forehead. Being an only child, I was always looking for playmates. I didn't care if they were four or forty. I seized the opportunity and said in German, "Wanna see my dive?"

"Sure, show me what you can do," the man said.

I proceeded to the deep side of the pool and jumped in, twisting my whole body like a spinning top.

"Excellent," he said. "You want to see mine?"

"Of course. What are you going to do?" I asked, excited that I had made a new friend.

"You'll see." He stepped up to the diving board, walked to the end, turned around, and dove in backward, arching his back beautifully. Just as he emerged through the water's surface, my mom came along wearing her polka-dot bikini and her hair in pigtails, making her look even younger than her thirty-two years. I noticed that she was swaying her hips more than usual as she approached.

"Mom, meet my new friend!"

She lowered her eyes coyly. "I'm Trudy Schepper, and this is my daughter, Robin, whom you have already met."

"Your daughter is a strong swimmer," he said.

"Yes, she loves the water and doesn't always get the chance to be in a pool. We live in New York."

"New York? Whereabouts? I am on Fifty-Sixth and Seventh Avenue." He introduced himself as Lars.

"On the Upper East Side, in Yorkville." My mom was an experienced New Yorker, always on guard to not reveal too much information.

A DIFFERENT KIND OF FAMILY

1968

I don't know how it exactly happened, but a few days later, my mom broke the news to me that Lars's ex-wife needed a live-in nanny for their son, Little Lars, and that we'd be moving in with her. He said she lived in New York in a huge apartment on West End Avenue off Seventy-Sixth Street.

"What do you think?" Mom asked as she started taking stuff out of drawers and arranging them in neat piles.

"What about our home and all my stuff?" I didn't like the sound of this plan, but I always wanted to please her. I knew she was worried about work after being let go from Air France; we had been on welfare for a couple of months earlier in the year while we were in Florida, and she did not like that at all.

"I promise we will talk to Bud, who is subletting the apartment, and ask to go back to collect your favorite things to take with us."

"But what about our apartment? Will we ever go live there?" I didn't like the idea of leaving my old neighborhood.

"The sublet with Bud is month to month, so we will go back there sometime." She stroked my head and continued. "Sh, Schatzi, watch your show now. I will pack everything up, so we are ready tomorrow."

The new neighborhood was so different from Yorkville. On the day we arrived, we were greeted by a doorman in a uniform and then an elevator operator, who used a lever to move the elevator up and down. The building was elegant and spacious. There were only four apartments on each floor.

We were greeted by Lars's ex-wife, Jeannette. She was tall—probably five feet eleven. She had blond hair, blue eyes, and delicate features, and I found out later she had been a model, like my mom. She was effusive and hugged me on the spot. She also spoke German.

"I always wanted to have a daughter! How perfect! Welcome! Let me show you to your room and introduce you to Little Lars." I could tell, when she pushed me toward him, that Little Lars was even shyer than me. He had blond curls, sky-blue eyes, and long eyelashes. I sensed he was very kind but also scared. I was scared too, but I knew I had to make the best of the situation because my mom and I had nowhere else to live. Mom also loved the idea of us living where Nana couldn't find us.

I tried to start the conversation in English. "You want to see my bunny rabbit?" I asked. I extended my white stuffed animal and searched for every English word I knew.

He took it and looked at it. "It's nice," he said and gave it back to me, his eyes still downcast. I checked out his room. There was a view of the Hudson River through huge windows and twin beds on opposing walls. The bedspreads were yellow gingham, and I could see a bunch of orange tracks in the corner.

"Hot Wheels!" I exclaimed. I had always wanted Hot Wheels, but since I was a girl, my mom never got them for me.

"You like Hot Wheels?" Little Lars asked. He got the box out, and we started to build a track from the top of the radiator under the window all the way to the other side of the room.

From that day on, we developed a routine. Every school-day morning, Mom would take us on the crosstown bus to Little Lars's school on the East Side, and then she and I would either take the bus or walk to my school. Little Lars and I each took the bus back home by ourselves at the end of the day, and Mom cooked dinner for us every night. Jeannette worked as a journalist, so we mostly saw her at dinner and on the weekends.

It was fun to have a pseudobrother. Little Lars introduced me to *Star Trek*, which I loved, and on Sunday nights, we would watch *Wild Kingdom* and *The Wonderful World of Disney*. My English began to vastly improve since I was speaking English at home now. When Big Lars would come for his scheduled visits, he would take my mom,

Little Lars, and me to Jones Beach, and we'd eat Carvel ice cream on the way home. It sometimes felt like we were a little family.

I thought this arrangement would go on forever, but then one night my mom came into my room and said we were leaving.

I started to cry. "But why? We have only been here for less than a year!"

"Schatzi, it's a grown-up thing. Big Lars and I have fallen in love, and it's not right for you and me to stay here. I have packed my things already, and I am going to pack your things now." She stood up and started going through my drawers and folding things as I had seen her do before.

"Will I see Little Lars again? I like having a brother!" I could feel the tears in my eyes.

"Don't worry, we are a family now. You will see Big Lars all the time. I know he is going to marry me. And you will see Little Lars frequently too." I started putting my stuffed animals in my backpack, dreaming of being one big family. But I wondered what would happen with Jeannette. I liked her. *Will she be part of this new family? And what will Nana think? Will we see her again?*

BLOND IS BETTER

1970

We moved back to our apartment on Seventy-Ninth Street in 1969, which we had previously sublet. Even though Big Lars loved my mom, they were not getting married, so he stayed in his apartment in Midtown. Mom got a new job, and I was able to walk to my Catholic school from home.

And we had started to see Nana again. She had already hired a private detective to find me and had occasionally shown up at my school once we were living back on the East Side again. I was always confused about how to act whenever she appeared: I loved her and missed her, but my mom hated her. Now that we were living a few buildings away from Nana again, she was officially back in my life, although it was rare that all three of us were ever together. It had to take a special occasion.

One of those special occasions was my Holy Communion. I was in second grade, and I had been practicing all week with my schoolmates. The night before the big day, I was in my room, finishing my spelling words, when my mom yelled from the bathroom.

"Schatzi, I have a surprise for you!"

She walked into my room holding a small box displaying an image of a lady with blond hair. Then my mom sat on my bed. "We're going to dye your hair tonight." My mom stood up and motioned for me to follow her back to the bathroom.

I was confused. When I was a baby, my hair had been light, and then in kindergarten it turned a dark blond. I struggled to come up with the right question to ask.

"Mom, don't you like my hair color now?" She motioned for me to take off my clothes and checked the bathtub water temperature.

"Of course I do, Schatzi. I love everything about you. I just want to help you get back to the color you should be, naturally."

I thought the hair color I had *was* natural. But I remembered Father Haskins and Sister Francis Marion reminding us about the Ten Commandments and that we needed to obey our parents. I didn't ask any more questions. I went ahead and took off all my clothes and gingerly checked the temperature of the water with my toes. It was warm and inviting, so I stepped in. My mom expertly massaged the dye into my hair, put a plastic cap on my head, and told me to wait twenty minutes. Then we rinsed out the dye, and my mom wrapped my head in a towel.

I stepped out of the tub and stood in front of the mirror. My mom took the towel off my head.

"Ta-da!"

I stared in the mirror and tried not to cry.

"Mom, it does not look blond. It looks red!" I leaned closer to the mirror, hoping I was mistaken. My mom looked concerned, but she assured me quickly. "No, it's strawberry blond, and it will be even lighter once it dries."

I kept staring in the mirror, wondering if my hair would suddenly turn the pale blond of my baby pictures as it dried. I wanted to hurry it up, so I took the towel and placed it on my head again to rub the moisture out.

"Don't dry it too much; we are doing rag curls tonight," my mom said. We proceeded into the living room, where I noticed a pile of long, white strips of fabric on her platform bed. "Sit," she commanded.

With a wide-tooth comb, she worked out the tangles in my hair. She parted my hair down the middle and then separated it into small sections, tying each with a strip of cloth. After twenty minutes, I looked like Medusa with white snakes coming out of my head. I still could not see the color of my hair, save for my scalp, and that looked red to me. But I never got a chance to check, because my mom sent me to bed, rags and all.

I woke up early the next day, and my first chore was to turn on the electric coffee percolator that my mom had prepared the night before.

I then ran into the bathroom and started unraveling the rags. As each strip fell to the floor, I saw my new hair was indeed reddish blond. It was not the blond of my youth or the dark blond of yesterday. I assumed we could wash it out easily, but I had so much to do in preparation for my ceremony. I went back into my room and started getting dressed, pulling the white dress over my head and then putting on my white socks and white patent-leather shoes.

Mom came into my room to help me with my veil. "Your hair looks beautiful," she said, although she was clearly fighting back tears. "You know, this was my wedding veil."

"It was?"

She had told me very little about her short marriage to Charlie, which took place about two years before I was born. They had originally gotten married in a twenty-four-hour chapel in Reno in 1961, but her parents had demanded a proper wedding, which she and Charlie arranged in New York a month later. The marriage didn't last, and she petitioned the Catholic Church six months later for an annulment, which she explained made it as if the marriage never happened. As a child, I never understood how annulments worked. *How can you erase history?*

My mom straightened the folds in my Communion dress with her delicate hands and told me again that I looked beautiful. "Now, go over to Nana's apartment. She is going to take you to church in a taxi because you have to get there early. I will meet you there."

I walked over and rang the doorbell. When she opened the door, I saw that Nana also looked beautiful, dressed in forest green and wearing clip-on gold-ball earrings.

"Come, Engelein, let me look at you," she said as she took my hand and pulled me inside. Normally, Nana wore a kerchief on her head, but not on this day. I could tell she had been to the hairdresser. Her hair was coiffed, and she was wearing makeup, including her signature coral lipstick. Her fingernails were even painted a matching color.

"And you, what happened to your hair?" She took my curls in her hands to examine them.

"Mom used this formula to bring back my natural color." I proudly parroted the explanation my mother had given me last night. "Do you like it?"

Nana started to put on her camel-hair coat and shook her head. "Bring back your natural color? That's nonsense. Your hair color was perfect before. Why did your mother have to change it? Anyway, you are my beautiful angel always."

Nana grabbed her purse and escorted me down to the lobby and out the front door.

"Let's hail a cab and get to church. Where is your mother?"

"She's meeting us there," I said.

CHILDREN OF GOD

1970

There were sixty-six second graders waiting for the First Communion ceremony: thirty-three boys and thirty-three girls filling up the first ten pews in the magnificent St. Ignatius Loyola Church. When I turned around, I saw Nana and my mom sitting behind us with other proud parents, grandparents, and siblings. Most of my classmates were Irish and came from large families of five or six brothers and sisters.

Father Haskins arrived at the altar with his gold-and-white vestments and lifted his hands up toward the church's vaulted ceiling. On his cue, we all stood up and opened our hymnbooks. The first notes came to life from the organ on the balcony behind us, and we started to sing the hymns we had practiced for the past month. I loved the sound of everyone singing; it filled me with oxygen and made me feel like I would be lifted up to Jesus Himself.

Thirty girls were in line to receive Communion before me, as I was one of the tallest girls in my class and we were arranged by height. I was nervous, and questions swirled in my head. *What if I trip? What if the wafer falls out of my mouth? What if I accidentally bite Father Haskins when his fingers are in my mouth?* I wanted to wipe the sweat off my palms onto my dress, but everyone was watching, so I just kept stepping forward, closer and closer to the front of the church. When I finally arrived at the designated spot, I stood as straight as possible, keeping my hands clasped in prayer, and I tilted my head back and opened my mouth. Father Haskins placed the wafer on my tongue. I could feel it get soggy and start to dissolve. As I walked back to my pew, I thought about how grown-up I was now because I could receive Communion like the other adults at Mass. I had no idea exactly how my seven-year-old soul could have become tainted and need confession, but I had a sense that all the running away from Nana, and even our relationship with Big Lars, might be considered off kilter in the eyes of the Lord. It also meant that I had to go to confession on the first Friday of every month to cleanse my soul, because now Jesus was in me. I walked past the pew where Mom and Nana sat, and as I briefly undid my hands in prayer to wave to them, I noticed a big cardboard box next to my mom. I suspected it was my Communion gift. I wondered what could be that big.

After exiting through the large church doors, my classmates and I quickly ran down the thirty front steps and poured onto the sidewalk of Park Avenue. We all knew there was a reception in the school cafeteria next to the church, but we just wanted to run around and play tag after sitting for so long. I looked around to see my boy buddies. David had pulled down his tie, and Paul's shirt hung outside his pants as he chased Kevin up the street. I smiled as I watched, wanting to run and play tag as well, when suddenly two of the cool girls, Jenny and Geraldine, walked right up to me.

"You dyed your hair!"

It felt like an accusation, and I suddenly felt ashamed. Without thinking, I just said, "No, I didn't. It's my natural color. I just washed it with lemons." My mom had coached me to say that line in anticipation that someone would notice, but I didn't understand why it was wrong to color your hair; Nana had been doing that ever since hers had started turning gray. But as with so many things, my mom was perpetually worried about what others would think or say. This was just another of the many secrets I had to keep.

The girls skipped past me on the way to the reception, singing in unison. "Robin dyed her hair! Robin dyed her hair!" I wanted to disappear. When my mom and grandmother finally appeared, they could see the tears in my eyes.

"What's the matter, Schatzi?" my mom asked as she put the box down and gave me a hug.

"Nothing." I couldn't tell her. "These are happy tears because I made my First Communion." I stood in between her and Nana, eyeing the box.

"I have something that will cheer you up," my mom softly said. "Why don't you come closer and look?" She grinned, and my grandmother started to laugh.

I bent over to look inside the box. Two brown eyes stared up at me, and a tail thumped against the cardboard. Looking at my mom for permission, I reached in for the tiny ball of brown-and-black fur. I held the puppy against my body, and it licked my hands and tried to lick my face. I giggled and placed her on the ground between my legs, holding on to the yellow leash affixed to her collar.

"Thank you, thank you, thank you!" I crouched down to her height and nuzzled my nose into the puppy's face.

"Gin Gin," I blurted. "That's what I want to name her, just like in *I Dream of Jeannie.*"

Nana asked my mom if we were going to the reception. "What are we going to do with the dog?"

"I don't want to go to the party in the basement," I said. "I just want to go home and play with Gin Gin."

"It's your day, Schatzi." Mom smiled, picking up the now empty box.

"Why don't I go to *Kleine Konditorei* and get some slices of *Schwarzwälder Kirschtorte*? We can celebrate at your house," Nana said.

Mom agreed, and as I guided my new puppy on her leash back to our apartment, I completely forgot about my new hair color.

FATHERLESS

1971

The fact that I didn't have a dad was a sensitive subject we didn't talk about at home, but occasionally I got the nerve to ask my mom about it. I had found one of my old passports, and it had a strange name stamped in it.

"Mom, how come my passport says 'Robin Francisca Schepper Auren'? How did I get the name Auren on my passport? You are Schepper, and Nana is Schepper, and at school I am Schepper."

Her expression told me that she had been expecting this question. She took me by the hand and sat me down beside her at our dining room table.

"Schatzi," she started. "Remember I told you that you were born in San Francisco?" I could see the tension around her mouth as she spoke.

"Yes, and you told me I was almost born in a Porsche," I responded gleefully. "A red 1962 Roadster, right?" Nana, my mom, and I all loved cars. We used to walk along the street seeing which one of us could spot and name the greatest variety—BMW, VW, Mercedes, Cadillac, Ford, Dodge, and Fiat. Since I was almost born in a Porsche, I felt like sports cars in particular were part of my being.

But my mom had never mentioned a father in her recounting of my birth story. Now she straightened her hands on her lap and looked at me briefly before glancing away again.

"Well, when I was a stewardess for Pan Am, I met your father, and his name was Robert Auren. That's how you got the name Auren. That's it."

She pushed back her chair to leave the table. I stared at her, but I could not catch her eyes as she walked into our tiny kitchen. I could tell she was trying to evade me, but I followed her. I had to know more.

"But where is he? If he's my father, how come he's not here? Doesn't he want to know who I am?" I didn't understand why a father would not want to see his own flesh and blood. *I'm a good kid,* I thought to myself. *Who would not want to meet me?*

"Schatzi, I love you very much, and so does Nana." My mom paused and put water in a pot to boil. "Robert was already married, so he couldn't marry me. He lived in California, and he told me he was going to leave his wife, but he didn't." She began to peel potatoes as she talked. "There was no life for us in California, and I couldn't work anymore as a stewardess because, in those days, you could not be married, or have a child, and be a stewardess. That's why I came back to New York. That's why we are here." She placed the potatoes in the pot and turned to face me. "That's the story; there's nothing more to say. Don't ask me again, OK, Schatzi? Now, go set the table."

I had plenty more questions, but I did not want to make her sad or mad. I hoped she would tell me more when I got older.

Years later, my son Shokhan started to have tough questions of his own, and we encountered some of them together with the help of a therapist. At one session, we talked about perfectionism and why Shokhan sometimes did not talk much for fear of saying something wrong. The therapist noted that I was a perfectionist too, and asked why I thought this was the case.

"Well, I think it started when I was little," I said. "I was called a bastard child in the Catholic Church because my mom had me without a husband. It's not a big deal nowadays to be a single mother, but in the 1960s it was frowned upon, especially in the eyes of religious institutions. Plus, I received mixed messages from my mom. Sometimes she would say, 'Why do I still have to pay for the biggest mistake of my life?' even though other times she would say I was the best thing that ever happened to her. I knew my mom loved me, but I also knew her life was harder because of me. So I guess I felt like I had to prove to her and the world that I was worthy of being alive and worthy of the hardship she went through. I worked as hard as I could to be perfect and would continue to do so throughout my life, striving for both personal acceptance and career success. There was no other option."

Shokhan asked why I cared so much about what the Church called me. I told him that times were different back when I was a child and went to Catholic school. "My life was dominated by what the priests and nuns said. I cared because I wanted to fit in. But now, I feel differently. Being the child of a single mom is my badge of honor. I am proud of her that she took the chance and raised me on her own. She was strong to do that; she was the first feminist I ever knew. She did the best she could, and I wouldn't be the fighter I am today if I hadn't started my life as the child of a single mom."

Shokhan squeezed my hand as a lump formed in my throat.

"What do you think now, Mom? Are there still bastards?"

"I think the word should be erased from the dictionary. Who cares if a child was conceived in a marriage or outside a marriage? Life is precious, and if two people create a child, that child should not be burdened with a name that's demeaning. That child should be honored and nurtured and given every chance to succeed."

Shokhan said nothing, but something about his expression or body language prompted the therapist to interject. "Seems like you relate to what your mother said."

"Yes, I agree with my mom," he said. We looked at each other, and our connection was so great at that moment that I knew, somehow, it was the universe that had led Eric and me to adopt our two children—two souls who have expanded my heart beyond recognition. I have never loved anyone so much as Shokhan and Marat. I would do anything for them—anything to protect them, nurture them, guide them, and, above all, love them.

PENNIES FOR MARIA

1974

As a kid, I woke up every weekday at 6:30 a.m. to my clock radio tuned to the rock station 95.5 FM WPLJ to start my morning ritual.

"Rise and shine, porcupine," I'd say to my sweet Ginny, who slept at the foot of my bed.

My school uniform consisted of a white blouse with a rounded collar, a plaid cross tie underneath the collar, and a plaid pleated skirt. By fifth grade, I was twisting the waistband to make the skirt a little shorter than the nuns' required length of below the knee. But I was still wearing a tank top underneath my blouse even though some girls were already wearing bras.

After getting dressed, I'd head out to take the dog for a walk, unbolting the two locks quietly so I wouldn't wake up my mom. Some days, I decided to walk down the seven flights of stairs to the lobby, instead of waiting for the elevator. By the time we were outside, the street was always busy with traffic.

My route took us past my bank, where I would sometimes peer in through the window and wonder how much babysitting money I'd be able to deposit that month. Then we headed downtown past the pharmacy, the Hungarian deli with the great salami, and my favorite bakery. As we walked past the local grocery store, the A&P, I thought about what groceries I needed to buy after school. I had been managing our twenty-five-dollar weekly food budget since the third grade. I often went to the store twice a week after school, looking for bargains. It helped with my addition and subtraction.

Back at our apartment, I fed the dog, finished getting ready for school, and poured a cup of coffee for my mom, adding just the right amount of milk and sugar.

"Rise and shine, porcupine," I'd then say to her, handing her the steaming cup. And then I was out the door once again, on my own for the rest of the day.

I raced across the street to catch my bus, flashed my pass to the driver, and found a seat. I rode with my bright-red canvas rucksack with white leather straps in my lap. The kids at school teased me about it because it wasn't the fashionable army-green backpack that everyone else had, but I didn't care. It was red and different, and Nana had bought it for me in Germany.

My school was on the west side of Eighty-Fourth Street, which was closed in the morning before school started, and again during lunchtime, so the students had space to run around and play. Every morning, as I walked from the bus stop to the school, I was greeted by a cacophony of noise from all the uniformed children. I found my friends, dropped my rucksack along with the other backpacks, and joined in a game of tag; Mother, may I; or red light, green light.

Once each month, Sister Francis Marion, my old and strict fifth-grade homeroom teacher, told us to get out our jars without talking. She was relatively thin and probably eighty, and her skin was wrinkled like a prune. A rosary dangled from the belt around her waist, and she still wore a habit even though the Second Vatican Council had said, back in 1965, that nuns could wear their hair uncovered and short.

My mom and I didn't have much money, but I was able to save three to five dollars every month in a glass jar that I brought to school for this tradition. I loved taking out the brown coin wrappers, folding one end, and inserting the pennies I'd collected. Even at that age, it felt good to know I was making a difference in someone's life. *Maybe it can offset some of the shame I carry with me to confession each week.*

"OK, let's see how well you know your addition. How much do you all have?" Sister Francis Marion said one day.

I sat upright every time she called on someone. You never knew if she was going to swish around in her long skirt and crack her pointer on someone's hands or take her knuckles to someone's temples. I tried very hard to behave; I did not want to experience her wrath. But it was even harder to watch her picking on someone else. I hated that.

Next, she narrowed her eyes and called on Jenny. "Have you brought enough to cover for all your sinful ways?"

When Jenny reported that she had brought two dollars, Sister Francis Marion wasn't satisfied.

"I think next month you will have to do better than that, given your behavior in the past week."

She then called on one of the boys to go to the front of the class to read a letter the class had received. The student got up from his seat and walked to the front of the class, his face bright red. She knew that he always had trouble reading, and I didn't understand why she would be so cruel. She handed him the letter, and as he grasped it in both hands, he was visibly shaking.

> *Dear Sister Francis Marion,*
>
> *Thank you so much for your donation of $40. We have sponsored a little girl in your class's honor and her name is Maria. With the $40 you sent, she can get two meals a day and all the vaccines she needs to keep many diseases at bay.*
>
> *Thank you.*
> *Father Pedro*
> *Catholic Charities, Mexico*

We all clapped. Even Sister Francis Marion smiled for a minute before striking her stick on the desk, which meant it was time to be quiet.

"Does anyone have any more to say?" she asked.

I was so moved by the letter and the thought that forty dollars could make such an impact on a child's life. I decided to express what I was feeling, even if she got mad at me.

"Yes, I have something to say. When I get older, I am going to have a child and adopt a second child from a poor country," I said proudly.

I already knew I wanted a big family, with me, a mom; a dad; and at least two kids to create the environment I never had. When that chance finally came, decades later, it wasn't exactly how I had imagined it, but it certainly brought back those feelings of concern I'd had for Maria in the fifth grade. We adopted Marat and Shokhan from orphanages in Kazakhstan, where babies and small children were living because their families didn't have enough money to support them.

TRAVELS WITH NANA

1975

As a child, I spent several summers with Nana in Germany, and I loved it. Traveling on airplanes was one of my favorite things to do. We flew on Lufthansa, and I'd settle into my window seat in economy class, pull out my books from my rucksack, and place them in the seat-back pocket of the seat in front of me. Then I'd smooth out my travel shirt, sweater, and skirt and click the metal seatbelt into place.

My grandmother always got dressed up for the plane. One time, I looked over and noticed her hair was out of place, which I knew she wouldn't like.

"Nana, can I fix your hair?"

"Oh, yes, straighten it out," she said. "We don't want anyone to think it's not my real hair." I took the bobby pins out and straightened out her headband so that Nana's natural hair and fake hair looked like they were connected. Nana suddenly stuck her tongue out.

"You are really good. You could be a hairdresser," she said.

I laughed. "Nana, I told you I am going to college to become a photojournalist." I was serious about this.

"Oh, yes, I forgot, Engelein," she said, and then she asked me to find her lipstick in her bag and put it on her lips because she didn't have a mirror. She said to select the one that I thought would make her the most beautiful. "You never know who you could meet while traveling." Nana grinned and winked at me, but then her eyes became sad. "Every woman needs a man, and your grandfather died and left me alone."

"But, Nana! You have money and your own business. Why do you need a man too?"

My mom and I lived in a home without a man, but talking about men made my mom sad too. *Why does every woman seem to think she needs a man?*

"Love, Engelein; we all need love," Nana said. I told her that maybe we would meet someone for her at the airport when we landed.

The air in Germany smelled different from New York—crisper and cleaner. Gone was the underground smell of spices, garbage, and urine that I was accustomed to back home. In the Germany I knew, there were no skyscrapers, no yellow taxis, no smelly buses.

We then took the train to a little town called Buchholz in der Nordheide, right outside Hamburg, and stayed near the edge of the woods, where there was a communal swimming pool nearby. I had lots of kids to play with every day. Nana did all the cooking and cleaning, so I could just be a kid. I had no chores: no walking the dog, no shopping, no making dinner. But sometimes I would accompany Nana, with her wicker basket on her arm, to the local market for fresh bread, eggs, milk, and whatever meat she would cook that day.

Onkel Paul was Nana's oldest brother. He had to have been at least ten years older than her because she was the tenth child and he was the first. Her mother, Oma, had popped out thirteen kids, one right after the other. Two of them had died. Nana was the youngest girl, and her brother Eric was the youngest boy.

Onkel Paul was usually very kind to me and Nana. He had playful blue eyes and wrinkly skin, and he hunched over when he walked. For some reason, he liked to help Nana scrub my white socks after I played in the dirt. His apartment had two bedrooms, and Nana and I stayed in the spare one. Every morning, Nana would open the windows and drape our feather beds over the windowsill to air them out during the day. When I went to sleep at night, I could smell the forest in my bed.

One day, on my walk back from the market, I reached Onkel Paul's apartment and heard yelling coming from inside. I carefully turned the knob and silently entered the kitchen. Onkel Paul and Nana were in the living room talking very loudly. Nana seemed to be crying, which was very rare for her.

"How could you invite them here?" Nana yelled.

"They are your brothers," Onkel Paul said. I wondered who they were talking about.

"They did terrible things to me," she said. "And I will never forgive them. I never told you what they did, but I hate them." Nana's voice trembled as she shouted. Meanwhile, I wondered what these unnamed people had done to my strong grandmother. I could not imagine anyone getting her so angry.

"I know, Greta, but that was a long time ago," Onkel Paul continued in a calm voice.

"If you knew what they did to me, then why didn't you protect me? You are my oldest brother. You could have done something." I heard her footsteps pacing.

"But I did do something. I saw how they looked at you. If I had said anything, Mama and Papa would have never believed it, so I just convinced Mama that you should go to New York to be with Anna," Onkel Paul said.

"I always thought Mama sent me to New York because I ran away with Johan one night," Nana said.

"Well, she *was* mad about that, so I took advantage of the situation. She didn't know what to do with you, and she wouldn't even have believed me if I had told her what they did to you, so I just told her she should grant your wish to be with your oldest sister and buy your ticket for travel."

I stood as silently as I could, hoping to hear more.

"I don't know whether to thank you or not. But I still don't want to be here if they come," Nana said.

"Can't you forgive them after all these years? It happened forty-five years ago." Onkel Paul's voice seemed higher than usual. I wondered if he was crying as well.

"No. Tell me when they are coming, and I'll take the little one on a trip or something, and we'll come back after they're gone." I heard her footsteps and the swishing of her dress against her legs as she came toward the kitchen, where I still stood, frozen. I couldn't pretend I had just come in. I looked around and saw my coloring book on the bench by the window. I quickly grabbed it and sat down at the table and started filling in the colors with my watercolor pencils. I looked down when she came into the doorway of the kitchen, pretending that I had not heard a thing.

"I didn't hear you come in," she said.

I could feel her looking at me, but I kept coloring in my book, afraid to meet her eyes. "I put the milk in the refrigerator, Nana, but I forgot the butter."

"Don't worry. I need to go shopping for lunch anyway. Plus, we need to go down to the travel agent to get some train tickets." She said it matter-of-factly, as if this had been the plan all along. She slid her hands down the sides of her skirt.

"Train tickets?" I asked, as guilelessly as I could. I finally looked up at her and saw her red eyes. She continued to putter around the kitchen, taking out plates from the cabinet and silverware from the drawer.

"Yes, I thought we would take a little adventure to Bad Kissingen or somewhere I can go for a cure. I need to soak in some mineral water."

"OK, Nana." I grabbed an apple off the counter and walked out the door toward the playground.

I wondered what Nana's brothers had done to her, only piecing it together years later in the same way I had to piece together bits of my mom's past. It made me so sad for my nana that she could not be safe in her own house. It was no wonder she emigrated to the United States. I've since wished I had just hugged her when she came into the kitchen that day. At the time, I think I was too scared to know how to react.

What began as a painful experience, with that kitchen scene, ended up being one of the funniest adventures I ever had with my grandma. We ended up getting first-class Eurail passes for a month, which allowed us to travel anywhere in Europe on the train.

It was quite a treat. The seats were covered with red plush fabric, and we rode in a compartment with a door and a half window. We had more privacy than the passengers in the economy section, where the seats were all out in the open.

Originally, I thought we were going to Bavaria, to a place with hot springs and strong women who gave massages. But instead, we were going to Sicily. I took out the map next to my window seat and traced my finger on the line that represented the train tracks. I was so excited: we were going to be riding through Germany, Switzerland, Austria, Northern Italy, and all the way down to the sea. I wondered what I would be able to see from the window. *Mountains? Lakes? Churches?*

After the train had been sitting in the station for a long time, Nana wondered what the problem was. By then she had changed into a flower-patterned dress with a neckline that revealed her deep cleavage. I looked down at my chest, wondering if I would be like her or my mom, who was almost flat chested, when I grew up. Nana also wore clip-on pearl earrings and her signature coral lipstick.

"Maybe there's a strike. Don't Italians always go on strike?" I asked, laughing.

"Nonsense, that's just our German relatives poking fun at the Italians. Maybe there's a crew change," Nana said.

I begged her to let me go see what I could find out. "I promise I will be very careful." I stood up, smoothed out my blue gingham dress, and gave her my best mischievous smile.

"Promise you won't leave this car," she said, and then she nodded to show she trusted me. It was amazing how much we communicated through a nod and a smile.

Even though I didn't speak Italian, I could decipher some words here and there, and I could watch gestures to interpret what people were saying. I walked down the aisle looking for anyone official looking. I finally saw someone in a uniform, and remembering that many people didn't like German tourists, I decided to address him in English.

"Excuse me, when is the train leaving?"

He looked at me and shook his head, motioning *no*. I didn't understand what he then said, even as he tried to communicate with hand signals. Somehow, I came to understand that the train was not going to move. I ran back to Nana's compartment, afraid that I had been away from her for too long and knowing she would worry.

As it turned out, I had been right. There *was* a strike. We got off the train and finished our journey by bus. There were only a few people left on the bus when we arrived in Messina. Not the most popular destination, I guessed.

"Our bags aren't here," Nana announced after we got off the bus.

The driver shrugged. "You probably just have to go back to Rome to find them."

One of the passengers then came up to Nana and me.

"I overheard your conversation. I am sorry about your luggage. We Italians are not the most efficient. Please, allow me to be of assistance. Come along with me to my home; my mother will make you lunch, and you can rest. I can call the authorities and find out what happened to your bags."

I took a good look at this man wearing beige slacks, a blue blazer, and a pale-blue oxford shirt. I was deeply suspicious. I knew, from my Italian school friends in New York, that Sicily was home to the Mafia, and it seemed to me that he was studying my grandmother with hungry eyes. "Your daughter is so beautiful," he then said, glancing at me. Now I was mad.

But Nana's eyelashes fluttered as she placed her hand on her chest. "Oh no, this is my *grand*daughter."

"You must have been a teenager when you became a mother," he said with a grin, his eyes transfixed back on her.

She laughed, and I tried to grab her hand to pull her away. Visions of murderers that you read about in the *New York Post* gathered in my head. I was scared that we were walking into a trap.

Then Nana said, "We would love to. You are so kind."

Oh great, I thought. *Here we go.*

He introduced himself as Giuseppe and said how pleased his family would be to meet us. Nana tilted her head flirtatiously. "Thank you for the hospitality. My name is Greta, and this is Robin."

Giuseppe looked like he was maybe thirty-five. My grandmother was over fifty. *What is he doing flirting with her?*

We followed him to his car and got in. As he drove along, they kept talking and laughing in the front seats. I, meanwhile, was trying to observe everything on the drive so I would know how to get back to the bus station if something happened. That's what you learn in New York: never trust anybody. Giuseppe suddenly took a right turn off the main road and onto a dirt road, and then I really started to worry. *Is he looking for a quiet place to dump our bodies?*

We stopped at a simple concrete-block house, and a swarm of children came up to the car. I was relieved to realize that Giuseppe was not an axe murderer, but I also felt nervous because ten little kids started touching me. Then suddenly someone pulled my hair.

"Ouch," I yelled, and Giuseppe shooed the kids away.

"I'm sorry, Robin. We don't get many tourists here—especially not ones with long blond hair. They want to know if it's real."

"Well, the hair is real!" I said. Little did he know that Mom had dyed it that color right before I left with Nana, so I would still be her little blond daughter. Or that some of Nana's hair was fake.

We followed Giuseppe into his house, and he introduced us to his mother, Anna. After she welcomed us and invited us to rest, he led us through the kitchen and past the dining room table to another room that had an enormous bed with blue satin sheets.

"Your home is simple outside. You would never know the beauty that is inside," Nana said as she looked around.

"Yes, we do that on purpose. We are not rich, but we have saved some for certain luxuries, and if we keep it discreet, no one bothers us—especially the tax authorities." He winked at my grandmother.

She smiled. "Yes, I know about being discreet. It is part of my business." I had no idea what Nana was talking about, especially in reference to the tax authorities, but I did reflect on how she always had me erasing messages from her answering machine. So something was suspicious.

Giuseppe said he would come back for us in about an hour for lunch. Once he left, I asked Nana what we were doing there.

"You could have gotten us killed. We don't know him, and we went in his car. What were you thinking?"

I tried not to speak too loudly, but I was speaking in German, so I doubted anyone would understand me anyway.

"Relax! Don't be like your mother, always worrying. I knew it would be OK. I saw it in the cards." I thought about how my mom had described Nana as impulsive and not thinking about consequences. I guessed I was experiencing it firsthand.

Nana started to lie down on the bed, her weight sinking into the satin sheets.

"The cards? You saw it in the cards?" My grandmother believed in something akin to tarot, and I often watched her lay the cards. I played along, not knowing whether I believed in her predictions or not.

Later, we went downstairs and discovered ten place settings at the long dining table. Everyone stood behind their chairs until the old lady motioned with her hand for us all to sit down. After Giuseppe explained to us, in English, what we would be eating, Nana asked how he learned to speak English so well. Her blue eyes sparkled, and she held out her pinky as she drank wine from her glass. I could tell she wanted to look like she was a fancy woman.

Giuseppe laughed and translated the question for everyone at the table. He explained that he'd learned English from watching American movies with Italian subtitles and listening to tourists. He said he sometimes worked as a tour guide and a taxi driver, which also helped. Nana flashed her big smile again, and as she exhaled a big breath, the cleavage in her dress moved up and down. She was flirting again. I wished she would just stop it.

Giuseppe then told us he'd found out about our luggage. It had never been loaded on the bus and was being held at the train station in Rome. Nana gave me a look, warning me not to say anything about Italian inefficiency. I kept my mouth shut other than to ask if that meant we would return to Rome soon. I enjoyed the food, and the family was very kind, but Nana's flirting was too much for me.

But to my disappointment, Giuseppe asked us to stay for the night and said he would take us to the station the next day. He eyed my grandmother as he sipped his wine.

"OK, you've convinced us," she said, now blushing. Everyone at the table seemed to understand because they were clapping. I glared at Nana, but she was avoiding me. Instead, she was smiling at Giuseppe. *I bet she'll be sleeping in his room tonight,* I thought.

PART 2

DISCOVERING THE WORLD

ESCAPE FROM NEW YORK

1975

By the summer of 1975, I was twelve years old. I had just finished sixth grade, but I already felt like a high schooler. My body had developed, and I could pass for seventeen or eighteen years old. My hair was still long and dyed blond, and instead of using bottled color at home, I was now volunteering to let new stylists at the Vidal Sassoon Salon on Madison Avenue practice their techniques on my hair. The way that men looked at me on the street made me realize I was no longer a little girl but an object of desire. It made me feel like I had power over them, but at the same time, it filled me with fear since I had no idea how to use or control this power. I had no male guidance: with Big Lars always traveling and Little Lars living with his mom, I hardly saw either of them. I had no manual or anyone to offer advice on how I should react to men in my life.

Mom and Nana's relationship had fallen into the usual pattern. They would argue about something, and Mom would cut off contact until she needed a favor. The final straw that summer was when Nana asked to borrow Mom's beloved Volkswagen Beetle and then totaled the car.

"Nana is so irresponsible," she said to me one day. "She has not even offered to pay for the car. It's so typical of her. She likes to have fun, but when things go bad, she walks away and never faces the consequences." I reminded her that the car had been insured, and also that Nana had a cast because of that accident and would be on crutches for two months.

Ironically, Mom made friends with one of Nana's former clients—
or as my grandmother liked to call them, one of her former *patients*.
Alex had a basement apartment in Port Washington, on Long Island,
where we'd be staying for the summer. She didn't want me staying
alone all day in the city while she worked, and with limited resources,
she couldn't afford summer camp for me. Mom was still in love with
Lars, but by that time he had started working for the US government
and was constantly going on six-month tours to countries like Syria,
Romania, and the Soviet Union. He spoke six languages, and I was convinced he was a spy, but he said he was working for the Department
of Commerce overseas promoting American businesses. There were
times we didn't see him for over a year, and my mom couldn't count
on him helping us. I rarely saw Little Lars anymore; he lived with his
mom in New York for a few years after we lived with them, but at some
point, Jeannette got remarried, and they moved to Colorado. My fan-
tasies of having a brother dissolved when that happened.

One evening in late summer, Mom and I heard a knock on the
door as we ate our spaghetti dinner. We didn't know anyone there except Alex. *Who can it be?*

Ginny ran to the door and barked. I tried to shush her.

Mom quietly went to a side window and peeked through the cur-
tains. It was Nana, and my mom didn't want to talk to her. "Why is she
here?" she whispered.

"I'll handle it," I said, motioning for Mom to hide in the front room.

I opened the door, and Nana barged in, pushing me aside with her
strong body.

"Hello, Engelein. Tell me where she is."

I was shocked at her abrupt attitude. When I was younger, she'd
always pick me up and swirl me in a circle when she saw me. But this
time she was on a mission. I moved forward to hug her, trying to soften
the situation, to no avail.

"Nana, what are you doing here?"

"I want to know: Why does she have this place? Alex is *my* patient,
my friend. I need a summer place too, you know." Like everyone else in
New York, Nana always wanted to escape the heat. She couldn't afford
the Hamptons or Martha's Vineyard, but a place near the beach on
Long Island would have satisfied her desire.

Nana peered into every corner of the room looking for Mom.

"Nana, what does it matter? I am off from school. We have no money for camp or travel. Remember, you were supposed to take me to Germany!"

I hoped to divert her attention.

"I am so sorry, Engelein, but it did not work out this year. I will take you another time. But I want to talk to her right now." She stomped her foot.

"Nana, I think you should leave. Mom is very tired, and there is nothing you can do to kick us out. And there certainly isn't enough room for all of us."

Usually, I saw the two of them separately, and it was difficult to handle both of their emotions at the same time. Mom seemed scared of Nana, and I felt obligated to take her side, especially in light of all the stories she'd told me about her childhood, including her father beating her with a belt at Nana's insistence.

"Me, leave? *She* should leave. She has always been a spoiled conniver, and now she's turning you against me too. She did that with her father as well."

Nana snarled as she ventured further into the apartment. I stepped in front of her to block her path, and she bumped into me.

"Robin, Engel, this is not about you. Get out of the way. I know she is here."

With my heart pounding, I suddenly shoved her backward. She was much bigger and stronger than I was, and one push from her would have sent me down to the floor. But instead of retaliating, she recoiled.

Tears filled my eyes as she retreated toward the door.

"I will go for now, but this is not over!"

She stormed out and slammed the door behind her.

My mom thanked me for sending her away, but inside I felt torn apart, as though my heart had cracked wide open. I had only two people in my family, and they each hated the other. And there I was, standing in the middle.

ON GUARD

1976

Although my family life was a mess, I felt like New York was my constant companion. I knew it well, and whenever I was sad or upset, the familiarity of my neighborhood reassured me that some things were strong and constant. I had my favorite block, my favorite route to school up Park Avenue, and my favorite stores to walk by. And I walked wherever I could, usually with Ginny at my side. On days when my mom was crying about Lars not marrying her, I left the house for hours to walk the streets and escape my reality. The city felt like my friend.

But I also knew New York was considered a dangerous place in the 1960s and 1970s, and it wasn't just robbery I needed to worry about. I always had my guard up, even when I was with Ginny, and was on the lookout for predators that might snatch me and pull me into an alley. I was a young girl alone, and this chronic undercurrent of fear probably added to my stress.

Some of the older boys at St. Ignatius had created their own Irish gang; they called themselves the Eighty-Third Street Gang. I made sure they all knew me, and I went out of my way to be friendly in case I ever needed their help. I knew I could run to the brownstone stoop where they gathered, and they would protect me.

But one day I became too confused to ask for help. I was walking just a couple of blocks from home when two boys walked toward me and suddenly split apart. They then came up on either side of me, and as they passed, they reached up under my plaid uniform skirt. Each of them grabbed one of my buttocks and laughed. I was mortified. As I hurried to the corner to get away, I kept thinking, *Why would they do that? Who gave them the right to touch me?* I didn't know a lot about sex at that point in my life, but I did know, after that incident, that I needed to keep my hands to the sides of my body when I walked so I could hold my skirt down if anyone ever tried to do that to me again.

Some days I didn't go straight home. Instead, I headed to Nana's apartment after school. I loved her building, which dated back to the 1920s and exuded both class and elegance. I was always greeted by the doorman with the weekday shift and the elevator operator, who waited for passengers in front of the Otis elevator with the gold-colored gate.

Nana's place, which she called "the Studio," was on the first floor, and she always welcomed me with her wide smile and her usual bear hug whenever I came for a visit. Sometimes she would pull out her deck of playing cards and read them as if they were tarot cards. She taught me how to use them, explaining that I had the gift of "sight." I practiced laying cards, and when I once told my friends what I saw when I placed the cards for them—divorce, love affairs, and death (death!)—they were flabbergasted. And I was scared. Their shock, and my embarrassment, kept me from ever wanting to lay the cards again myself, but I was happy to indulge Nana when I visited. It was her way of connecting with me.

One day, she carefully placed each card: seven cards across and four rows down. I eagerly watched for the queen of diamonds, which represented me, and for the queens of spades and hearts, representing Nana and my mom, respectively. When she turned over my card, she used her thick knuckle to point to it.

"I see romance, Robin. Who is your boyfriend now—the Irish kid whose father is the super? Or the Italian whose family owns all the grocery stores?"

"Oh, Nana, I can't decide. The Irish kid is Paul. I've known him since I was little. He has beautiful blue eyes. But Walter, the Italian one—he is a little more mysterious."

Nana laughed. "Mystery is more fun, and Walter's family is rich. If you can get a rich one, you won't have to work like I do. Look at your mother. She could have had plenty of rich guys. She's beautiful. I sent her to 'finishing' school in Switzerland, for goodness' sake, and after that she traveled all over the world as a stewardess. She could have anyone, but she holds out for that Swede who won't even marry her, and that's why she must work so hard. You both should be living on Park Avenue in a co-op instead of a rent-controlled apartment down the block from me. But she won't listen to me."

"What else do you see?" I asked, impatient with her diatribe.

"No, tell me what *you* see. I know you can read the cards just as well as I can, even if you refuse."

Suddenly the doorbell buzzed. Nana quickly arranged the cards in a pile and motioned for me to get up and go into the kitchen.

"Hurry, hurry, Engelein. I forgot; we have a new patient. A referral from one of the lawyers that comes here. I must make a good impression. Get in the kitchen so he doesn't see you."

I quickly ran into the kitchen like I had always done since I was a little girl. But on that day for some reason, I wanted to know more. I left the door ajar so I could hear them and sneak a peek.

The guy wore a well-tailored suit with a pale-blue shirt and a red-striped tie. His eyes locked onto mine, which made me feel very strange, like he could see right through me. I felt unsafe. And then, as he sauntered toward the treatment room, I heard what he said to my grandmother.

"I want her."

Nana stiffened. She grabbed his elbow to usher him down the hall. "No, one of my girls will take care of you. That girl is not an option. She is my granddaughter."

I waited for the treatment room door to close and then quietly slipped out of the apartment. I tried to walk quickly and calmly past the elevator operator and the doorman so that I wouldn't arouse any suspicion, but my mind was spinning with questions. *Why does Nana always have wads of cash? Why doesn't she have a checking account? Why are all the young masseuses who work for her so extremely beautiful? Why does she give "enemas" to her patients? Why does she never want me to meet them?*

And then, suddenly, it all made sense. I realized what her business was all about. My suspicions were confirmed: Nana did more than massage.

LIKE MOTHER, LIKE DAUGHTER

1976

When I was thirteen, I wanted to find out more about my grand-mother, my mom, and my origins—including more about my father. One afternoon, my mom and I were sitting on her bed looking through her old Pan Am scrapbook. I asked her to tell me stories about her time there.

"Oh, Schatzi, I have told you the stories before. You want to hear them again?"

"Yes, yes, please." I tried to sit quietly, and I put my hands underneath my butt to contain my excitement.

In the first photo, my very young-looking mom was wearing an elegant dress and was seated at a table with a young man and another couple.

"The first airline I worked for was Capital Airlines, and I was based in DC and Chicago." Part of her training, she said, was learning how to entertain at dinners whenever she had twenty-four- and forty-eight-hour layovers so she could represent the airline well. I thought about how exciting that must have been. Twirling her hair as she talked, she went on to say how much she loved the airlines and all the important people she had met, like Adlai Stevenson when he was running against President Eisenhower in 1956.

"Then one day, I heard Pan Am was looking for stewardesses, especially ones with language skills. You had to be twenty-one, which I had turned in 1956. I knew German, and because of the two years I had at the finishing school in Lausanne, I spoke French too. Plus, they liked my looks. So I got hired."

We had been eating pasta while looking through her photo albums, and now she smiled as she looked down at her fork. It was one she had saved from the first-class cabin at Pan Am all those years ago. She didn't realize I had set that fork out intentionally.

Mom continued. "Those were great days. We wore beautiful silk uniforms, and I worked in the first-class cabin where we used linens, silver cutlery, and porcelain dishes on our transatlantic and transpacific flights. I know I don't cook now, but back then I would make roasts in the oven on the plane. We also had a film projector on board for movies. It was very elegant. People dressed up to get on the plane, and almost all the passengers in first class were men on business trips." She grinned. "Let's just say I got a lot of attention back then."

I imagined Mom sashaying up and down the aisle and then recalled how she had once been upset that I walked too much like a boy. She had placed a book on my head and told me to walk back and forth in the hallway by putting one foot in front of the other. I thought it was stupid; my feet went in parallel lines, not along an invisible tightrope. But she told me your hips swayed more if you put one foot in front of the other.

I flipped to another picture. "Mom, what about this one?" She was in a bathing suit and high heels, standing next to a ship's wheel.

"Pan Am encouraged us to take part in beauty contests when we were on our forty-eight-hour layovers." Again, I imagined my mom walking across the stage while exaggerating her hips. "The layovers were so that we had the opportunity to rest between flights. When we weren't entertaining, we Pan Am girls would enter beauty pageants with the local girls. In this one, we were in Italy." Mom pointed to the ship's wheel in the photo. Its insignia read *Italia*. "We were initially twenty girls, and then it came down to three. I won third place. The blondes always won first place."

Mom kept turning the pages. In another photo, she wore a pearl choker, a black 1950s-style dress, and a sheer black shawl over her shoulders.

Mom exhaled deeply. "This was the time of my life. Dr. Sukarno was the Indonesian president, and he chartered a Pan Am airliner in 1958 for a forty-one-day trip to what were called 'the capitals of uncommitted countries'—otherwise known as neutral countries. Don't ask me what that means because I can't remember. I never was a good history student."

I figured it likely had something to do with the Cold War and meant the countries they visited weren't part of NATO or the Soviet alliance.

"We deadheaded the plane from New York to Calcutta and met Dr. Sukarno there with his traveling party. He was wearing his traditional hat and sunglasses like in all the pictures I had seen of him from the papers."

I had seen those pictures too, and what I remembered about him was that he was a dictator. Then I tried to imagine my mom actually liking him. *Ugh, how could she?*

"His traveling party was all men, and Dr. Sukarno took an instant liking to me. Our first stop was a visit with Prime Minister Pandit Nehru in New Delhi." She described how crowded the streets of India were and all the beggars that she saw. She was too afraid to get out of the limousine. I, on the other hand, would have gladly gotten out and interviewed everyone around me, trying to find out more about their lives.

Mom sighed as she remembered more details from that trip, like tasting curry for the first time and feeling as though her mouth were on fire. They visited the Taj Mahal, and they went on to Sri Lanka, only a decade earlier known as Ceylon, for twenty-four hours and drank a lot of tea. When she noted that there wasn't any alcohol on the trip because Dr. Sukarno was Muslim, I wondered if he knew she drank alcohol back home or if she kept it secret from him in the same way I was currently keeping it secret from her that I was in charge of buying beer for my friends because I looked the oldest.

She reminisced about the time their plane was flying over the Red Sea and the crew heard a loud, screaming whine.

"We looked out the windows, and what did we see? Russian MiGs on either side of our plane! It still gives me chills. You know what the Russians did to Grandpa's family in Austria."

Luckily, the Russians were just escorting her plane to Cairo, where she then met General Gamal Nasser.

"I felt like I was a president's wife or a movie star."

She had a wistful look in her eyes as she talked about Luxor, a barge down the Nile, Damascus, West Pakistan, Burma, and Angkor Wat in Cambodia. It seemed as though she wished she were back there being a stewardess instead of having a pasta dinner with me.

At one point, Dr. Sukarno bought her a purple gemstone ring in Alexandria.

"He was always trying to get more personal with me. I had to walk the fine line of being a welcoming ambassador for Pan Am without getting caught in a compromising position. His chief of staff delivered numerous notes to me from the president, but I said to reply that I was unable to meet him. I was not about to get involved with a head of state. What was the future in that? And of course, he was later killed in a coup."

I thought about all that. If Dr. Sukarno had been successful in his advances toward my mom, she might have become one of his wives—and I would have never existed.

Later, as we were washing dishes and cleaning up the kitchen, she reemphasized how impressed she had been to meet all those heads of state but also how hard it had been to believe they could be such ruthless leaders. "You can't imagine how personable and charming they were to me," she said.

"Mom, people liked Nixon too, until Watergate."

After a pause, she said I must go and see some of these sights when I got older. "In fact, you need to travel the world and get it out of your system before you're married and have kids."

"Mom, that's why I'm going to be an international photojournalist. So I can travel the world and take photos."

That night, while doing homework, I considered how a scholarship to a private school could be my ticket to any kind of life outside our little apartment, and I made a vow to myself. I would travel like my mom had when I grew up. Neither of us could possibly have imagined at that time, however, all the people I would meet, and the places I'd visit, when I finally grew up.

Many of my jobs would ultimately take me far and wide, and like my mom, I would also meet heads of state. But it's hard to imagine anything better than having an office in the East Wing working for the First Lady of the United States, Michelle Obama. I had spent the previous four years wearing leggings, T-shirts, fleece jackets, and sneakers in my work as a life coach, and suddenly I had been recruited to lead the First Lady's Let's Move! campaign to combat childhood obesity. Some things never change, and in the same way that my mom had to dress in a certain way for her role as a Pan Am stewardess, I dressed for success on my first day in a purple Eileen Fisher dress with a matching jacket, control-top pantyhose, uncomfortable beige high-heeled pumps, and a long necklace that I quickly learned could easily become entangled with the White House ID tag hanging around my neck.

I sometimes think about my mom, and all the luxurious places she visited, when I reminisce about my time at the White House. After my first weekly staff meeting with the First Lady of the United States, I found myself walking downstairs past the Family Theater and making my way through the East Colonnade. Glancing at the pictures lining the walls of all the previous presidents, I wanted to pinch myself. *Is this real?* The sound of my heels clicking on the marble floor and the murmur of voices confirmed that it indeed was. When I encountered a tour guide leading a group of visitors through the public sector of the White House, I thought about how cool it would be for them to get a glimpse of Marine One on the lawn. *Maybe I will too.*

The East Wing, the West Wing, and the Residence were not built at the same time, but many rooms connect the different buildings. My daily route took me past the East Garden Room and the busts of historical figures, the White House Library decorated in dark-red tones, and the Vermeil Room with its huge painting of Jackie Kennedy Onassis in a long, flowing dress. I gazed at her portrait on my first day and every day thereafter as I made my way through the White House. Imagine that: I was walking in the same rooms, and taking the same footsteps, as presidents, First Ladies, and foreign dignitaries had. *How does a child of a single mom, whose first language wasn't English, end up walking past this portrait of a woman who embodied American high class and nobility every day on her way to work?* Surely, it had something to do with the same good fortune my mom had when she visited all those dignitaries years ago.

AN EARLY LESSON IN
FAMILY PLANNING

1976

During the summer after seventh grade, I got a job as a nanny for the twin three-year-old boys of a famous conductor for the Metropolitan Opera. They had a wonderful home in Rhinecliff, New York, on the Hudson River. I played with those boys on their lush grass lawn and down by the river almost every day. It was a relief not to be in the midst of all that concrete for a New York summer.

I became friends with one of the girls in town named Crissy. She was fifteen, with blond curly hair and blue eyes, and she wore cutoff denim shorts and tube tops of different colors that showcased her bronzed arms and chest. She had a boyfriend named Chuck, and he had a motorcycle. I often saw Crissy riding on the back of his bike through town with the wind in her hair.

One week I didn't see her for a few days, so I went to her house in the working-class part of town and knocked on her door. Her mother, a woman in her forties with hard eyes and dyed platinum-blond hair, slowly opened the door and scanned me up and down with what felt like disdain. I didn't dress like the other girls in town; my khaki shorts came down to midthigh, and my navy-blue polo shirt was nothing like the tube tops all the other girls wore that summer. I had been taught to cover my body and "leave more to the imagination."

Crissy's mom asked what I wanted. "Are you that snooty girl from the city?"

I sheepishly told her my name and asked if I could see Crissy. Her mom yelled for her, and when Crissy came to the door, I saw that she had transformed. Her blond curls were flat and oily. She wore a baggy nightgown. And she had a black eye. My mouth must have dropped in shock because she immediately closed the front door behind her and guided me to the bench in their front yard.

"What happened?" I asked. My eyes scanned her arms and legs to see if she had any other bruises. I wanted to give her a hug, but her body seemed tense and became erect, and I didn't know how she'd react.

Her eyes focused on the grass. "I fell down the stairs," she told me, tightly holding her hands in her lap.

I tried to meet her eyes.

"I was really upset; I had just told my mother that I was pregnant, and she got mad at me. I must have slipped."

Then Crissy started to cry. I wrapped one arm around her shoulder.

"Pregnant? How?"

Crissy looked at me condescendingly.

"I mean, I know how it works, but how did it happen? Didn't you use birth control?"

Crissy nodded and spoke through her tears.

"Yes, we used rubbers, but I guess we didn't use them every time."

She sighed and held both arms over her stomach, clutching the sides of her torso. "Mom tells me I can't go to school in the fall because New York doesn't let pregnant girls in high school. She also told me I can't have an abortion because we're Catholic, so I guess I am going to be a mother at fifteen." Now she started sobbing, and I held her close and let her cry. I didn't know what to do or how I could help.

After we had been sitting together for thirty minutes, her mom called her inside. I never saw her again that summer and found out later that her mother pushed her down the stairs again, hoping she would have a spontaneous miscarriage. She didn't.

Crissy's experience marked me for life. While my friends were experimenting with foreplay and sex, I kept everything I did with boys above the waist. I did *not* want to end up like her. I needed to go through high school and on to college. I was determined to get more education than my mom, who only had a high school diploma. I kept hearing my grandmother's voice: *Education is key, my love.*

As soon as I was back in New York, I went to the local Planned Parenthood and met with a counselor who told me about birth control and the mechanics of my body. I learned about ovulation cycles, condoms, IUDs, diaphragms, and the pill. I knew I wanted to be a parent one day, but I didn't want to be poor and uneducated.

"Joey told me that if we have sex standing up, I can't become pregnant because gravity keeps the sperm from reaching the egg," my friend Jean told me one day while we were walking out to recess the next school year.

I shook my head no. "You can still get pregnant. Gravity isn't enough to deter the sperm. You need birth control—a condom, a diaphragm, something! Do you want to tell your parents you're pregnant? Imagine what Sister Elizabeth would say—you'd get kicked out before we graduate from eighth grade." I looked at her with indignation. I hoped she got the point.

Even though I wasn't having sex with anyone yet, I had become the expert on pregnancy and birth control for my eighth-grade classes. Female classmates would seek me out when the nuns weren't looking and ask me questions, like whether pulling out would work.

And as with Jean, I would shake my head no, wondering why they didn't ask their moms or why they didn't go to Planned Parenthood. But then I remembered that I didn't talk to my mom or my grandmother about these things either. I was determined that none of the girls in my school would get pregnant. None did, as far as I knew.

BREAKING AWAY

1977

So much of my life had always revolved around St. Ignatius. I was at school five days a week. I went to church on Sundays. I played basketball with my friends in the school auditorium every Saturday morning.

However, I lived in a building where almost everyone was Jewish. They didn't all go to temple, but I remember one neighbor telling me that being Jewish was not just a religion; it was a culture. I started to see being Catholic in the same way: learning the lessons from the Baltimore Catechism and remembering the teachings of Jesus in my daily life made it seem that being Catholic was also more than a religion. I didn't like the institution of the Church and all the man-made rules that seemed particularly unfair to women. But I did like what Jesus said in the Bible: love thy neighbor, treat others how you want to be treated, help the poor, and use the gifts God gave you to make the world a better place. Those were the lessons that stuck with me. I especially didn't like the Old Testament. All that "eye for an eye" stuff was too harsh. Jesus was about love, and I believed that love could cure most problems in the world.

I always felt so small whenever my classmates and I filed into the enormous church with its large marble columns and majesty. It seemed as though the church was so much stronger than us, and we couldn't rebel or else we'd be crushed. I had trouble paying attention to the priest because my eyes always fixated on the enormous gold cross with Jesus hanging on it, or on the twelve Stations of the Cross depicting the last moments of Jesus on earth, or the stained-glass windows that told stories of different saints.

But when the sound of the organ pipes filled up the church, my whole being reverberated with the vibrations. And when my classmates opened their hymnals and began to sing, their voices mingled together to envelop me in a feeling of oneness, a feeling of belonging. My favorite part of Mass was the moment we said, "Peace be with you" and shook hands with the people around us. I longed for more of that fleeting feeling of connection.

But this sense of goodness and fellowship was constantly tested by meanness and cruelty, which created an enormous conflict in my soul. One time, I was sitting in my eighth-grade class at attention. I had my long braids pulled back and secured by a blue elastic band that matched my navy-blue socks, just as the nuns had instructed.

I diligently copied the grammar diagram Sister Elizabeth had written on the blackboard: subject, verb, direct object. She drilled grammar rules into us, and although I didn't like those lessons at the time, I must admit that they did help me later in life when I was studying French, Spanish, and Greek.

Sister Elizabeth's voice was shaky from age, and she was stern. She constantly pursed her lips like something bitter was in her mouth. She wore a dark-blue dress with a white rim at the neckline, a little like a priest's collar, and sensible flat shoes. As she slowly walked up and down the aisles between our desks to check our sentence diagrams, I waited patiently, proud and ready to show her my work because I was good at grammar. I also had beautiful penmanship. When she stopped at my desk, I was certain she was going to compliment me.

I was wrong.

"Miss Robin, are you trying to anger the Lord?"

I was surprised by her reaction, but I answered confidently and smiled. "No, Sister Elizabeth, I am trying to please him."

"Then take those rings off your fingers. You suffer from the sin of pride, and you look like a hussy, a gypsy, a harlot. You are deliberately attempting to entice the boys in this room!" She was now yelling at me. "I know about you. I can't have you in this room. Take those rings off and go down to the principal's office and think about why you are deliberately offending the Lord!" Her eyes were daggers, ready to strike me down.

I ran out of the room, wiping tears from my face. Nana had given me those turquoise rings when she returned from a Mexican vacation, and I thought they were beautiful. I didn't understand why Sister Elizabeth was so angry.

I sat in the principal's office for the rest of the day. My penance was writing two phrases one hundred times in my notebook: *Vanity and pride are sins. I will not offend the Lord.* While I wrote, I tried to remember where the lessons about pride and vanity were in the Bible. *If God created everything, didn't He create turquoise too? The nuns wear wedding bands, so why can't I wear rings?* I concluded that the nuns didn't want to see any individuality from any of us. Our uniforms made us all look alike. Through our obedience, we would never call attention to ourselves.

But I knew that God gave me intelligence and creativity. And He had made everything, like silver ore and turquoise. I would try to behave in school, but outside of school, I was going to be my own person and not a carbon copy of anyone else. I would not be a sheep with no unique thoughts.

As the year progressed, I became bolder, searching for my voice and realizing that I wanted to stand up not only for myself but also for those who had no voice, whether it was animals, children, or the environment. When I was younger, I had sent a letter to President Nixon asking him about pollution in the Hudson River and on the land, and he had written back telling me how he had founded the Environmental Protection Agency. That had been my first time being an activist, but it was not the last.

One of the things that bothered me about our school's rules was the gym uniform that girls were forced to wear: hospital-green gym dresses with bloomers. They looked ridiculous. The dresses had to go down past our knees, and the bloomers puffed out underneath the dresses in a way that made us look like we were wearing balloons. *How are we supposed to run with long dresses on?* I longed to wear the gym uniforms that the boys wore: shorts and T-shirts with our school's emblem.

Another rule I hated was that I wasn't allowed to play basketball because the team was only for boys. I wanted to join it so badly. I practiced with the boys on weekends. My legs were strong and fast, and I was as tall as the boys, so I could steal the ball, especially after one of them attempted to make a basket and missed. Rebounds were my specialty, and I'd dribble the ball under my long fingers as fast as I could to the other end of the court. Sometimes I'd attempt a layup, but most times I'd pass the ball to a teammate and let him make the shot. I thought it was so unfair that I wasn't allowed to play just because I was a girl.

Although Title IX had been enacted by then, which banned discrimination in sports programs on the basis of sex, the rule didn't apply to my school because it didn't receive federal funds. In the future, most Catholic and private schools would follow the law and ensure that boys and girls had the same athletic opportunities, but this early experience of gender discrimination gnawed at me. I couldn't understand why I wasn't allowed to play even though I was clearly capable. The boys' coach often told me he would love to have me on the team, especially for defense, but rules were rules, and I would probably have to wait until high school before I joined a basketball team. I vowed that it would be different then.

For years, I had seen kids in New York wearing school uniforms different from those worn by the Catholic-school kids. We wore plaid, and we all knew the different plaids from each of the Catholic schools, like the Scots know the tartans from different clans. The private-school uniforms were plainer and seemed crisp and expensive. I knew my mom couldn't afford to send me to private school, but by eighth grade, one of my older classmates, Maria, was attending the Chapin School, and she told me that she had gotten a full scholarship. If she could do it, so could I.

I started my research. First, I opened the Yellow Pages at home and found the address and phone number of the Chapin School. I called the number and, using my most adult voice, talked to the receptionist and asked if they could send a brochure. She said of course and asked for my address. This became a ritual, and for the next several days, I would call another private school when I came home in the afternoon. I called the Nightingale-Bamford School, the Brearley School, Trinity

School, the Spence School, and the Dalton School. There were other private schools, like Horace Mann, Friends Seminary, and Riverdale Country School, but they were too far away. I limited my calls to schools that I could walk to from my apartment.

I filled out all the applications for these schools, including the financial aid applications. I was accepted to each one. This fact made me very proud, but only one, the Spence School, offered a full scholarship. So that was that. I'd be going to Spence the following year.

Of the sixty-six students in my graduating class at St. Ignatius, I was one of two that was going to a private, non-Catholic school. Tina, one of my classmates who arrived at school in a limousine every day, was also going to Spence in the fall. I think her father was a Colombian diplomat or businessman. They had an incredible two-story apartment on Central Park South in a beautiful art deco building.

The excitement built in me every month as I got closer to graduation from eighth grade. I knew Spence would set me free and also teach me lots of new things. But my mom had other ideas.

SCHEPPER BECOMES LOFAS

1977

Shortly after my eighth-grade graduation, my mom shared with me that after nine years of dating Lars, they were finally getting married. She had been spending more and more time visiting him in DC, and I was spending more time with my friends. I think she persuaded him that he needed to marry her. I also found out that Lars had consulted his astrologer, Morrison, and upon his advice, my mom and Lars picked July 26 for their wedding because the stars were aligned for their union on that day. I later learned that they wanted to get married in a place where Nana and Jeannette couldn't crash the wedding because they lived in fear of both women.

I was invited to the wedding, and so was Little Lars, and Lars's parents, who lived in Sweden. I was my mom's bridesmaid, ensuring that she was pampered and looked beautiful. I pinned daisies in her hair as she gingerly placed her fake eyelashes on her eyelids. Her bouquet included dried edelweiss, her favorite flower, which she had long ago collected on hikes in Austria and Switzerland. She said the flower was a connection to her past, and since her father hadn't lived long enough to see her marry Lars, these flowers meant he was still there with her somehow.

"You look beautiful, Mom," I said.

She stood up to admire our handiwork, tracing her hands over her cream-colored dress, and said she'd been waiting for this day for a long time. "Nine years to be exact. Now everything will be perfect." She leaned over and hugged me. "You look beautiful too, my little maid of honor."

When we went downstairs, Dad was waiting for us. I had become comfortable referring to Lars by that term, although I still felt awkward using it around his parents and his son. He was flanked by his mother and father, Marta and Alf. I had not seen them since meeting them at the pool in Florida in 1967, when I'd also first met Lars. They both wore thick glasses, and Alf smoked a pipe, which made me think he smelled academic for some reason. Although I called them Grandma and Grandpa Lofas, I sensed they didn't really like me but rather tolerated me because of my mom. Still, I wanted to have grandparents—anything to make my little family bigger.

Little Lars now stood almost six feet tall. We had only seen each other two or three times since he moved away from the West Side where we lived as children. We were friendly with each other, but we had no bond. That would come decades later when we both became parents.

We gathered in the judge's chambers in London's city hall. I had never even been to city hall in New York, and I didn't know what to expect. Windows filled the room with light, and the judge had a great English accent, kind of like James Bond. There were only six of us, and no priest, even though my mom was a practicing Catholic. There were also no flowers except for my mom's bouquet and our corsages.

Standing next to Mom, I thought about how this was probably the smallest wedding I would ever attend. It was also strange to me that Nana wasn't there. *I would want my mom at my wedding.* But my mom still didn't get along with Nana, and she'd even forbidden me to talk about the wedding to Nana or anyone else. Years later I found out that Nana had written to Marta and Alf and told them that Lars was sexually abusing me, just as she had once called the police to accuse my mom of child abuse. That sure would have made me want to keep my mom away from my new in-laws. I also learned, years later, that Nana had experienced some of her own traumas, and it saddens me that she didn't get counseling at a younger age. I believe her emotional wounds made her relationship with her daughter toxic and kept me from having a healthy bond with both of them.

But ours wasn't the only secret. Little Lars had been instructed to tell his mother that his visit to Europe was just his annual visit to see his Swedish grandparents. And there was also a secret about money: getting married in London would allow my mom to still file her taxes in the United States as a single parent.

The judge asked the pertinent questions once the ceremony began.

"Do you, Trudy, take Lars to be your lawfully wedded husband, in sickness and in health, until death do you part?"

"I do." Mom looked up into Dad's eyes and grasped his hands.

"Do you, Lars, take Trudy to be your lawfully wedded wife, in sickness and in health, until death do you part?"

"I do." Lars's voice cracked a little, but he smiled.

By the power invested in him by the City of London, the judge pronounced them husband and wife and told Dad he could kiss Mom. Dad bent down, held her by the shoulders, and kissed her on the lips. Mom cried and buried her head in his arms. They turned and hugged Marta and Alf, and then Little Lars, and finally me.

"We are all family now," Dad said. "Let's go celebrate."

MISS SPENCE'S SCHOOL FOR YOUNG LADIES

1977

When I started at the Spence School in September 1977, I was intimidated. Formerly known as Miss Spence's School, it offered kindergarten through twelfth grade. It was housed in a beautiful building off Madison Avenue on Ninety-First, right next to an old Carnegie mansion that is now the Cooper Hewitt Museum. When I first opened the red doors to my school, I thought, *This is it, Robin. This is your ticket to a different future.*

During my nine years in Catholic school, I had known my place in the pecking order of my class. I was smart, athletic, pretty, and popular with the boys. But at Spence, I had no idea how I was going to fit in. *How will they judge me?*

I was relieved that we had uniforms, and the moment I put on my ironed white oxford button-down shirt and crisp skirt, I was transformed. With this uniform, I would be one of the private-school girls walking in New York. The ones who had wealth and privilege. With this uniform, no one could tell I was a Catholic scholarship kid with no money and no father.

My secret would be safe. But even so, being a new girl in ninth grade was a challenge. I had never been around such wealth before. I could spot the nuances: the macramé bracelets around the other girls' wrists and their tasteful, small gold or diamond-stud earrings. There is an ease about people when they don't have to worry about money. I didn't have that ease and tried to hide this from my classmates.

Mary, another new girl, was my closest friend during the first few months of school. Her family was well off, but, like me, she was different from the other students. In her case, she was different because she was Jewish. Her family also lived on the West Side, and many of the school parents would not let their daughters leave the safety of the Upper East Side.

Mary and I bonded because we were two of the few girls who didn't belong to a white, Anglo-Saxon, Protestant family, commonly known as WASPs. Someone later told me that Spence hadn't admitted Catholic students until the 1960s, when John F. Kennedy was president, and then years later they allowed the first Jews. Following the trends of society, they finally admitted a Puerto Rican girl and a Black girl, both from Harlem, when I came along in 1977. The three of us were the scholarship students: all not WASPs and all poor.

One day, Mary and I were walking up the stairs to our English literature class when one of our classmates, Jennifer, bumped into us on her way down to the first floor. Jennifer was cool: she smoked, she drank, she dressed like a hippie, and she was one of the "old" girls, having been at Spence since kindergarten.

"Mick Jagger is in the building!" she yelled.

Mary and I squealed at each other. "Mick Jagger!" We nodded at each other conspiratorially, knowing that we'd get tardy slips if we were late to class.

"But it's Mick Jagger!" Mary said. "And if we see him and no one else does, we will be part of the 'in crowd' instantly. Think about that!"

At the bottom of the stairs, the three of us saw another student hiding behind one of the marble columns and trying to peer into the admissions director's office. Then we heard screams coming from the second floor. That could only mean one thing: he was somewhere else in the building. We all bolted up the stairs and were told by yet another student that she'd spotted him in the elevator.

"He said 'Excuse me' in the best British accent ever, and I almost fainted," she said.

The fact that a rock star was in our school was exciting, but equally exhilarating was how, without even meeting him, he was bringing students together. We raced to the cafeteria and peeked in through the French doors. There he stood with his daughter Jade, gazing at the mural on the east wall of the cafeteria. Spence loved having celebrity students, and Jade Jagger eventually went to Spence, as did the actors Gwyneth Paltrow and Kerry Washington, years after me.

When we finally slipped into English class, a discussion was underway about Shakespeare. A student said she thought he was making comparisons with Queen Elizabeth's court without specifically naming anyone directly, and the teacher praised her analysis.

"I want you all to think about that when you're reading Shakespeare. It's not just about the stories, but about the politics of what was going on around him. He was very clever to write about the times and also clever enough to *not* offend the queen and get arrested. For your homework, I want you to pick three sonnets, compare the metaphors, and write me a paper by Friday."

She then dismissed the class. I was confused about the assignment, so I mustered up the courage to ask her a question about it. In Catholic school, I had written book reports and studied the catechism, but we didn't look for hidden meaning in anyone's writing. We were taught that what we read was dogma, no questions asked. No nuance. No metaphors. I sheepishly told her I didn't understand the homework.

"It's not about what I think; it's what *you* think," she said. "Use your imagination. A metaphor is the understanding of one concept in terms of another. For example, 'Your insincere apology just *added fuel to the fire.*' Shakespeare used metaphors throughout his sonnets. It's like he was creating little pictures in your head for you to understand his meaning. So be creative."

All this creativity was making my head hurt. At St. Ignatius, everything had been black and white, right and wrong, sin and no sin. I could diagram a sentence. I also knew my grammar, which I really appreciated in later years when I studied other languages, especially when I realized how so many American students have a hard time with other languages because they were never taught grammar. Even though I did not like the rigidity of a Catholic education, I did have to thank the nuns for giving me a strong foundation in math, science, and grammar.

At Spence, there were so many options and expectations that I felt overwhelmed. I did not write well—not like the other girls who had been going to private school for years. But I needed to excel and keep my grades up, partly because I was on scholarship, but also because, although I didn't fully understand it at the time, I knew instinctually that going to Spence was going to be the opportunity that would launch me into a life far different from the one I'd lived so far.

WHERE I BELONG

1978

I settled into my new school. It was strange being with just girls all day, with no boys in sight. Mom was spending more and more time in DC with Lars, who still worked for the government and was based there. I was discovering that I liked boys, but I wasn't sure what to do, and my mom was no help in this area.

I still saw my male buddies from St. Ignatius. They had gone to Catholic high schools, and I went to a few dances at one of those schools. I also attended the annual Gold and Silver Ball in ninth grade that was held for private-school kids at the Waldorf Astoria, but the boys who accompanied me just didn't feel like the right fit. Even though I didn't know what I wanted, I did know that boys my age were immature and couldn't appreciate me.

I liked guys who would talk to me like an intelligent person about things like world events and politics, not just about getting drunk or high and sports. When I was a sophomore, I met a gorgeous guy in my neighborhood, Peter. He was in eleventh grade at the Lycée Français, a private K–12 bilingual school a few blocks from Spence. He was tall and blond with blue eyes, and when we were together, we got along so easily that I felt like he was another girlfriend. I never considered him a boyfriend; he was a friend that happened to be a boy. In retrospect, I think he was probably gay, but that wasn't something we talked about at the time. The best part about him was that he loved dancing as much as I did, and he could get us into the hottest discos in New York.

When my mom was away visiting Lars in DC for the weekend,

Peter and I often hit the clubs. When she came home, I never told her about my adventures—yet another secret between us. One time she came home and asked me about my weekend while I was preparing dinner. I placed two steaming plates of boiled potatoes and paprikash on the table. We bowed our heads in silent grace, made the sign of the cross, and started eating. And then I told her about winning the basketball game on Saturday, and doing homework, and walking Ginny. I completely left out the part about going to Studio 54 with Peter and coming home at four in the morning. If I'd revealed those details, I would have been grounded for life.

I asked her about her weekend, and she told me she and Lars went to the Kennedy Center with free tickets. Then she rearranged the napkin on her lap and took a sip of water.

"But I have to tell you the most exciting news. Daddy wants us to move to DC and live with him. We talked, and we decided that it was silly to live apart now that we're married. We don't have to hide anymore. There are good Catholic schools you can go to, and I was thinking you should come down to DC in two weeks so you can see for yourself." Mom was happy.

But I was in shock. She was prioritizing her life, not mine. I was not going to leave one of the best schools in the country where I had a scholarship. I had gone to DC on one of my mom's many trips to visit Dad, and I hated how small and provincial it was. It didn't have the same vibrant energy as New York. No way.

I struggled to find the right words. I wanted her to be happy even if I had no intention of moving.

"Sure, Mom, I'll come with you to visit Daddy."

It was then that I realized I needed to come up with a plan to stay in New York, whatever it took.

There is a time and a place for moving, and 1978 wasn't the right time for me to leave New York. My sense of place was important to my well-being then, and it has been important to me ever since. As I grew older and matured, I discovered that a connection to the natural landscape was more important to me than a vibrant urban scene. I first realized this when I went to college in coastal California, and I discovered it again as an adult when my husband, Eric, and I decided to uproot ourselves and our two young sons and move out of DC, where my career had ironically taken me years after I refused to move there with my mom.

Eric had been raised in Colorado, and he'd always vowed we would move back to the Rocky Mountains. We took a few vacations to Steamboat Springs so the kids could learn how to ski and we could see where Eric had spent part of his youth. While I had been learning how to navigate the nuances of private school in the ninth and tenth grades, he had spent those formative years living on a ranch with his family in Phippsburg, a small town about thirty minutes south of Steamboat. After we got married, he and I bought property north of Steamboat, intending to build a vacation home. We never had enough money to build the house, but we never gave up on that dream.

Nearly a decade later, we spent a week at a dude ranch in the area and decided to spend a few extra days in town. I had just left the White House and was exhausted, but I loved looking at property. We still had our land but had started to discuss how much easier it would be to buy a house that was already built.

One day, we put the kids in a vacation day camp on the ski mountain and visited several homes. When we visited one that had a view of the valley and the Flat Tops mountain range, Eric began to tear up. The Flat Tops were where he and his brothers had camped and hiked as children. He wanted the same type of life for our kids.

I don't remember what got into me, but something sure did.

"Well, maybe we should buy this house and move here. There's an airport, so we could commute to DC every month and live here instead."

An hour later we were signing papers to make an offer on the house. I couldn't believe we were doing it. We rented the place from October to June and set the wheels in motion to sell our house in DC, convince our clients that we could work remotely, and finally move our life to the great outdoors in Colorado.

Of course, we would be moving our kids away from their familiar and comfortable home, just as my mom had wanted to displace me. But Marat and Shokhan were younger than I'd been.

We all settled in quickly. Steamboat Springs felt safe, and I loved that I could send the boys out to play without having to worry about them as my mom had worried about me in New York. They went to the public school, joined sports teams, and hung out at the local pool. In the fall, I enrolled them both in an alpine ski club, which was especially fulfilling because Marat's ski coach back east had said he had the potential to be a ski racer one day.

The rhythm of our life was slower and more manageable in this new place, and the joy of being outside permeated our bones. We hiked and biked in the summer and skied in the winter. The other benefit of moving to Steamboat was that we were closer to several family members. Eric's mother, Pauline, lived in southern Colorado and regularly visited us, allowing my kids to have a relationship with a least one grandparent. My stepbrother, Lars, and his family lived in Denver, so my kids finally got to spend time with their three cousins. It made me so happy to see them together.

PRESSING MATTERS

1978

My lifelong dream of building a close-knit family in a beautiful place would finally come to fruition far into the future, but when I was in ninth grade, I was focused on more immediate concerns.

The first was about my real father. *Who is he? Where is he? Why doesn't he want to know me?* All the secrecy about him had left a void, like a crater in a desert landscape, and every so often, I tried to find a way to fill that void. I imagined my biological father as having blond hair with blue eyes because I learned in biology that you can only have blue eyes if both your parents have the recessive gene for blue. Since my mom's eyes were brown, it was likely his were blue. I also pictured him being tall and good-looking. *But what about his character, his personality, his sense of humor? Did any of that end up in my DNA? Does he have my sense of truth and justice? Or is that only a learned behavior?* My mom sure didn't endow me with my social conscience.

When I thought about what he smelled like or how he talked or even walked, I drew a blank. Maybe that emptiness was the hole I was trying to fill with a boyfriend, but my romantic relationships had so far been unsuccessful. Nana wasn't around much anymore, ever since the awful letter she had written to Dad's parents. I missed her laughter and her love for me, but I didn't want to anger or sadden my mom, so I stayed clear of Nana.

Unfortunately, my stomach pains got worse over the years due to the stress of the lies my mom asked me to tell and the secrets I had to keep about Nana's profession, who my biological father was, and so much more. I don't think it ever occurred to my mom what toll all those secrets would take on my body. By the time the proposal to move to DC came up, I had already told her that I would no longer lie for her if people asked me questions about my biological dad. I would say I had a stepfather but didn't know who my real father was.

"Robin, there will be too many questions if you say that," she had said. From her perspective, since I had a stepfather, why did I need a biological father?

I would later find out, at the ripe old age of seventeen, that I had developed the beginnings of an ulcer because of her insistence that I protect her secrets. Dad supported her, often reminding me that I was the strong one and Mom was "fragile," but all I knew was that I was in pain—and there was no physical explanation for it.

It wasn't that Dad was bad to us; he was in fact good to my mom. And she was proud of him: he was good-looking and from a success-ful family, and he had a master's degree from the Swedish military academy. I sometimes wondered what our relationship would have been like if he had married my mom after they first met in late 1967 when Mom really needed him most, rather than after so many years. But that wasn't what happened, and whenever she told stories to other people about him raising me, I grimaced. She wanted to create an image that we were a normal family and that he had participated in child-rearing, which he hadn't—at least not much. Yes, he read me *Grimm's Fairy Tales* in German, and he caught the mumps from me when I was in second grade. He was a presence, but he was not a full-time parent. He wasn't around long enough to help me with my homework, know the names of my friends, or interview the boys who wanted to date me. He was frequently gone, working for the US gov-ernment on special commercial projects around the world. He did *not* raise me, and I hated the lying.

I didn't have the language to articulate why I needed more than what he could offer. I knew the relationship between my mom and grandmother was frayed, and my mom and stepdad were too absorbed with their own needs. As a young teen, I wanted a father who could teach me about relationships. A father who would take me on vaca-tions in the summer or away on weekends during the year. A father who loved me, who was honest with me, and who wanted whatever was best for me. I sometimes fantasized that my biological father *was* part of my life and just lived separately from us, like other divorced dads I knew or heard about.

I also wondered if having a relationship with my biological father would tell me more about myself. My mom and grandmother's memories have been the flashlight on my journey; because of them I have strong tethers tying me to New York and to Germany, and also to other immigrants. *Would knowing the other side of my parentage provide me with something else I need on the journey of life? If I met my father, would he be my new North Star?* With my current flashlight, I felt like I had guidance but no idea what direction to go in.

Sometimes, when I thought too long or too hard about my father on my lonely weekends, I despaired. I knew I would never meet him because my mom would never tell me enough for me to find him. It wasn't in her interest to find him; it was in her interest to keep him hidden from me. Then my despair would turn to anger at my stepfather. *Why can't he behave more like a real dad, going to the father-daughter dances, helping with my homework, telling me about love and life? Why didn't he marry my mom sooner so that Little Lars would have been more like a sibling to me?* I even wondered if I'd have felt less alone in this world if he and my mom had had another child. One thing was certain: I could not live in a fantasy about my biological dad.

It was also clear that Mom was moving to DC no matter what, and I needed to make her understand that I was not moving with her. I reminded her that I had a scholarship to a top school in New York. I was also learning to exploit her weaknesses, and so although I thought astrology was bullshit, I told her that as an Aries and the first sign in the zodiac, I was a pioneer. It was my calling to forge my own path, which I could do by staying behind. I also played up the fact that I was so responsible. After all, I had been cooking dinner every night since the second grade; I had saved money from babysitting, dog walking, and wallpapering. She and I both knew that I would figure out a way to go to college.

And most of all, I appealed to her romantic notions: if I stayed here in New York, she would finally have time alone with her new husband.

The toughest part about my scheme to stay in New York was figuring out what to do about Ginny. The apartment building in DC didn't allow pets, so my mom couldn't take the dog. But there was no way I could keep her with my school and sports schedule. It broke my heart that no one would be there to greet me when I came home from school each day and that I wouldn't have my ball of fur sleeping with me every night. Luckily, one of my grandmother's "girls" loved Ginny and said she would adopt her. It was hard for me to give her up, but I felt grateful she went to a loving home.

And now I needed a home. My mom arranged for me to stay with a lovely couple on the tenth floor of our building. Henry was from Switzerland and owned some type of fashion business in the Garment District. His wife, Carole, was much younger, always wore flawless makeup, and dressed impeccably. She tried to be a surrogate mother to me, which was very kind, but I never really felt that way about her.

During the nine months I lived with them, I saw my mom and stepdad maybe twice. I took the Greyhound bus to DC for Christmas, and my stepdad came up from DC for my sixteenth birthday in April and took me out for dinner. I called them every Sunday because long-distance calls were cheaper on that day of the week.

But aside from that limited contact with them, I was really on my own.

I continued to get good grades, and I played varsity basketball. I spent hours in Central Park and thanked my lucky stars that I was still in New York. I went to some school dances, but I wasn't attracted to anyone. Until I met Jean-Marc at the end of ninth grade.

We started dating that spring and stayed together throughout high school except for summer breaks, when he went home to France.

"Cherie, let's be realistic," he said as the first summer approached. "You are pretty, and I am handsome. We will have people who want to be with us, so let's be honest, have our romances, and then come back together after Labor Day."

He seemed so mature and practical to me—and very French. He was intelligent, curious, and polite. He believed that the working class needed to have a bigger voice in politics, and I think he wore green fatigues to resemble Cuban revolutionaries. He gave me a red keffiyeh, a scarf associated with Palestinian Marxists, and he shared his belief that there needed to be a two-state solution in the Middle East for the

Israelis and Palestinians to have the same rights and access to water and land.

I loved Jean-Marc's mind and how he treated me. He was the first man with whom I had intelligent conversations, and I think he set me on the path of always being attracted to smart men. And I loved how honest we were with each other: no pretenses, no games, just an acceptance that human beings are flawed and that monogamy is difficult between two teenagers.

At the end of tenth grade, it became clear that Carole and Henry no longer wanted me living in their apartment. My romance with Jean-Marc was getting serious, and they didn't want to be responsible. My mom threatened to force me to move to DC, but I was determined to stay in New York. I had already found a summer job as a camp counselor with the city's Fresh Air Fund.

This program was originally set up to introduce underprivileged kids to the outdoors, with campers coming from economically distressed neighborhoods all over New York. Most of them had at least one parent who abused alcohol or drugs or parents who were otherwise unavailable. These kids were precocious and knew so much about life. Their world was the opposite of what my privileged classmates at Spence knew.

I headed to the Fishkill, New York, camp in late June and was assigned to the youngest girls, the Chickadees, who were six to seven years old. At first, I was a little scared that I wouldn't know what to do, but I developed an easy relationship with all of them. They wanted time and attention that I was all too happy to give. I even learned how to cornrow, and when some of the young girls needed upkeep on their hair, I enlisted the older Black girls to help me. They admonished, "Pull tighter, pull tighter!" I was afraid that if I pulled tighter, I would hurt them, and they had already been hurt so much in their young lives.

I was also the nature counselor and took different age groups out every day for hikes on the two thousand acres of our camp, called the Sharpe Reservation. I loved hiking with them. I pointed out different trees and plants, and in between we sang songs popularized by James Taylor and Carole King as well as songs from the musicals *Hair* and *Godspell*. Some of the kids knew the songs from the radio, and others learned the words quickly and joined the chorus. I often thought that

I could have been one of these kids with a poor single mother. Their circumstances were similar to mine, but they were also different. My mom valued education, and—I'm sure in no small part thanks to her race and her own privileged background—she was able to talk her way into apartments in good neighborhoods and to surround me with opportunity, even though we had very little money.

I don't think she realized how much I absorbed simply by watching our neighbors on the Upper East Side. I was a sponge, sucking in every detail: how they walked, how they talked, and what their mannerisms were. The kids in my camp had likewise learned from their surroundings, and they'd become proficient at being tough and suspicious of others. I wondered how they would have turned out if they had lived in a different zip code and gotten a scholarship to a private school. *Would their lives be different? Or would their families doom them to repeat the patterns of their parents, regardless of any educational opportunities?*

That summer set me up for a future of helping kids. When I ultimately ran Let's Move! for Michelle Obama, many years later, I organized lots of different experiences for kids on the White House lawn, like climbing walls and riding mountain bikes. I worked with local sports leagues to offer free clinics to underprivileged kids from tough neighborhoods in DC, Maryland, and Virginia so they could try out baseball, football, basketball, tennis, and soccer. My hope was that if these kids knew about sports and other opportunities that might be available to them, they'd be more motivated to do well in school and go on to college or some type of certification. I had been the product of those opportunities, and a great education showed me what was possible.

At camp, I was determined to open that path to as many kids as I could, and so after that summer ended, I became a nanny for a divorced mother named Ally and her two lovely children. One of them, Genevieve, was about to go into seventh grade at Spence, which meant we'd be going to school together. She had a little brother, Oscar, who was in the second grade and who I also cared for.

Their apartment was spacious and gorgeous. The small maid's room off the kitchen became my room. It fit a single bed and a very small desk. I also had my own tiny bathroom.

Ally was a former model and now an editor at an art magazine.

Modern art and photos of her modeling work hung on the walls throughout the apartment. Her friends included the famous artist Christo, and she had the mannerisms of someone who always had money. There was an easiness and confidence that people with money had, unlike the nervousness of people who lived paycheck to paycheck.

The conscientiousness I'd developed when I was younger set me up well for this job. I made breakfast every day for the kids, accompanied them to school, made dinner every night during the week, helped them with their homework, and tucked them into bed. I became very close to Genevieve, as if I were her older sister, and taught her about menstruation, puberty, and birth control. I even told her that the first time she had sex had to be with someone she loved.

PART 3

NAVIGATING ADULTHOOD

PUSHING THE
UNWRITTEN BOUNDARIES

1981

As the years passed at Spence, I became more comfortable in private school. My grades improved every year, and I spoke up in class, no longer afraid that I would be betraying my humble origins.

Then Nana bought a mobile home and started spending the weekends on the Jersey Shore. It was ironic that I was attending an expensive private school in New York, yet I was visiting my grandmother in a trailer park. None of my classmates would ever set foot in a place like that; they had homes on Martha's Vineyard and in the Hamptons. One classmate's family even owned an island in the Caribbean; they would take a helicopter from the helipad on the East River to the airport and then take a private jet to the island. I couldn't even imagine that kind of wealth.

But Nana taught me some valuable lessons with her move. First, it didn't matter what other people thought. She had fallen in love with the Jersey Shore years earlier, and a trailer there was the most she could afford. Second, I no longer had to tell my mom my whereabouts, which meant I didn't need to tell her when I visited Nana or get in between the two of them, who still weren't on speaking terms. And finally, I learned we shouldn't always feel compelled to follow silly or unnecessary rules. When Nana offered me a plate of strudel topped with whipped cream before dinner, and I questioned her about it, she had the perfect response.

"Life is short," she said. "Eat dessert first. We'll eat dinner later."

Life is funny in other ways too. I was president of my class in twelfth grade, and I honestly don't really know how that happened because of all the trouble I'd had fitting in, in addition to my being the daughter of a single, Catholic mom who lived hundreds of miles away while I worked as a nanny for another Spence family.

Now, as a senior in a leadership position, I had the chance to make a difference. Ever since my experience with Crissy in Rhinecliff, I had been obsessed with teenage pregnancy and wanted to ensure that none of my friends or classmates got pregnant before they were ready. I don't know where I got the gumption, but I guess I understood what single parenthood looked like, and I didn't want it for my classmates or for their children. I don't think I fully comprehended that if an affluent girl got pregnant, there were ways of taking care of it. But even if rich families could pay for abortions, didn't young ladies deserve to know how their bodies worked as much as they needed to read Flaubert, Goethe, and O'Connor?

I had previously talked to Madame Schmemann, our headmistress, about adding more sex education to our curriculum.

"Young ladies at Spence do not engage in that behavior, so what we provide is adequate," she had said. "We will not discuss this again."

But I was not going to back down. Spence didn't teach sex education until eleventh grade, and this incensed me. I knew girls who were having sex before then. I had just read about Martin Luther King Jr., Gandhi, and the concept of civil disobedience, which we had discussed in American history class. Now I wondered if I could influence Madame Schmemann to change her mind if we protested in some way.

Prior to one Wednesday morning assembly, I waited for the auditorium to fill and asked my classmates to wait in the senior lounge until all the other grades were seated on the floor. I had also asked every senior to bring a pillow to school that day. While we were waiting, I asked everyone to stuff their pillows under their shirts to make it look like we were all pregnant. Exaggerating our gaits, we waddled to our chairs in the auditorium and then extended our hands and arms onto the seats to illustrate that we needed assistance sitting down. Some of our teachers nodded in solidarity with us, but Madame Schmemann's face was red with anger. We listened to the weekly speaker with our hands folded on our "bellies" and our feet crossed at our ankles. After the speaker finished, we waddled back out the door the same way we had come in, single file, to our senior lounge. Some of the younger girls giggled and waved at us. We quickly put the pillows in our lockers and headed to our different classes.

As a scholarship girl, it was risky for me to organize a demonstration like that, but I had become more confident in my beliefs. Sure enough, during my next class I was summoned to the headmistress's office.

I walked up the flight of stairs. Her secretary told me to go in. The pale-yellow walls, silk drapes, old English-walnut furniture, and flowered sofas made the room look more like an elegant sitting room than a school office. Madame Schmemann, who motioned for me to sit, was already seated with her hands neatly clasped in her lap and her graceful legs crossed at the ankles. She started talking in her faintly French-accented English.

"Miss Schepper, what was that all about at assembly? Was that appropriate Spence behavior?"

"I apologize for the disruption, but I was trying to make the point that if we don't get proper sex education, we might have girls who end up pregnant." I mustered up the firmest voice I could, even though I was so nervous I could almost feel my toes curling in my loafers.

She briefly touched the pearl necklace at her throat and then leaned forward. "As I've already told you, we do not have to worry about this at Spence. Our girls are the smartest in the country, and their families will always make sure they have everything they need to be successful in life."

Listening to her, I felt like she was saying something else, but I wasn't sure what that might be.

"Yes, I understand," I replied, even if I didn't. "But we don't get sex education until the eleventh grade, and for many girls that is too late. I know personally that there are girls experimenting even earlier than that, and I am afraid for them."

She glared at me but did not respond to my concern.

"Miss Schepper, I would advise you to stick to more important priorities as class president, like organizing the flowers and the reception for your graduation. Leave the curriculum to me." She stood up and straightened her skirt with her long arms. Following her lead, I stood and straightened my own skirt, and then I gingerly made my way between the couch and the coffee table and out of her office.

No changes were made to the curriculum that year, but I found out after I'd gone to college that Spence expanded the sex education curriculum to lower grades. I hoped that I had played a part in preventing at least one more teenager from getting pregnant before she got her high school diploma. The horrible irony was that all this didn't help me.

COLLEGE AMBITIONS

1981

At Spence it was expected that every student would go to college, mostly to the Ivy League schools and other private liberal arts colleges in New England. Since I was the first one in my family to even consider college, it was all a mystery to me, and I needed to figure out how to pay for advanced studies. When my mom moved to DC, I asked her to let me become an emancipated minor, which would work if she didn't record me as a dependent on her taxes or pay for me in any way. I also asked my godmother, Annie, who was an old friend of my mom who lived in the East Bay in California, if I could start using her address as my permanent address. I had figured out that if I had residency in California, I could go to a California public university and only pay in-state tuition. Besides, Annie had worked for Trans World Airlines when my mom worked for Pan Am, and I thought maybe I could learn more about my dad if I stayed with her and went to college in the state of my birth.

"Robin, please come in and sit down," Madame Schmemann said one day after summoning me yet again to her office. I worried that she was going to continue to reprimand me about the pregnancy stunt at the assembly. As usual, her makeup was discreet and flawless, her lips natural looking and full. Her pale-yellow cashmere sweater looked ironed, and it was accompanied by her standard plain pencil skirt, comfortable brown pumps, and short strand of pearls that always adorned her neck.

I preemptively thanked her for calling me in and said that I wanted to talk to her about our graduation planning, which was one of my duties as president of the senior class.

"Yes, yes, of course," she said. "But let's talk about your college choice first."

"I decided I'm going to the University of California at Santa Cruz," I said proudly. I had visited UCSC with my mom the summer before and loved the open space, the ocean nearby, and the great language program.

She sternly said she'd heard about my decision. "I would like you to reconsider."

"Reconsider? I already accepted." I fidgeted and then folded my hands in my lap, fearful they would become too expressive with her.

"I realize that, but things can be arranged. Why didn't you consider Smith College? It's a good school, and it would be good for you."

I searched for the right words. "Well, Madame Schmemann, I really wanted to go to Stanford because I want to go back to California; that's where I was born. But having only an 89 percent grade point average, I am in the bottom third of the class. And I didn't do so well on the SATs." I hadn't had the funds for test prep classes. Moreover, if I had been in a public school, I would likely have been in the top 5 percent with my grades, but private schools in New York were designed to prepare you for the rigors of an Ivy League education with advanced classes, which impact the grading curve.

"So I didn't get into Stanford. Also, as you know, I am a scholarship student, and I will be paying for college myself. I can't afford to take out any loans, so I need to go somewhere that is affordable for me. That means a state school." I shifted uneasily in my chair.

"Is there no one in your family that can help you with money—an aunt, an uncle, your grandparents? Because I must tell you, it looks very bad for you to go to a state school. Spence is one of the best schools in the country, if not *the* best. Our alumna, not to mention our board, expect that each young lady goes to an Ivy League school such as Harvard or Columbia. If you must go west, then it should be to Stanford, but if you can't get into *any* of those schools, Smith or Vassar are acceptable choices." She folded her arms across her chest when she finished.

I swallowed my pride hard, realizing that I wanted something from her. I tried to be as humble as I could.

"Yes, I understand. I do not want to let Spence down; the school has done so much for me. I hope you will understand that there is no one in my family who can help. My family consists of only my grandmother, my mom, and me. No one has money, and I will have to repay any loans myself. Instead of paying twenty thousand dollars a year for a school like Smith, I will pay $365 each quarter at UCSC, plus living expenses. I have to be practical. I take our school's motto very seriously: 'Not for school, but for life we learn.' I am sure that after I have finished my studies, Spence will be proud of my accomplishments." I straightened in my chair to show a composed posture even though, on the inside, I was on the verge of tears. Years later, as I helped my son with his college applications, I wondered why no one at Spence had told me that I would have been eligible for financial aid. I often wonder how my trajectory would have changed if I had gone to Smith on a scholarship and was active in sports like rowing, soccer, or field hockey. It would have fulfilled my dream of intellectual rigor and athletic achievement.

"Well, I don't like it, but I have to respect your situation," said Madame Schmemann. She put on her tortoiseshell-rimmed glasses and looked at the papers on her desk, indicating that our meeting was about to end. "Now, what was it that you wanted to discuss about your graduation? We've been doing it the same way since Miss Spence founded our school in 1892. I can't imagine what sort of question you might have for me."

I told her that our class wanted to change the flowers from red roses to wild spring blossoms, thinking it fitting for a class of blossoming young ladies. I tried to gauge her reaction.

"We have always had red roses. When you look at the wall of pictures, every class has had red roses since the founding," she said sternly. Yes, and all those graduation photos made all former Spence graduates look like virgins being offered up for slaughter. But I couldn't say that out loud.

I searched for something diplomatic to say instead. "Madame, we all believe in tradition—that is what makes Spence so great—and I promise that it will be tasteful. I can bring you a sample from the florist next week if you like."

"Is there anything else you want to change?" She peered at me over her glasses.

"No, madame, just that," I lied. I wished I could have changed so much more, like having the graduation in a secular setting and not in a church since we had Jewish girls in our class, but I knew *that* tradition would be nearly impossible to break.

I also would have liked to change the grading scheme and the overall system of support for students. Whenever my classmates took advanced placement classes, they would get overall grades for the year higher than 100 percent. It was great for them, but it was not so good for people like me who got less than 90 percent in regular classes. Spence really had no concept of what it meant to come from a modest background; a scholarship to attend school was not enough if you wanted to provide a successful future for a child. We were constantly told about Spence women's achievements, but we needed mentorship and a road map on how to plan for what lay ahead. If scholarship kids like me had access to the resources that most of our classmates had, like SAT prep classes or private tutors their parents paid for, we might have done better. We also surely would have benefited from taking the SAT more than once, but we didn't have the money to pay for additional tests. If I'd had tutors—or parents—checking my homework, explaining concepts along the way, and helping me write my college essay, I probably could have gotten into Stanford. Instead, I had to fill out college applications in longhand in the maid's room at Ally's house and use the money I got from taking care of Genevieve and Oscar to pay for the application fees.

I knew I needed to go to college for my own sake, but I also wanted to show everyone what was possible for a scholarship kid.

"Very well, Robin. Bring me the arrangement next week, and I will let you know what I think." She stood up, signaling that it was time for me to leave. I bowed my head, thanked her, and left.

I may not have changed the entire system, but at least I had a small victory with the graduation flowers, and my classmates would be happy I got her to say yes. How I went from the most unpopular girl in ninth grade to the president of the class baffled me, but perhaps it was preparation for the future.

YOU'RE HIRED!

1981

As the spring of my senior year approached, I knew I had to find a job for the summer. Ally told me that although the kids were going to Maine for the summer, I was welcome to stay in her apartment until I left for college in the fall. But she couldn't pay me.

At least I knew I had a free place to stay. I couldn't stay with Mom and Lars that summer because they were moving to Moscow, where he was going to be the commercial attaché at the US embassy.

One Friday after school, I applied at Bergdorf's. They said no. I headed over to Bloomingdale's and even Alexander's, which was not as sophisticated but still a department store. Everyone said no. I worried that I wouldn't be able to find a job and have money for food over the summer. I decided to walk over to First Avenue; I knew there were some boutiques there.

As I reached Sixty-Fourth, I saw a white awning and a boutique called Grecophilia. I took a deep breath and turned the handle of the door. The moment I entered, I heard laughter. A young woman looked over and greeted me.

I was so nervous that I stood clenching my shoulder bag. I reminded myself how much I needed a job.

"I was wondering if you needed any help this summer. I'm looking for a summer job."

She studied me for a moment. "Yes, I do. You're hired." She began to laugh again, and her whole body seemed to laugh with her.

I couldn't believe what I was hearing. "What? You don't want to know my retail experience?"

"Nah. I work on gut instinct, and I can tell you are going to be good for business. By the way," she said as she walked through the store and checked on merchandise arrangements, "where do you go to school? Hunter College? Columbia? NYU?"

"Actually, I go to Spence," I said, swallowing my fear that she wouldn't hire me once she realized I was only seventeen.

"Spence? Is that a small college?"

"Yes, it's a small school, but actually it's a K–12 prep school. I'm in my senior year, and I start college in the fall."

"I thought you were older, but no matter. I just wanted to know. If you are going to one of those chic private schools, why do you need to work? Don't your parents have money to give you?"

"I go to Spence on scholarship. My mom used to be a receptionist but now lives in DC. I live with a divorced mom and her two kids, and I take care of them after school, helping them with their homework and making dinner every night. I don't come from money; I need to *make* money."

I sighed. I had never been so blunt with anyone before. Honesty felt so much better than lying about who I was.

"I like it! I like your story! Good—you know how to work hard."

We introduced ourselves properly to each other, and then she introduced me to her Greek family.

"So I will see you Saturday at 10:00 a.m.," she said, opening the door for me. "And don't forget to dress up. *Filakia!*"

I beamed as I walked out the door. Not only did I have a summer job, but I had a spring job. I had forgotten to ask how much it paid, but I didn't care. It was something, and it meant I could find a way to afford to live in New York for the summer.

A HIT TO MY HEART

1981

I woke up feeling so awful one morning that I couldn't even make breakfast for the kids. Genevieve found me crawling on the floor from my room to the kitchen, which was no easy task since I had broken my wrist roller-skating at the Roxy disco and had a cast extending from my left elbow to my fingers. I was trying to get to the refrigerator to get some bread for toast to soothe my stomach. Genevieve took over. Now in eighth grade, she loved that she had a friend who was a senior. I think I was the first Spence girl to be a nanny to another Spence girl while attending school.

The toast helped, and I managed to get us to school. I decided to visit Nana afterward at the Studio. I flipped through German magazines to pass the time until Nana was finished with her patient. We still had not discussed that I knew about her business, although I think she knew that I knew.

"Engelein, how are you?" Nana burst into the waiting room. She rushed over for her usual greeting, wrapped her arms around me, and lifted me off the floor. We still spoke easily in a mixture of German and English.

"I'm fine, Nana. I am almost done with high school and excited that I am going to California for college, back to where I was born."

"I can see you're happy. You are glowing. I am so proud of you, the first one in our family to go to university." She reached over to the side table and got her trusted deck of cards wrapped in a rubber band.

"Let's see what the cards tell us about your future." She shuffled the deck and placed it on the coffee table for me to cut.

"Very interesting," she said a few moments later when she turned over the queen of diamonds.

My patience was waning. I didn't want to waste time on the cards; I had come over to talk with her about the phone call she'd had with her doctor the previous night. It had sounded ominous when she mentioned it.

"Yes, yes, I will tell you in a moment," she said, her eyes fixated on the cards. "See here? There is a king of diamonds close to you as well as the ten of hearts. This means great love. Is it that French communist still, or did you come to your senses and start dating that grocery-chain owner's son? He has money and good teeth."

"Nana, please." She was avoiding the subject. I glanced around the room at the dried candle wax on the wall near her altar of rice, pennies, and water. She had burned a green candle, which meant she had been praying for money. How she reconciled being a Catholic with all this voodoo stuff always amazed me, but I guessed that any type of prayer was her way of hoping her dreams would come true.

Then her eyes glistened. "Here's a seven of hearts—I am not sure what that could be. It usually represents a child, but it can't be referring to you since you started menstruating. You are a queen of diamonds, a woman. Hmmm . . . maybe you will have a child soon with your king of diamonds. That's one way to snag a rich husband."

"Tell me what the doctor said, Nana."

I had changed the subject, but her statement about a child piqued a thought. Perhaps my upset stomach had been morning sickness. *How ironic it would be if I got pregnant after all that effort to get sex education taught earlier at Spence, the counsel I gave to my classmates, and my trips to Planned Parenthood!* I had always been careful with my diaphragm, but no contraception was 100 percent effective.

Keeping her gaze on the cards, Nana made an announcement. "Engelein, I have cancer." Then she gathered the cards and shuffled them.

I froze. "Cancer? What kind? How far along? How come?" I tried to make eye contact, but she kept attending to her cards and refused to look at me.

Nana then put the cards down and lifted her blouse. "I have lumps near my left breast." She pointed to two lumps next to each other under her armpit. They were blue and the size of silver dollars. "They say I need a mastectomy, chemotherapy, and radiation so it won't spread."

It was rare to see my Nana cry, but now her eyes were tearing up. I could tell she was fighting them back.

"I know doctors. I was a nurse for damn sake. They make mistakes; they are not gods. I am not chopping off my breast for some cancer. Lay the cards for me, Engelein, and we'll see what they say." She scooped up the deck and handed it to me.

"Nana, you know I hate laying the cards," I said, trying to keep my voice calm. "It's your health we are talking about, and the cards can't solve that problem. Can I talk to the doctor? Will you let me talk to him?"

She took a long, deep breath and then, finally, met my gaze. "OK, you can call him, but tell me first what the cards say."

Despite the gloom of her diagnosis, Nana's sky-blue eyes twinkled. I could not refuse her, even though I still didn't want to believe I had the gift of seeing with the cards ever since that overwhelming experience in eighth grade. I laid them, but my sadness overwhelmed me when I saw black cards indicating sickness and death. My throat was so constricted in fear that I said nothing. She saw the same cards as me.

My heart broke as I thought of a world without Nana. She was quirky, crazy, unpredictable. But she loved me, and I loved her, and she made me laugh. She believed I could do or be anything—a lawyer, a doctor, whatever I wanted. She was my biggest cheerleader, especially now that I was alone in New York. I needed her.

STRAIGHT FROM THE SOURCE

1981

Once Nana had told me about the cancer, I was determined to find out more from her doctor. Neither she nor my mom was good with accurate details. This was one of the times I really wished I had a father. I imagined calling him, telling him about Nana's cancer, and asking him to call the doctor with me so we could find out the truth. But instead, I was alone again, facing grown-up problems by myself. I would have to find the confidence to call her doctor and act older so he would disclose the truth to me.

The seniors were allowed to leave school at lunchtime to eat out, and one day some of my classmates went to a nearby restaurant for hamburgers. I couldn't afford to eat out, and I wasn't hungry anyway. I had been feeling nauseated again that morning. So I went off to find a phone booth.

I placed my quarter in the pay phone and waited for someone on the other end of the line to pick up. In my most mature voice, I asked to speak to Dr. Greenspan. After a slight pause, a woman asked who was calling.

"This is Margaret Schepper's granddaughter," I said. "She's one of your patients."

I heard a click and waited on hold, listening to Muzak's instrumental version of a Beatles song. It was a crime, I thought, to take good music and turn it into what I was hearing.

Suddenly I heard a man's voice. The doctor.

"Margaret's granddaughter, I have heard a lot about you."

"Thanks. My name is Robin, and my grandmother said she has breast cancer and needs a mastectomy but won't do it. I wanted to get the facts from you." The words rushed out as I tried to sound as grown-up as possible.

He sighed. "Your grandmother is a tough one; she is strong. But the cancer is in her lymph nodes under her left arm, and she needs to get the breast removed. If she gets it removed, there is a good chance she will survive, but if she doesn't, it could spread. And then I can't tell you how long it would take before she . . . um . . . If she wants to live, she needs the operation." Dr. Greenspan cleared his throat.

My eyes welled with tears, but I could not let him hear my voice break. I tightened my fists and asked how quickly he could schedule the operation.

"I have it on the books for next week," he said. "Wednesday at 9:00 a.m. here at Presbyterian Hospital. Can you get her here by seven for prep? I know she loves you more than life itself, so I'm hoping you can convince her to show up."

I tried to keep my voice even. "Please keep it on the books. I will get her there. Thank you."

Tears began to stream down my face as he thanked me and said he'd see us next week, and my hand shook as I dialed the number I had known by heart since I was five years old.

"Studio," Nana answered in her German accent.

"Nana, it's me," I said, again trying to sound normal. I was staring at the yellow taxis on Madison Avenue to help keep me from crying again.

"Engelein, how are you? Why aren't you in school?" I heard her chewing something—probably a bacon, lettuce, and tomato sandwich from her favorite deli on Third Avenue.

"I am. It's our lunch break." I paused for a moment. "I called your doctor, and he told me about your cancer."

"And?" she asked.

"Nana, you must get the operation. He told me that it has spread to your lymph nodes, and it will spread further if you don't have the operation." My voice cracked. "Nana, if you don't want to do it for yourself, do it for me. I can't lose you, OK?" By now, the tears were coming down so hard I could no longer see anything clearly.

"Oh, Engelein, don't cry," she said. "I am not going anywhere. I want to see you graduate from college and get married. I'll go, I'll go. For you, I'll go. But now I have a patient at the door, so we will talk later, OK?"

I heard the click, and Nana was gone. I breathed in and out deliberately to control my tears. Without a pocket mirror, I wondered what I looked like. I was happy I had succeeded in getting her to go, but still my heart felt heavy that her days on earth were numbered. I had never really thought about her—or Mom—dying. Without them, I would be an orphan. There was no one else who cared what happened to me. Nana needed to survive, at least until I could find someone else to be part of my family.

OPPORTUNITIES AND OBSTACLES

1981

I asked Mom and Dad to come up from DC to see my graduation from Spence. It was so rare for me to see them that I wanted to make sure they would come for this special occasion.

But even though I was achieving something academically significant, Mom seemed to care far more about how I looked. Perhaps she had the same dreams for me that her mother had had for her: that I would use my beauty to snag a rich husband. And she did know how to make me beautiful. When she came for my graduation, she brought the most stunning blouse, which she had made herself. The material came from her first wedding dress, a very expensive silk organza that she'd bought in Hong Kong in 1959. I'd seen a photo once of her first wedding, but she never gave me any details about her first husband or her special day. Now, the blouse she created for me had a high neck, a gathered waist, and covered buttons down the back.

On the night before my graduation, she wrapped my long hair in rags like she had done when I was a little kid. When I woke up in the morning, I had Shirley Temple ringlets. She styled my hair on top of my head like Audrey Hepburn's and then let some tendrils loose to drape next to my face. When I looked in the mirror, I saw a charming young woman. I put on some mascara and berry-colored lip gloss.

"You look so beautiful," she said. "You are glowing!"

It was hard not to burst out and tell her that I was glowing because I was pregnant. A urine test at Planned Parenthood had confirmed what I'd suspected. As much as I wanted to share the news, I didn't tell her, and I didn't tell Nana either. I didn't want to give them another reason to get into a fight. I was also scared, embarrassed, and sad all at the same time, and I was afraid to find out what each of them would say. If either said I should keep the baby, I would have felt pressured to cancel my plans of going to school. Nana was more likely to do so; she was so interested in bloodlines that I thought she would have offered to raise the baby herself. My mom, on the other hand, was starting a new chapter in the Soviet Union with Lars and would probably have encouraged an abortion.

When I got to the church and saw my thirty-two classmates dressed all in white with their spring-flower bouquets, I started laughing to myself. I highly doubted there had ever been a Spence girl graduating as president of her class with a broken wrist in a cast and pregnant. Being a scholarship kid, I knew I couldn't let anyone know. Just another poor, pregnant Catholic girl having a shotgun wedding at eighteen—my education would have been for nothing. No, I was not going to prove them right.

I had invited my friend and coworker Valerie to the ceremony; she was the first person who knew I was pregnant. She helped me talk through how I felt and ultimately make the decision to have an abortion. It wasn't easy. Somewhere inside, I still felt Catholic. I could have had the baby and put it up for adoption. *But where will I live for eight months? How can I support myself until then?* Being on my own was hard enough, and becoming pregnant made my problems seem insurmountable. Mom and Dad would be in Moscow, and now Nana was saying she planned to go back to Germany to live with her sister.

Graduation was supposed to mean a whole new world awaited me, and I had already secured grants at UCSC. I also had a place to live out there. So in the end, there really was no choice. I kept my secret on graduation day, knowing I had to have an abortion if I wanted a future. I could always have a baby later when the time was right. Right?

GRETA'S SCAR

1981

Soon after graduation, Nana had her mastectomy, and she forbade me to visit her in the hospital. So I called every day to talk to her after she was discharged. I offered to come visit, but she kept saying no. Until one day she said yes.

I'd always loved looking at all the apartment buildings, and the exterior art on their upper floors, as I walked from school to her place. I especially loved the older ones; the more modern buildings were so boring, with shiny bricks and balconies, but no character, no gargoyles.

I was relieved, upon my arrival, to see Nana so healthy. Her face looked bright, even though she hadn't had her hair done in weeks and gray streaks were showing. But I was surprised to find there were no cards on the coffee table to read. Not having her cards nearby normally made her feel out of sorts, so I knew something was off.

"Does it hurt?" I asked, not knowing what else I could say. I felt guilty that I had asked her to go through with this operation, but selfishly I was happy she was still alive. *How can I live without her impulsive antics? Who else has a grandmother that will go on a roller coaster and then put on a leopard dress with no underwear for an evening out? She always tells me she likes the breeze between her legs; it makes her feel free and rebellious.* I wondered if her carefree spirit would be lost after this operation, if she'd be a different woman.

"No, Engelein, it doesn't hurt in my body," she said. "But how am I going to find a husband looking like this?" She pulled up her blouse. A thick, pink scar ran horizontally across her chest. The stitches were gone, and the surrounding skin was virgin white, never touched by the sun. The remaining breast sagged, almost down to her waist, its nipple pointing toward the floor after so many years of aging and breastfeeding. It seemed lonely and out of place without its twin. I didn't want to stare. I wanted to look into her eyes, but hers wouldn't meet mine.

"See what those butchers did to me? No man will want me without a breast. And how can I wear my push-up bras? How do I show my cleavage in my leopard dresses? My breasts were my best asset."

Nana's shoulders slumped, and I finally understood that losing her breast was not just physical. To her, it meant she was no longer desirable and sexy. Her hopes of finding a husband were dashed, and I think she thought that maybe her business would disappear too. I knew she was feeling bad, and I was grasping for anything to cheer her up, knowing that I would soon be the one in need of lifting up.

RIPPED APART

1981

My face was wet, and I could taste the salty tears in my mouth. I felt the pain in my body, the emptiness. I felt naked, despite the gown draped over me. I tried to reposition myself, but an IV pinched my arm. I wrapped my free arm around my stomach and quietly sobbed into the pillow.

"Your first, right?" the woman next to me asked. I hadn't noticed her until just then. My throat was dry, and I didn't know how to respond to the question.

"Yes," I blurted out. "And it's my last; this is never happening again." The pain in my pelvis sharpened, and I scrunched into the fetal position. The woman kept talking, even though she saw I was in pain.

"Me, it's my third," she said. "What can I say? I'm really fertile." She rolled onto her side toward me. "I've already got two at home. I can't have any more."

I was speechless. *Who could do this more than once?* I had just ended a potential life and had no desire to talk. And I knew *I* couldn't ever do this again.

I was only eighteen, and I was all alone. I still had not told my mom. Or Nana, who was still undergoing radiation and chemotherapy. If I had told her, she would have been devastated, all her dreams for me shattered. I never told either of them, ever.

It had been hard to tell Jean-Marc at first, and when I finally did, I told him over the phone because he was away on a biking trip. He didn't say anything for a few seconds. I could hear the beeps from the pay phone indicating he needed to add more coins, which he did. And then he said I shouldn't worry.

"It's going to be OK." I curled the phone cord in my fingers. "I have some money," he added. "I can help take care of it."

To him, it wasn't even a question. He was finishing his degree at NYU and then heading to law school in France. I'd known he would agree that we weren't equipped to be parents.

"When you're ready, you'll be a great mother," he assured me. "You've had so much practice taking care of kids already." His voice was like oxygen. He calmed me. "I wish I could be there to hold you. When do you think you'll go?"

I told him my appointment was the following week and that Valerie would be coming with me. I spoke into the phone quietly, hoping that no one else in Ally's apartment could hear me.

He asked if I needed the money right away, but I was crying too hard at this point to respond. "Cherie, I love you. Don't cry."

I couldn't talk to him anymore. It was too painful. I asked him to be safe in his travels and hung up.

When Jean-Marc did return, he reimbursed me for the abortion. But I couldn't be with him anymore. I couldn't face the intimacy and the possibilities that had been shattered. Every time I looked at him, I imagined the child we could have had, and it made me feel broken and empty. It was as though my love for him had evaporated on the gurney in the clinic. He left a few weeks later for Cannes to see his relatives, and I didn't see him again for many years. I put my feelings for him in a box that I never opened again.

Something else snapped inside me that summer, and I decided there would be no more boyfriends and no more commitments. Valerie and I went out to the bars and met a lot of guys, and I discovered just how quickly I could get someone to ask me to dance. I had power over men—but what I really wanted was love. Conquests were fun for a night, but my heart needed validation.

Then, within weeks, I fell head over heels for another man—an unlikely one. Kostas was my boss and a Greek immigrant. He was also forty years old.

EMBRACING THE GREEKS

1981

I had seen Kostas many times when he'd come to check on the store where I now worked. He was always friendly and polite, but initially I didn't find him attractive. He was too old for me.

But then one day, he invited Valerie and me to the Garment District to learn more about how the clothes we sold at Grecophilia were made in the Greek tradition. In the factory, there were rows of women sitting at sewing machines, pressing on pedals, and handling the Greek cotton. It was the first time I learned about the supply chain and how much it costs to create a piece of clothing, run a store, and sell garments. I think Kostas wanted us to appreciate all the work it took to run his business. I asked questions about how much the fabric cost, how much he paid the seamstresses, and how much rent he paid at his two stores. He was intrigued that someone so young had so many questions, and he invited me to dinner to explain even more.

We went to a Greek restaurant on the East Side called Estia. That restaurant was the opposite of the old German bakery I frequented as a little girl. The sounds of live Greek music overwhelmed me as soon as I stepped inside, along with the smells of garlic, olive oil, tomatoes, and fish. Tables of four, six, and eight were filled with people laughing and speaking loudly. The host and the waiters all seemed to know Kostas, each nodding hello or saying *yassas* as we walked to our table. I felt their eyes on us—on me. I did look older than I really was; maybe I could pass for early twenties. I could have been his daughter. But clearly, I wasn't. He did in fact have a daughter who was ten years old, and an ex-wife.

He also had a fascinating life story. He had traveled through Europe selling counterfeit Swiss watches and later spent time in jail for that enterprise. While imprisoned, he learned French and German, and then later he landed in New York with no money. He worked as a waiter in a Greek restaurant and, thanks to his charm, magnetism, and language skills, was promoted to maître d'. Eventually, he saved enough money to start his Greek clothing import business and open two stores.

Being with Kostas made me feel like part of a family. We hosted lots of large dinners with his friends, and I loved the energy and noise of all these people laughing together. I also loved how he looked at me with adoring eyes. Our conversations were effortless; we talked about politics, traveling, languages, cultures, and the Greek way of life. We never ran out of topics, and he wanted to know my opinions on so many issues. Once he learned that I spoke German and French, we alternated among three languages.

I never realized until I met Kostas how my days had been so filled with worry while growing up. *Do we have enough money for the rent? Is Lars going to marry Mom? How am I going to find the money for college? How can I keep my grandmother and mom apart so there won't be another explosive fight? How can I convince Nana to get cancer treatment? How can I find a way to live in New York with Mom living in DC or Moscow?*

It was refreshing to be with someone so gregarious and successful. Someone who wasn't worried about tomorrow. Living for today was what mattered to Kostas the most; for him, every day was about devouring life and all it had to offer. I believe his days in jail made him appreciate his time on this planet. And being Greek helped. At my first Greek Easter with him, I met so many vibrant Greeks that I wanted to change my nationality. I loved what I saw in this friendly and happy culture.

Kostas showed me a new way to look at the world. He was not a father figure per se, but he did teach me so much about life and about relationships—things that perhaps I would have already learned if I'd had a father. One night we returned to his apartment after a party, and

I was mad about something. The only way I knew how to be mad was to give him the silent treatment, the way my mom had always done to me.

"Stop being so German," Kostas said when I went into the kitchen for a drink of water. He came up to hug me from behind, but I pulled away and sulked on the couch. Later, he placed a pile of dishes on the kitchen table.

"Ella tho," he said. "Come here."

I was still mad but approached, slowly.

"We have a tradition in Greece: we throw plates on the floor when we dance, like this." He tossed a small white plate onto the kitchen floor, and it shattered into pieces. I could feel my mouth open wide, agape in shock. "You try," he said, offering me a plate.

I looked at the broken pieces on the floor and the unbroken plate now in my hand.

"No, I couldn't. Plates cost money. This is wasteful." I placed the plate back on the table.

He picked it up and threw it on the floor, and I watched more pieces shatter.

"The cost of the plate is nothing compared to easing your anger," Kostas said. Smiling, he handed me another plate. This time I threw it, and he laughed.

"Good. Do it again." He handed me another plate. I threw it and found I enjoyed the sound of the clatter.

Suddenly my words came pouring out. "I saw you talking to that pretty woman at the party. You were flirting. I thought you loved me." Tears fell as I threw more plates.

"I will always flirt, but it is you I love," he said. *"S'agapo.* I love you so much I want you to move in with me. You can stay here, and we can be together. I will pay for you to go to Columbia." He wrapped his strong arms around me. He was only a few inches taller than me, and our bodies fit together so well.

I held him close. I had fallen for him. But I could not stay in New York. A voice inside me reminded me that I had to leave. I had to go to California.

The plate throwing worked, though. I was no longer mad. Kostas had freed me, and I loved him for it. I would always have a place in my heart for him. He gave me so much, including an introduction to Greece—a place I grew to love even more down the road.

Sixteen years later, I got a phone call from George Stephanopoulos, who by then was a colleague of mine in the political arena. He was putting a team together to help Gianna Angelopoulos-Daskalaki, a wealthy Greek woman, win the bid on behalf of Athens to be the host for the 2004 Olympic Games. He asked me to join the team and help with media.

I didn't need convincing. My personal life was a mess at the time, so I packed up a suitcase and flew business class to Athens.

I quickly learned how to work with the Greeks, which included dealing with men who were not accustomed to women rebuffing their sexual advances. We worked hard, using our knowledge of American campaign strategies, to win over the international media. We also worked to convince the African and American representatives on the International Olympic Committee (IOC) to vote for Athens as their first or second choice. Nelson Mandela was promoting Cape Town, and I cried listening to him talk. Rome almost won. But in the end, victory was ours. Athens, the home of the ancient Olympics and the first modern Olympic Games in 1896, was going to host the 2004 Summer Olympic Games.

Athens was awash with celebration, with people lining the streets and cheering in victory. While Gianna spoke to the thousands gathered in the square near the Hellenic Parliament, I stood backstage with tears streaming down my face. By then, my old boyfriend Kostas had died a painful death from ALS, but now it seemed he was talking to me from the afterlife: *Agapi mou, my love, I told you that you were part Greek. I am so proud of you. You helped bring the Olympics back home.*

I still have his love letters written on yellow legal paper in a box in my office, and he continued to inhabit my heart as the date for the Olympic Games approached a few years later. I briefly ended up in Athens to help with organizing the games, and I later accompanied Gianna to South Africa so she could give a speech and share her knowledge on how to win an Olympic bid. An all-expenses-paid trip to Cape Town was too good to refuse. I even got to meet Nelson Mandela at his home and play with his grandchildren in his garden—yet another opportunity afforded to me by my beloved Greeks.

THE CITY ON THE HILL

1981

I started at UCSC in the fall of 1981. Unlike all the students around me, I arrived at college by myself, with no mom or dad to unpack with me. By this time, I had been living on my own for three years.

UCSC is called "the city on the hill" by the locals because it overlooks the seaside town of Santa Cruz. I often sat in different parts of the campus, in fields of dried grass, and looked at the ocean. It seemed like a luxury to see this incredible beauty after growing up with concrete buildings outside my window. Soon enough, I fell in love with nature, and I wondered if I could ever live in a congested city like New York again.

With all my credits from Spence and good grades on my exams, I entered university with almost enough credits to be a sophomore. My classes were fascinating, and UCSC was the epicenter of nascent programs like women's studies at that time. I didn't really understand what that meant, but I joined all the other students flocking to the assembly hall to see the sponsored speakers, including the Black feminist Angela Davis. I became more interested in politics, and one of the many political groups organized a march on campus protesting the UC Board of Regents' investments in the South African Krugerrand during apartheid. We demanded they withdraw their money. We were unsuccessful then, but in 1986 the board did withdraw three billion dollars of financing from South Africa. I liked to think we started the pressure campaign.

I was not interested in drugs or alcohol, but I was interested in boys. My mom and Nana had always emphasized the importance of having a man in their lives, so I thought that if I wanted to create a new life in California, I would need a man too. I found myself a stereotypical beach boy: blond, tall, strong, and funny with an infectious smile. Phil had grown up in Southern California with a single mom and had already spent five years in the navy. He was a twenty-three-year-old freshman, going to school on the G.I. Bill. He knew how to throw great parties and organize fun events on campus, like beer tasting. He made me laugh and embrace the California lifestyle; we went swimming and bodysurfing almost every weekend, except when the water was too cold.

By my sophomore year, I was living off campus in a rental with Phil and other students on West Cliff Drive. Our bedroom window gave us a perfect view of the Pacific Ocean, and I fell more in love with it, and the beach, every day through our early morning ritual: we put on our bathrobes over our naked bodies, went down to the rocky beach, and jumped into an inlet where the water was deep enough. All our senses were startled awake, which prepared us for the day way better than coffee ever would.

I applied for a junior year abroad in France. As I was gathering my paperwork, Nana came to visit. She was planning on a long stay in Germany and wanted to see me before she left.

We were relaxing in my room when she saw a pile of papers on my desk. She asked about them, and I told her that in order to get my student visa to live in France for a year, I had to get recommendation letters from my university professors. I also needed a notarized copy of my birth certificate.

She riffled through the papers. "Engelein, why is Robert Auren listed on your birth certificate as your father?"

Why is she asking me about this? She surely knew the story even though we had never discussed it.

"Well, he's my biological father," I said. "Mom never wanted to talk about it, but apparently she was in love with him, and he got her pregnant. He was already married, though, and wouldn't marry her." She once showed me a picture of him holding me when I was a baby.

Nana made a *tsk-tsk* sound. "Your mother—why does she do this? She always fell for married men. After all I did for her. But, Engelein,

I don't know why she told you that Robert Auren was your father. He wasn't. Ray Hulz is your father. A good Bavarian, but he never gave her any money for you."

I felt my face flush. I had hoped we wouldn't fight about my mom while Nana was visiting, but this was a bombshell; I couldn't avoid getting upset.

"Nana, I don't believe you. You're trying to start a fight again about Mom. You always do that. Why do you lie?"

"Engelein, why would I lie? I have nothing to gain. Ask her yourself. You will see I am not lying."

She had a point. I didn't want to fight with her; I wanted the facts. I let it drop and focused on my final moments with her. After her cancer, I knew I had to cherish every second.

After she left town the next day, I searched for my mom's telephone number in Moscow. I could call her collect. I had no idea what time it was there, but I had to know the truth. Now.

My mom accepted the charges, and the operator connected us.

"What's wrong, Schatzi? I said you could only use this number for emergencies." Her voice sounded concerned but also tentative. As I'd been living on my own since the age of fifteen, I rarely called about any issues, so she knew it had to be something big.

I didn't know where to start. I did my best to stay calm, but I was already sniffling. "Mom?"

"Yes, Schatzi. Are you all right? Are you crying?" Her tone softened.

I stared at the ocean from my window and breathed deeply. "Nana just came for a visit and saw my birth certificate. She asked why Robert Auren was listed as my birth father. She told me some guy named Ray Hulz is my real father. I figured she was lying to start a fight, and I told her that I didn't believe her and that you were telling the truth. You told me the truth, right?"

Mom sighed deeply into the phone. "Schatzi, you know it was a long time ago, but Nana is right. Ray Hulz is your father."

"What?" Now anger started to rear its ugly head.

"I was so in love with Robert Auren, and I wanted him to be your father. But I met him when I was already three months pregnant. When you were born, I put Robert's name on your birth certificate, hoping he would leave his wife and marry me," she said. Her voice was so matter of fact, as though this act of manipulation and the lie she'd been telling me for all these years weren't problems whatsoever.

My anger escalated. "How could you? This is my life, my records, my permanent record, my birth certificate, my passport. I lied for you for years, telling everyone that Lars was my father so no one would ask questions about why you weren't married and why I didn't have a father. And you let me think for years that Robert Auren was my father; you even showed me a picture of him holding me! And now, after always saying that Nana is crazy and lying, it turns out *she* is the one telling the truth and *you're* the liar! I am never going to believe you anymore. I can't believe you. My whole life is a lie." I slammed the phone down and cried into my pillow. *Will I ever know the whole truth?*

BREAD CRUMBS

1982

"You got a letter," Phil said as he handed me a blue airmail envelope. As soon as I saw it, I knew it was from my stepdad. He had very distinctive handwriting—block letters in all caps. It was short and to the point.

> *Dear Robin,*
>   *I thought you might want this.*

The note listed an address for Ray Hulz in Valencia, and then he signed off.

> *Love, Dad*

I held the letter in my hand, thinking that Dad was trying to make things right with Mom and me. I was still mad at her for lying all these years. He must have used his government contacts to find out Ray's address. I immediately walked across the room to my desk and sat down, found the red-leather pouch my mom had had in finishing school in Switzerland, and pulled out a sheet of blue airmail stationery.

> *Dear Ray,*
>   *You don't know me, but my name is Robin Francisca Schepper, and my mom is Trudy Schepper. You knew her in the early 1960s in San Francisco. I just found out that you are my biological father. I know that this might*

come as a shock. It did to me too. I don't want anything from you. I don't want money or anything else. I would just like to know more about you, about what you do, and anything you can remember about the early 1960s in San Francisco. My mom doesn't like to talk about it, so my history is a blank page of my life. If you have the time, I would love to meet you or talk to you on the phone so I would know a little more about who I am.

I am not too far from you. I live in California. In fact, I go to the University of California at Santa Cruz, and I could easily come to Valencia to see you. I speak German too. My grandmother told me that you are originally from Nuremberg.

Please contact me so we can get to know each other a little. I promise to be discreet if you have a new family.

I signed off with my contact information and said I hoped to hear from him, and then I ran downstairs, hopped on my motorcycle, and rode to the post office downtown to get it into the mailbox before the 5:00 p.m. collections. I didn't want to wait for the postman the next day.

I knew I had to call Nana next. She hadn't meant to hurt me. She had just been telling me the truth.

"Nana, I wanted to apologize. You were right. Ray Hulz is my father, and Mom finally told me. I am sorry I didn't believe you." I stared at my fingers as I talked.

"Engelein, do not worry. Your mother is a little crazy. It doesn't matter. You will find a nice husband in California or when you go to France, and it won't matter who your father is. She was always focused on the goal." But then there was a pause. "I have a favor to ask you."

"Sure, what is it?"

"Well, I am going to Dorsten to be with Tante Trude, and with the time zones it is going to be difficult to keep up with the Studio. I am going to give your number to the girls in case they need someone to talk to while I am gone. OK?"

I was shocked. Nana knew that I knew about her business, but we never talked about it. I didn't know the details and didn't know how I could help.

"Sure, Nana," I blurted out. "Is there anything I should know?"

"No, the girls are pretty good but sometimes they fight. Just talk to them and everything will be all right."

As if the drama surrounding my biological origin wasn't enough to deal with, I got a call two weeks later from one of Nana's girls. She said that some of the girls wanted to do house calls to make more money, which was against Nana's rules of operating her business. I didn't know exactly what to do, but I channeled my grandmother and guessed what she would say.

"You tell them that my grandmother will be very upset if they go to any clients' apartments. It is too risky. If they won't listen, I will tell my grandmother to fire them." What I proposed must have worked because I didn't hear from them again. Problem solved. In fact, Nana later told me that the business ran so well without her that she might take another trip to Germany soon to find a permanent apartment.

REBUFFED

1983

A few weeks before my sophomore year ended, a letter with no return address, but with a Valencia postmark, arrived. As I rushed upstairs to open it, my stomach fluttered with butterflies of anticipation. The handwriting was feminine.

> *Dear Robin,*
> *We got your letter and need to inform you that Ray Hulz is not your father. I am sure you are a nice young woman who is very beautiful and smart, but your mother has misinformed you. Ray Hulz is not your father.*
> *Please do not contact us again.*
> *Sincerely,*
> *Beate Hulz*

I threw the letter on my bed so my tears wouldn't stain the ink. I wondered if Ray even saw my letter or if Beate had intercepted it. I imagined driving down there and showing up on their doorstep and demanding to talk to him. My sadness increased. *Why doesn't he want to meet me? Wouldn't a normal person want to meet their flesh and blood?* I stared at the wooden floor of my bedroom as the truth swelled inside. I would never meet him. I would always have a hole in my heart that nothing could fill. I would always be a bastard child. I no longer considered myself a Catholic, but my catechism lessons still filled my thoughts: I would never be worthy in God's eyes because my conception was a sin. I would never be considered a full human being.

DISAPPOINTING ROOTS

1983

My despair was somewhat abated when my mom and dad invited me to spend the summer in Vienna before my junior year started in France. Dad had been transferred there for a three-year assignment, and I think they saw this summer sojourn as an opportunity to get to know me better after so much time apart.

A year earlier, they had tried to create a family unit with my stepbrother and me on another family trip. Even though I had not seen Little Lars in years, I had been eager to join them in Sweden, to spend some time with Dad's relatives, and then on to Moscow. I had always wanted us to be a foursome, but it had been hard to create relationships out of thin air.

When we were in Moscow, they showed me where all the expats lived—a large compound composed of many apartment buildings behind a gate. Mom told me the apartment was bugged, so she and Dad could only have meaningful conversations on the sidewalk. She also told me that we were followed whenever we left the city, and that KGB agents would enter all the foreign diplomats' apartments whenever they left for a weekend. The agents would unplug the refrigerator or rearrange the decorations on a table just to let the diplomats know they were being watched.

When it came time to visit them in Vienna in 1983, however, it was a much different experience. This was my family's homeland, with my grandfather hailing from a tiny farm village south of Vienna. I liked the idea of spending that summer exploring my roots, improving my

German, and repairing my relationship with my mom. Soon after we arrived, my mom told me we were going to Burgenland to see her first cousins and extended family.

As we drove into the town, I saw the sign that said Punitz, population one hundred. In the distance you could see the tower that marked the Hungarian border. Guards and razor wire still marked the border back then, and I heard stories on the news about people from Hungary trying to jump the fence into Austria to escape communism. Some made it and others did not. It felt eerie being so close to a heavily patrolled border; I had never experienced a police presence like that in New York or California, although it was reminiscent of my visit to Moscow.

We stopped at a bar in the center of town, and I walked in to ask for directions to the Schepper farm. The people there seemed suspicious of me. I spoke proper German, but they kept asking me questions. Luckily, my mom came into the bar when she started to wonder what was taking so long, and the German she spoke was different from the High German I had been taught. When she slipped into the Burgenland dialect, I could hardly understand a word.

We drove down a few dirt roads and pulled up to a whitewashed house with a thatched roof, parking between the chicken coop and the door. An old woman with gray hair pulled back in a bun appeared. She wore a long black dress and a white apron, and she looked strong despite her advanced years. Looking at me in the passenger seat, she seemed puzzled, but as soon as my mom got out of the car, she approached.

"Trude?"

My mom skipped over to her and gave her a big hug. "Resi Tante. How are you?" She started up again in the Burgenland dialect, and I guessed they were talking about me because Resi Tante kept looking at me and sizing me up.

After introductions, we went into the kitchen. As soon as we sat down, I heard footsteps coming up the stairs. Rudolf Onkel stood in the doorway, and he looked so much like my grandfather, except older. He and my mom hugged, and he twirled her around the kitchen. My mom reminded me that we had visited Burgenland when I was a toddler, and Rudolf Onkel said he took me for tractor rides and I laughed the whole time. I wondered why we had not visited again until now. More blood relatives that I didn't know.

Resi Tante asked how old I was. She called me by my middle name, Franziska, refusing to call me by my American name, Robin, because it was hard to pronounce and wasn't Austrian. Franziska was the feminine version of Franz, which was my grandfather's name, and it was also associated with Saint Francis of Assisi. All my Austrian relatives were very Catholic.

I told her I was twenty, as I gathered the bread crumbs around my plate with my hand.

"How come you aren't married?" she asked. "Is something wrong? You are pretty enough to get a husband." I blushed and could feel the heat in my face.

My mom quickly came to my defense. "She is going to university in Paris soon. We are very proud of her."

"University?" asked Resi Tante. "Why? Women don't need to go to university. Or is that how you will meet a husband? Do you want to marry a Frenchman? What's wrong with an Austrian?"

"I want an education, Resi Tante," I replied. "I want to become a photojournalist. I think photography and journalism are great ways to illustrate what is happening in the world."

Rudolf Onkel saw my discomfort and changed the subject, inviting us to stay for dinner and meet some of the cousins. When my mom accepted the invitation, Resi Tante put me to work.

"Go outside and pick some chickens for me, and you can help me prepare dinner."

"What do you mean, Resi Tante?" I asked, thinking I hadn't understood her German.

"Go in the chicken coop and see which ones are the plumpest," she said with exasperation, realizing I had no idea what came next or how things worked on a farm.

On my way to the chicken coop, I thought about how grateful I was that my grandfather had come to the United States. If he hadn't, he would have never met the attractive blond German girl in New York who became Nana, and neither my mom nor I would have ever been born.

My reverie was quickly broken by the swishing sound of the folds in Resi Tante's long black wool skirt. She surveyed the animals and then, in an instant, cornered the white hen with black splotches. Her large hands grabbed it, and she nestled it against her chest. I was about to pet the chicken when one of her hands grasped its neck. She quickly twisted it and then handed the dead bird to me.

"Hold this. We have more people coming to eat; I am going to get another one." I watched her wring the neck of another chicken as I tried to keep the bile from rising into my mouth.

She glared at me. "Happens to all you city folk; you don't know where your food comes from. I would have never thought Franz's granddaughter wouldn't know how to kill a chicken."

She stomped into the kitchen, and I made my way to the cow stalls where a baby calf had just been born. I didn't want to let anyone see me cry, so I let the calf suck on my hand while tears came streaming down my face. When Mom and I left the next day for Vienna, I didn't think I'd ever want to go back to Punitz.

WHEN LOVE ISN'T ENOUGH

1983–1986

Back in Vienna, my mom searched for other excursions we could take. We both loved to travel; it was a way for us to spend time together and focus on the sights without getting into any deep conversations.

At some point during the summer, Phil arrived from California. I had broken up with him earlier in my sophomore year because I had found him in bed with another woman. He apologized and begged me to stay at our rental home. But I told him I was leaving; I didn't trust him anymore, and we were done. When I left for Vienna, I never expected to see him again. But he showed up at my parents' apartment, unannounced, with an engagement ring. I felt bad he had traveled so far to ask me to marry him, because the answer was no.

After that, my mom and I went on one of her excursions. Toward the end of the trip, while wandering around a town on the Danube River and visiting the castle where Richard the Lionhearted had been held for ransom during the Crusades, we had to check our watches regularly. We didn't want to miss the boat back to Vienna. As we got closer to the departure time, we walked down to a grassy area near the dock. There were picnic tables where we could wait for the boat to appear.

"There's a photographer behind us whose lens has been following you," my mom said. "He is very handsome. I think he's close to your age. Why don't you go talk to him?"

"Mom, no way." I turned away from her.

I expected a response, and when none came, I discovered that she had already walked away, toward the photographer. I saw him shake his head, and then they both headed my way. I was mortified.

My mom introduced him in German.

"Robin, meet Claus."

He held out his hand, and I shook it.

"What are you photographing?" I asked. I couldn't help but notice his soft blue eyes.

"I am a photojournalist for an auto magazine, and there is a motorcycle rally here today, so I am reporting on it."

He had a really nice voice. He was tall and looked fit. He also had a warm smile, and one of his teeth was a little crooked, which made him even cuter.

"Your mom said you just arrived in Vienna from California. I live in Vienna—my family has for generations—and I would be honored to give you a tour of the city tonight."

Before I could say a word, my mom interjected that this was a great idea and told him we were staying in Blutgasse.

"Do you know it, by Stephansplatz and the cathedral?" She rummaged in her purse for a piece of paper and a pen, and then she wrote down our address and telephone number for him.

He took the paper. "I sure do. Thank you. See you tonight."

My mom took my elbow and guided me to the dock, and I grew angry as we walked.

"Mom, what are you doing? He could be a serial killer. Why did you give him your number and our address?" We walked toward the plank of the boat and showed the attendant our tickets.

"Don't worry so much, Robin," she said. "Live a little. We are not in New York. We are in Vienna. There are no serial killers. It will be fine."

As we sat on the boat, we watched the beautiful scenery glide by from the river, and I remembered my time with Nana in Sicily. Were all the Schepper women such risk-takers? Mom had obviously taken risks in her life by leaving home and moving to California to be a stewardess. I took a risk by staying in New York for school and later moving to California for university.

But taking risks with men was frightening because of how some incidents had turned out, and the image of one memory in particular flooded my brain while we walked on the deck.

I had been visiting my mom in DC. She had introduced me to a charming and good-looking stranger while we were ordering ice cream. She had asked him to give me a tour of DC and essentially pushed me into his car. He gave me a nighttime tour of the city, but it ended at his apartment where he forced himself on me. I did not fight back, for fear he would hurt me with a knife or a gun. I just succumbed, praying for it to be over quickly so that I could leave after he had gotten what he wanted.

Now, here in Vienna, I feared my mom was setting me up again for another disaster. I wanted more control and less risk.

When we arrived at the docking station in Vienna, I couldn't believe my eyes. Claus was waiting for us. He told us it was quicker to drive from Melk to Vienna than to take the boat, and he wanted to escort us to our apartment. I was reluctant until I saw his car. He had a green American jeep with no doors and no top. He took my mom's hand, led her to the passenger seat, and asked if I didn't mind sitting in the back.

As we dropped off Mom, Claus asked if I was interested in a tour of the city by night. He promised to have me home by ten. Something inside me told me I could trust him despite the fact that this seemed like a suspicious repeat of the experience I'd had in DC. As we drove, he told me about Austrian history, the Hapsburgs, and World War II. He told me about his family: his father was a gynecologist and his mom, a homemaker. At the end of the night, we shared a kiss under the statue of the Austrian queen. He kept his word and had me back at the apartment by ten.

Our romance blossomed quickly after that. Since I knew no one in Vienna and had no job, I had lots of free time. My German improved dramatically from speaking with him every day and interacting with merchants in the city. He introduced me to his friends, and they accepted me instantly. His parents were lovely and so happy that Claus and I were giggling all the time.

Claus was funny, kind, and smart, and at first, I expected that my romance with this Austrian photographer would be a summer fling and that we would part ways when I had to leave for university in

France. But he was devoted. He came up with a plan for us to take the jeep through Austria, Italy, and France, landing in Pau, in southwestern France, where we could live together while I studied for the first semester of my UCSC year abroad before going to Paris for the second semester. He had already talked to his editor about working from there. He would bring his typewriter and send his articles by post every week. I was touched. I was in love. Extending our relationship seemed inevitable.

We found an apartment in the old part of Pau and settled into an easy rhythm: I studied, and he wrote. We took adventures on the weekends through the Pyrenees mountains, and after four months, we moved to a tiny apartment in Paris. There, I continued my education and interned at a French magazine called *Le Point*, which was similar to *Time* magazine in the United States. I did the research in French, and the journalists turned my work into articles. I loved every minute of my internship and fantasized about a career as a journalist in Europe.

When it came time to return to California for my senior year, Claus found me not one job but three jobs in Vienna so I could stay with him. One was as a radio producer for the Austrian network Österreichischer Rundfunk on a show called *Blue Danube Radio* that was broadcast in English and French. They needed a producer who spoke English, French, and German. A second job was as a model; Claus was an excellent photographer and had sent photos of me to a modeling agency. I was too short to model clothing, but I did get assignments for my face and my hands. And lastly, I worked at a press agency, writing captions for photos in English and German. It was there that I met Evi, a young woman who became my best friend and soul sister. Thus, I told UCSC that I was taking a year off from school and would return in January of 1986 to finish my last two quarters. This was before gap years were popular.

My time in Vienna was fantastic. My parents were still there, and we celebrated holidays with Claus's parents. I bought an old VW Beetle for five hundred dollars and helped Claus test Maseratis, Renaults, Volvos, and other cars when he had to write an auto review. We lived in the apartment above his parents' rent-free, and I painted and wallpapered it to make it more our own. I became part of his family and close with his friends, and I was happy to be part of a community again, as I had been with Kostas and his people.

Claus asked me to marry him. I said yes. I envisioned our life together in Vienna and thought I had found paradise. I had found home.

But after a year of working at the radio station, reality set in. My work was fulfilling, but I wanted more opportunity, more responsibility. I listened to men read the news in English and French and knew I could do it too. I went to my boss, a British woman, one day. She was somewhere between forty and fifty years old and had worked in Vienna for several years.

"May I practice with you to prepare to read the news at the top of the hour in English and French?" I was so full of hope and excitement.

She gave me the once-over. "Women will never read the news. You can do some feature stories, like when the circus comes to town, but you can never read the news."

With that, I'd had enough. I realized that my opportunities for being a radio broadcaster or photojournalist in Austria were limited. In 1985, feminism had not yet reached the old country. So, I quit my job a few weeks later.

Soon after that, Claus and I were at a reception my parents were hosting at their apartment. The apartment was full of strategically placed photos that made it look like a perfect nuclear family lived there, and I overheard my mom talking to another guest as she showed a picture of the four of us: me, Little Lars, my stepdad, and her—all together like one happy family.

"Oh yes, we are very proud of our son, Lars. He finished his degree at Boston University, and now he is a musician in Boston."

Hearing my mom talk about Lars as if he were her son made my stomach cramp. I understood that she didn't want to create more questions from Dad's diplomatic colleagues, but by 1986, divorce was common, and I wished she had called Lars her stepson.

Her comments, and the expectation that I would go along with the "family story," reminded me why I got ulcers when I was seventeen. It made me physically ill when she was not honest. For her, it was no big deal, but for me, it was foundational. I knew living in an environment where I had to be careful of what I said about my past was not healthy for me. Even after all this time, it still ate away at me when she and Dad were not totally honest about our family. I felt ashamed, although I never said anything to her about it.

Instead, I devoted my attention to Claus, who agreed to come back with me to California. We left a few weeks later. He loved Santa Cruz: the ocean, the sky, the relaxed attitude, and the weather. We got a small apartment in Capitola, a town on the beach just down Highway 1 from Santa Cruz. He worked construction with the boyfriend of one of my classmates who had been in Pau with us. He also watched a lot of American comedy shows to improve his English. For almost three years, I had spent most of my time speaking German and French, and only English at work. When I came back to California, people asked where I was from—not because I had an accent, but because of where I placed the emphasis in my words.

I passed my oral dissertation in French and got my degree in language studies after two more quarters. I had gotten a job at the college radio station and at a bakery in Capitola, but once I graduated, we wanted to be in the big city. We moved to San Francisco, and I got a job at Burson-Marsteller, a public relations firm, as a temp.

After a few months, we learned that Claus's dad was sick. We needed to move back to Vienna to get married before his father died. Before we left, we decided to take our honeymoon even though we weren't married yet. We spent a month on Maui enjoying the sun and living in a studio apartment for twenty-five dollars a day. We played tennis every morning and bought used bikes to go to the beach and bodysurf. It was a nice break, but it wasn't reality. The time came for us to return to Vienna. Some part of me held back, though. I shipped many of my boxes to DC, where my parents were now stationed. I was still not sure I could live in Vienna permanently.

We returned to our same apartment in Vienna and started our lives again. I looked for a job, but my heart wasn't in it. I knew I couldn't have a serious career there. And as much as I loved Claus, I didn't want to live in his country. It was too hard after the sunshine and sense of freedom in California; Vienna was the opposite, especially with its many rules. In Austria there is a saying, *"Mann macht das nicht,"* which means "One does not do this." It applied to a lot of things: You had to put your window boxes with flowers out by April 1. You had to hang your wash out to dry on a given day. And you always had to defer to your elders, in contrast to what I learned in Santa Cruz—to question authority. This was not even an option in a Catholic, conservative, patriarchal country like Austria in 1986.

Right after Christmas, I broke my engagement with Claus. I told him I needed to go back to the States. He would have followed me, but he had started writing comedy and doing well, and it would have been hard to translate Austrian humor for American audiences. I took the train to Brussels on New Year's Eve, crying all the way. I had broken up with my fiancé, and I had also left my best friend, Evi, as well as Claus's parents and our community of friends. All I'd thought I'd ever wanted was intimacy and closeness and the energy of having a family and friends around me. I had that with Claus. But something inside me wanted even more. I was way more American than I had realized, and I wanted to be in a country where I could thrive. I was devastated. But I knew I had to start over.

NEW DIRECTIONS

1987

When I returned to the States, I went to live in DC, and it was hard: I had no friends, I found the town provincial, and I had no experience in politics, which is the currency of that city. I also had no money and no job. My parents had moved back by then and would be there for another year before my dad's job would send him overseas again, and I needed a safe and stable landing. So, I asked to stay with them at their apartment in Columbia Plaza, steps from the famous Watergate building on the Potomac River, for a little while until I could save enough to figure out my next move.

I reached out to a military recruiter one day, remembering my former boyfriend Phil saying his college education had been paid for by the navy. When they asked if I was interested in becoming an officer and whether I would commit to five years of service, I freaked out. It was not for me. I also sent my resume to temp agencies and learned that my typing speed wasn't fast enough to be a proper secretary. Besides, I didn't know shorthand. All these rejections were discouraging to hear. I spoke three languages fluently. I was smart. I was a hard worker, and I'd worked for a news magazine in France and a radio station in Austria. I didn't know what to do next.

But, like my mom and my grandmother, I embodied the phrase "Fake it till you make it." I'd made my way into Spence against all odds and expectations, and now the same willingness to take risks and venture into the unknown, in search of a better future, landed me a job at one of the most popular programs in the country, even though I had zero experience working on TV broadcasts.

Connections are helpful—and perhaps nowhere are they more necessary than in DC. One of my mom's neighbors had heard about a job at *The McLaughlin Group*, a Sunday talk show about politics. The star of the show, the famous pundit John McLaughlin, needed an executive assistant. I didn't know anything about the show, but I didn't care. I needed a job. I called the office manager using my mom's connection as an in; she asked me to come in that afternoon with my resume and sit for an interview.

She was impressed with my language skills and my knowledge of geography. I told her I knew nothing about American politics, and after looking me up and down, she told me not to worry. I would do fine if I was willing to learn about the politicians in power. I didn't have an interview with McLaughlin, but I got the job, and I simply showed up the next day at my desk outside his office. The office manager introduced me to the other staff: the booker, the producer, and the researchers. We were about five people in total.

On the very first day, McLaughlin called me into his office and told me to take some notes. I sat on the chair nervously; he asked me a few questions about myself and told me my deadlines. My dreams of being a proper journalist only grew now that I was signed on with a political TV show in DC.

After about two months with my parents, I saved enough for a rental deposit and moved into a rental house with two other women in Capitol Hill. We lived across the street from a crack house, but the dealers kept their neighbors safe. It was a whole new world for me.

The office was also in a "transitional" neighborhood, meaning it wasn't yet gentrified. On many mornings, I had to negotiate my steps around used condoms and syringes. I was often the first to arrive at the office in the mornings, and on Fridays, when we taped for the Sunday show, I had to be there at 5:00 a.m. Sometimes some of the ladies of the night were still on the street, posing suggestively in doorways. They made me think about Nana and her studio.

Every Friday morning, the staff wrote out McLaughlin's notes for the Sunday show on large, white poster boards, like the ones kids use for class projects, for his cue cards. He was frequently dissatisfied with

our work and told us we were idiots and stupid. The staff and his outside political consultant would practice the questions and possible answers from the panelists. I had nothing substantive to add, but I drank
all the information in. I felt like I was getting an advanced degree in
political science every Friday. This was the Reagan era, and the show
covered lots of scandals. One day, we had Oliver North on the show to
discuss the Iran-Contra debacle.

Once McLaughlin felt like he was ready, we'd take a caravan of
cars up to WRC-NBC studios on Nebraska Avenue, near American
University. He often had me sit in the back of the limo with him to go
over his one-liners that were supposed to be funny. All the security
guards knew us when we arrived at the studios. I think he loved ar-
riving with an entourage. He craved attention and the feeling of being
relevant.

As part of his staff, I would help prepare the set and make small
talk with the other usual panelists, including Jack Germond, a political columnist for the *Baltimore Sun*; Morton Kondracke from the *New
Republic*; and Eleanor Clift, a journalist with *Newsweek*. Sometimes
McLaughlin would switch out journalists to keep the show interesting
and lively. His show was one of the first political commentary shows,
and I watched with fascination, taking in every word from the various
viewpoints of the panelists.

Although he had initially been a Democrat and opposed the
Vietnam War, McLaughlin had become a Republican by the time
I worked for him. Originally from Rhode Island, he had also been a
Jesuit priest, served as a speechwriter in the Nixon White House, and
run for the US Senate for Rhode Island. He lost the election but married his campaign manager, Anne, who by then was the secretary of
labor.

Working for McLaughlin was challenging in more ways than one.
My office cubicle was right outside his door, and he would yell whenever he needed something. I oversaw his schedule and had to coordi-
nate with the booker, the producer, and the writer to ensure he would
get the guests he wanted on his show. I remember once, early on, he
yelled to "get the Speaker on the phone." I thought he was talking about
a speakerphone. Luckily, the other staffers helped me understand that
he meant the House Speaker, who was Jim Wright at the time. I started

reading the *Washington Post* religiously to learn more about DC, in part because I was interested and in part to keep my boss happy. I had never worked for someone so demanding.

Over time, I became more comfortable with politicians' names and who was a Democrat or a Republican. I learned about Congress and who the majority party was. I became familiar with titles like Speaker, Majority Leader, Minority Leader, and House Whip. And I followed the news—there was always news, such as President Reagan telling the Soviet leader Gorbachev to tear down the Berlin Wall, or the war in Nicaragua heating up.

Once, we all traveled to Pakistan to interview the military ruler President Zia. I will never forget landing in Islamabad and seeing military personnel with machine guns everywhere. The producer, Ali, and I were the only two women on the trip, and we wore scarves on our heads, long skirts, and long-sleeved blouses to be respectful. Even with head coverings, I felt very vulnerable as we traveled to the hotel and walked in the markets with our guide. My blue eyes and blond hair felt like magnets for glaring eyes.

When we plugged in our cameras and lights at the presidential palace, we blew a fuse. As several men ran for the breaker in another room, they made a point to give us a wide berth. They seemed nervous around us. Then I heard someone ask, in heavily accented English, if we were ready for the interview yet. I turned around to find President Zia standing there, staring into my eyes.

"Yes, sir, of course. Please take your seat."

His staff placed the microphone on his shirt because, as women, Ali and I weren't allowed to be that close to him. This experience made me reflect on my mom's own experience with the Indonesian president.

Although I loved all the travel and the opportunity to learn from McLaughlin and his team, tensions in the office were rising for me. I felt uncomfortable almost every day and never wanted to be alone with him in his office, but as I was his executive assistant, we had a meeting every day to go over his schedule and his assignments for me. Often, when I would sit in one of the chairs on the other side of his desk, he would say things like "I wonder what you would look like naked with just your high heels on." I would ignore him and try to focus on the task at hand.

Then it got worse. He was a big man, over six feet tall and probably close to two hundred pounds. Sometimes, as I started to leave his office, he would get to the door before me and shut it. He would slam his body on me, grinding against me and licking and kissing my neck or ears. I always wiggled out of the situation and was so uncomfortable. I needed a job, but I didn't want to put up with his grabbing and gyrating—with his assault. I threatened to quit if he didn't behave. He restrained himself for about two weeks, and during that time I started carrying a tape recorder in my pocket to record his lewd comments. As a young woman with no power in DC, I knew he could destroy me and my career. I needed evidence, even if I didn't know what I would do with it.

McLaughlin kept me in his employ with the lure of another foreign trip. He knew I spoke fluent German and asked me to come on a trip when he would interview the mayors of East Berlin and West Berlin. It was intoxicating to witness history being made right before my eyes, but my self-esteem was tanking. His verbal insults to me and the staff created a terrible dynamic in the office, and his constant sexual harassment was too much to bear. I gave two weeks' notice and quit. I later learned that I wasn't the only one he'd been assaulting, and he was sued two years later for sexual harassment by another executive assistant.

The prospect of being without work scared me. I had been on my own since I was fifteen, but I didn't have much in savings. Luckily, I connected with a former colleague from when I had worked in public relations briefly in San Francisco after graduating from college. Wally McGuire was in DC for work, and we met for a drink. He could tell something was wrong and asked me what was going on. His compassion made me feel safe, so I told him the whole story about McLaughlin and how I had quit and that I didn't know how I was going to support myself next.

Without hesitation, he invited me to work for him.

"I just got the contract with the Archdiocese of Los Angeles to organize Pope John Paul II's trip to the United States."

He had worked for President Jimmy Carter doing advance work, which meant setting up and producing events for the president domestically and internationally. He now had a business producing events;

one of his big ones had been Hands Across America in 1986, when more than five million people held hands across the United States to raise money and awareness to fight poverty and homelessness. He gave me his business card and told me to contact his assistant to arrange my flight.

I could not believe my luck. A few hours earlier, I'd had no job, and now I was suddenly moving to LA. Little did I know that this opportunity would change the trajectory of my career.

What I did know was that I was so excited to be back in California. This time, I was right in the middle of downtown Los Angeles, and our office was filled with people hurrying around and looking very important. Wally explained that I would be organizing the pope's trip to Los Angeles.

"We need to have every detail nailed down, and we need to be diplomatic at all times. You, as with all of our staff members, will be assigned a priest as a liaison to ensure that we follow Vatican protocols."

As I sat in the chair on the other side of his desk and listened to his every word, I took notes in my reporter's notebook, knowing I would not remember everything. There would be teams for transportation, constituency outreach, ticketing, event production, diplomatic relations, media relations, scheduling, and more. My job was to secure the correct hotel rooms for all the visiting cardinals, archbishops, and bishops, along with their staffs and security. Someone else would handle the logistics for the pope's lodgings. Together, our team would be organizing and scheduling every detail from the moment his plane landed at the airport to the moment he would leave.

"Nothing is left to chance," Wally said.

My mind reeled. I had never organized a large-scale event before. But I knew the Catholic Church, the hierarchy, and the difference between a bishop, an archbishop, and a cardinal. I was no longer a believer in Catholicism, or any organized religion, but I did recognize the one good part of the Catholic Church: the nuns and priests following their passion and helping the poor. I think perhaps their influence laid the foundation for me to care about social justice issues.

While doing the advance work for the pope, I periodically questioned whether I was a hypocrite working for the archdiocese and a religion I no longer respected, but when I became more acquainted with my coworkers, I learned their motivation was more about executing large events perfectly than about the religious aspects, and I adopted their philosophy.

We worked long hours, twelve to sixteen hours a day. With this intense schedule centered around a shared goal, it was easy to transform coworkers into friends. We worked all day; had meals together; and, when we could, went out in LA to have some fun. As the days and months passed, I once again felt like I was part of a community and befriended women who remained my very dear friends decades later.

I had originally met Robin Smith, who shared the same name as me, at Wally's training in San Francisco, where we had spent hours mapping out the train route for Tom Bradley's race for governor. In LA, we shared a room at the Los Angeles Athletic Club and became fast friends because of our time together twenty-four hours a day. She was originally from Berkeley, and she reminded me of the California girls I had met when I was at UCSC.

Maris, with her flawless skin and jet-black hair, was another friend. She was responsible for the youth event with the pope. And then there was Denise, with curly hair; she was originally from Iowa. They were all older than me, and I looked up to them for guidance, since organizing such a prestigious trip was intimidating to me.

As we got closer to the pope's arrival, we had countdown meetings every night where Wally would walk us through the events for each day, and we would make sure no detail was forgotten. The pope was coming in September, and we had been organizing since July. There were so many details and so much to learn, like how housing was political. If I gave one cardinal a corner suite in a hotel, for example, I would have to do the same for every other cardinal. It was like a puzzle ensuring that the hotel suites matched the power structure of the American Catholic Church.

Once the pope arrived, it was a frenzy. All his supporters in LA thronged the streets as his motorcade arrived at the cathedral. We all had our specific jobs to do, and since the guests had checked into the hotel rooms, I was dispatched to help at other events. I helped at the Dodger Stadium Mass, at the youth event, and at the airport when the pope arrived from Vatican City. Right after he came down the plane's staircase, he thanked each of us personally, taking our hands in his right hand and cupping his left hand over ours. When he looked into my eyes, I felt an incredible connection. He made you feel like you were the only one in the room. His assistant pressed a packet of rosary beads into each of our palms afterward, which I gave to my grandmother when I saw her again in New York months later, since she was the only practicing Catholic left in my family.

After the multiple papal events were over—and the rush of adrenaline had subsided—I worried about what to do next. I was afraid I'd return to loneliness and lose these wonderful women I had just met. I actually thought about driving to Valencia to knock on Ray Hulz's door and ask him to spend time with me. I thought if he saw me, and how successful I was, he would want to know me and be a part of my life. I never had the courage to take that drive.

Instead, what happened next was that Tom Flynn, one of Wally's colleagues, took me to lunch and told me I had promise as an organizer. He said I should work for a political campaign, even for one of the presidential candidates, organizing events and reaching out to potential supporters. It was now September 1987, and several presidential candidates were running for the Democratic nomination for the 1988 election: Senators Al Gore, Joe Biden, and Paul Simon; Governors Mike Dukakis and Bruce Babbitt; Rev. Jesse Jackson; and Representative Dick Gephardt. This group of candidates was also known, at the time, as the "seven dwarfs." Tom wrote down the number of his friend, Donna Brazile, who was working on the Gephardt for President campaign, and told me to go see her when I got back to DC.

POLITICAL DIRT

1987

In October of 1987, I returned to my group house in DC and set up a meeting with Donna Brazile. Donna ran the field operation for the Gephardt campaign, working in Iowa and New Hampshire to garner votes in the states that were the first to vote in the presidential election process. I knew nothing about presidential campaigns, and I didn't know much about Dick Gephardt either except that he was a congressman from Missouri and that everyone thought he was a good guy, an Eagle Scout.

A tall woman, Donna was intimidating. She had a lilting southern accent from her hometown of New Orleans, and she was known as an excellent community organizer who had worked for Reverend Jackson and Walter Mondale in the 1984 presidential election. Little did I know that years later, she would run Al Gore's presidential campaign in 2000 as the first female African American campaign manager. She even became chair of the Democratic National Committee (DNC). But on this day, everything sounded good until she asked me if I was willing to move to Iowa. I gave her a blank stare. She said I should try the advance operation instead of field organizing. I thanked her for seeing me and did as I was told.

Doing advance work is like being a movie producer: you go to a town, find a location for an event, build a crowd, work with the local media and the local politicians, and prepare everything for when the candidate and his staff arrive. The most important part was to create a backdrop for the photo, which had to convey the story of what the candidate was doing without any further context, regardless of what the accompanying caption or article said. It sounded very similar to what we had done in Los Angeles for the pope's trip.

I went to Iowa for four days to meet with the state's advance director, who was staying at the same hotel. I was nervous, feeling like an imposter. This was an important presidential campaign, not a one-off event.

I recognized him immediately. John Toohey didn't look like the other Iowans; he was tall and wore skinny black jeans, a blue jean shirt, aviator shades on his head, and a pack of cigarettes in his shirt pocket. Originally from Boston, he had a slight accent, and he put me at ease right away by telling me stories about the events he had just done in Iowa. He made it seem easy and fun. This was his third presidential campaign; he'd worked on the 1984 Gary Hart campaign during the primaries and then with Walter Mondale during the presidential campaign.

He handed me a pair of car keys and a stack of checks with carbon paper, and he said that the next morning I'd need to drive to Council Bluffs, on the Nebraska border, and work with the senior center there to create an event for Congressman Gephardt.

"You'll need to build a crowd of about fifty to one hundred people and borrow a microphone for the speakers. We can work together over the next few days to figure out who will introduce him." He said we'd have countdown meetings every night, and then he smirked. "When you go to the senior center, make sure you don't go during bingo. You never want to disturb seniors during their bingo."

He also explained that because I wasn't technically on the Iowa staff, I had to follow the four-day rule. "Which means, after the event, I need you to go to Omaha for the night, stay at a cheap hotel, get receipts, and then come back to Des Moines, unless I call you to send you somewhere else."

It all sounded suspicious to me, but I remembered every word.

I understood nothing about American politics, or the caucus system, wherein people gathered in gyms, church basements, and recreation halls in early February to decide which candidate would be best. It seemed like an arcane system and a very undemocratic one. *What if you work or have small kids? Who can devote four to five hours on a weeknight to decide on the best presidential candidate?* But since Gephardt was from Missouri, there was a serious chance that his campaign could win the Iowa caucus.

My first event in Council Bluffs was a learning experience. What surprised me was how unimpressed the senior center director was, given that presidential candidates came there all the time every four years. He pointed to the wall in his office displaying photos of him shaking hands with all of them. I thought I recognized Jimmy Carter in one of them.

I asked if he had American flags I could use as a backdrop. He did, and John told me to tape wire hangers behind the flags so each stripe would fan out better than if the flag were just hanging on the flagpole. I made flyers for the event and posted them around town wherever I thought seniors would be—the local diner, coffee shop, laundromat, and so on—hoping that lots of people would turn up a few days later.

The countdown meeting every night helped me. All the teams from different cities in Iowa were on the conference call, and I soaked it all in, learning to copy what others were doing. "Fake it till you make it," I was told. Just like my mother said.

On the fourth day, I had built a crowd of about seventy-five people. I met Congressman Gephardt at the entrance of the senior center and led him in. He had an entourage of only four staff plus some media; I learned later that October was early in the campaign and, come January, the size of the staff and the media would get bigger.

Following John's instructions, I spent that night in Omaha, across the border from Council Bluffs, using the drafts he had given me for expenses. While I was there, he called to ask if I could do another event. I said yes but reminded him I was only supposed to be in Iowa for four days.

"Are you having fun?" he asked.

I said yes. That was enough to get me to work on another event. He sent me to another county in Iowa, and I continued doing advance work all over the state every four days. I only had clothes for four days, which meant going to the local laundromat often.

Luckily, the campaign needed more advance staff for Iowa, as Gephardt was determined to visit all ninety-nine counties in the state. I reached out to my friend Denise, who had worked with me on the papal trip. She was from Iowa, and her parents still lived there. The campaign hired her, and we used her dad's car to get around. More importantly, she brought more clothes for me to wear. She was a few inches shorter than me, but I could wear her tops with the few pants that I had.

As the weeks progressed, the events grew bigger. By the end of November, the crowds had grown from as few as fifty people to two hundred. Although we had stacks of drafts, meaning plenty of campaign money, the campaign preferred that we stay at supporters' homes when possible. The families were always so kind, and I learned a lot about farming. One time, I stayed in a young boy's room, sleeping on Spider-Man sheets. I heard the cows mooing early the following morning. When I came down to breakfast, I had to ask why the cows were making so much noise. The family explained that it was time for them to be milked. In fact, the family had already been up since 5:00 a.m., milking the cows, and when I came down, they were eating their "second" breakfast. I must have seemed like an oddity as a young woman from New York, but we weren't so different at all. These families wanted many of the same things that people in New York wanted: the ability to continue their family business and not be bought or pushed out by big companies, affordable health care, education for their kids, and the ability to retire comfortably.

The more I traveled throughout Iowa, the more I learned the reasons all these politicians were running for president—or what I wanted to think were the reasons: they believed, under their leadership, they could help these families and others like them throughout the United States have a bright future.

Aside from working, I had started a budding romance with John. He had switched to the Simon campaign and was hopscotching throughout Iowa just like me. Many times, our candidates were in the same town, sometimes for debates against each other, and we would steal some time to meet up. It almost seemed illicit because we were working on rival campaigns.

John was not like anyone I had ever met. He was a political vagabond, working campaign to campaign, which I found out later was very normal. He was witty and smart, knew everything about the Kennedys, and had an edge that was extremely appealing to me. He reminded me of some punk rock band members I used to watch at shows in New York. He made me laugh and taught me so much about politics. I was smitten.

The campaign brought me back to DC for a few weeks around Thanksgiving to recruit more advance people. I guess my German organizing skills were useful! It was great to be back in my group rental where I was still paying rent. I called a list of friends and donors and asked if they knew any young people who wanted to go out on the road and work on the campaign. I worked closely with the campaign scheduler, Kiki Moore, who later became another lifelong friend. Together, we recruited many additional young people to join the campaign, and we all slept in a rented "flophouse" in Des Moines when transitioning to different parts of the state. We also met there every few weeks to swap receipts to "prove" that we had been out of state every four days so that the campaign wouldn't need to count our measly salaries of twenty five dollars a day against the Iowa campaign spending limits.

There are many parts of a political campaign, and scheduling and advance work were my specialties. The field operation was responsible for voter outreach, solidifying support, and getting people out to vote at the caucus in those states that had caucuses. The press staff worked with the national and state media and used our events to get the message out. Of course, there were always fundraising events too. Research was also key, especially gathering opposition research on the other candidates. The campaigns also had pollsters; media consultants that did the advertising for TV, radio, and print; and an overall national campaign manager. But the people who really make the money on campaigns are the media consultants because they get a percentage of the media buys for all the candidates they represent. A campaign spending $20 million on television ads would yield between 7 and 15 percent—or between $1.7 million and $3 million—for the consultant.

As the months progressed and we got closer to the Iowa caucuses, we started getting more attention, and the polls showed we might win Iowa. Because I was so involved, I saw Gephardt every four days, guiding him through each event and writing on index cards all the names of the politicians that would be there so he could thank them before his speech. Gephardt was a nice man, easy to talk to, and friendly with all of us staffers. I also became acquainted with the national media following the candidates. I was part of a community of people that cared about campaigns, and we all seemed to feed on adrenaline.

But I didn't get to see the Iowa caucus; a week before, I was sent to New Hampshire to help with the events for their primary. I watched the results of the Iowa caucus from a hotel bar in Manchester, along with loads of other campaign staffers from rival campaigns, including John.

Gephardt did in fact win Iowa. Gary Hart had dropped out because of a scandal involving a woman who wasn't his wife. Biden had dropped out because one of his speeches had contained exact language from a British politician. We were all on a high, thinking we might be on our way to the Democratic presidential nomination, and when Gephardt arrived in New Hampshire after Iowa was finished, he had rock-star status as a front-runner.

My first big event in New Hampshire was bringing him to an annual dog-sledding competition. His picture—a portrait of him with snow dusting his strawberry-blond eyebrows—ended up in *Time* magazine, which was always an accomplishment for an advance person. Sadly, Governor Mike Dukakis of Massachusetts ended up winning the New Hampshire primary.

I worked the final months of the presidential election in DC for twenty-five dollars a day. I "desked" the events, making sure the advance teams had what they needed on the road. But the campaign was running out of money, and after it looked like we would lose in Michigan, we were told they didn't have the funds to fly people home. I was angry that they considered us expendable, and I had to tell my teams in Michigan to take the rental cars and drive home because there would be no plane tickets for them. Most of the advance staff never got paid at the end of the campaign. I was still owed three thousand dollars, although I was sure the consultants got their fees. It did not seem fair.

My beautiful mother, Trudy, in her stewardess uniform.

My mom, second from left, with her Pan Am stewardess colleagues.

My mother with President Sukarno of Indonesia on his tour to meet international world leaders. His government chartered a Pan Am plane, and my mom was one of the flight staff that he invited to all his meetings (1958).

My grandmother and mother on one of their many sea voyages to Europe (circa 1960).

My first Holy Communion and the day I got my beloved dog, Gin Gin (1970).

In Central Park with my stepbrother, Lars, and his bike (circa 1973).

My headshot for modeling in Vienna, Austria. Photo credit: Claus Shoenhofer.

One of my mother's beaus, Jack Lentz, on his sailboat.

My mother and stepdad, Lars Lofas (circa 1968).

In front of my first car, a VW Beetle, with my Austrian boyfriend/fiancé, Claus (1984).

The White House advance team with President Bill Clinton after a successful visit to Berlin to commemorate the fiftieth anniversary of the Berlin airlift. Photo credit: United States Government Work (1998).

To Robin, Shokhan, and Marat—
Thank you for all you have done for us.
Best, Michelle Obama

First Lady Michelle Obama with me and my kids, Marat and Shokhan. Photo credit: United States Government Work (2011).

First Lady Michelle Obama with me and chef Sam Kass and Domestic Policy Council staff member Martha Coven. Photo credit: United States Government Work (2011).

Eric, Marat, Shokhan, and me (2021). Photo credit: Shannon Lukens.

LESSONS FROM POLITICS

1988

I was worried about not having a job after Gephardt's primary loss. Politics was fun, but not secure. Once again, my fear was short lived, though. Through my relationship with John Toohey, whom I had begun to call by his last name in accordance with our walkie-talkie "etiquette," I had become friends with a clique of advance-work warriors. While I was still packing up boxes in the Gephardt campaign's DC headquarters, I got a call from one of them, Laura Quinn, about another campaign opportunity, working for presidential candidate Rev. Jesse Jackson, who had been on the balcony when the Reverend Martin Luther King Jr. had been shot.

I got my first taste of the difference working for a Black politician connected to churches when I was sent alone to Upstate New York to organize an event. By this time, I was comfortable doing political event work. I knew how to borrow large American flags from car dealerships for the backdrop. I had learned how to use PVC piping and diaper pins to drape flags high in the air. Sometimes, I borrowed sound systems from churches or built stages and press risers from pallets and flatbed trucks.

When I arrived at the church, the minister hosting the event was not happy to meet me. He didn't understand why he had to organize a Jackson event with a young blond white woman. I was at a loss until I met his wife. I explained to her how we were trying to fill the church in three days, and that I needed their help getting the word out and letting media set up in a special section of the church so they could get a clear view of Jackson when he spoke. I also needed their help in creating a lineup of entertainment and speakers to warm up the crowd.

The minister's wife was amazing. "Leave it to me, sweetie; I will turn him around."

By that evening, the minister and his staff were helping me every step of the way. I didn't know what his wife said, but it worked. In all the subsequent events at Black churches, I met with the ministers' wives before meeting with anyone else.

When it was time for the New York caucuses in April, the seven dwarfs were down to three. Then Gore got crushed. Only Dukakis and Reverend Jackson were left. We were first sent to California, but there was some backlash about a bunch of white kids working for Reverend Jackson, so we ended up in Oregon, where we fanned out across the state, each of us in charge of a different event.

Jesse Jackson was a powerful speaker, and he appealed to more than just Black voters. His message was about lifting the poor out of poverty, creating systems for a more just and fair society, and investing in people so they could succeed. I can still hear his voice in my head: "Keep hope alive!" I loved his message, but the mechanics of his campaign were challenging. Two of his staffers were especially misogynistic toward the female press, and after working from March to June, I'd had enough. I quit.

Little did I know, but the ability to produce events was in demand in other fields. One of my Jackson campaign colleagues, Dennis Walto, called me up and asked if I would like to make two thousand dollars a week working for Universal Studios. I asked him what I would have to do, and he said that we would be responsible for advancing the release of the movie *The Last Temptation of Christ*. It was a controversial film because it depicted Jesus marrying Mary Magdalene, having children, and spreading the gospel as a father and husband, instead of dying as a martyr. I laughed, thinking that my Catholic upbringing seemed to follow me everywhere. *Or is it that religion is so pervasive in American life?* Because I hardly had any money and was still paying back my college loans, two thousand dollars a week seemed incredible. I didn't really care what the movie was about. I said yes.

The Jackson advance clique was back together: Dennis Walto, Laura Quinn, Rob Johnson, Charles Sweeney, Steve Rabinowitz, and me. John Toohey was there too, and we all met in Los Angeles at Universal Studios to get briefed by the marketing and promotion team. As part of our duties, we had to pick up the movie tins from the airport and protect the film. We would also work with the movie theaters to get security scanners like at the airport and with the local authorities as we admitted people to the theaters to watch the film. Even with that preparation, we were surprised by the extent of the wrath from the fundamentalist Christian movement against the movie, who considered it blasphemy, and by the number of people who took knives, switchblades, and guns to the showings. Years later, I was interviewed by Thomas Lindlof about my experiences with the film's release while he was doing research for his book *Hollywood under Siege: Martin Scorsese, the Religious Right, and the Culture Wars*.

When our work ended for Universal Studios at the end of the summer of 1988, I returned to politics and jumped on the Dukakis bandwagon as the advance team lead. I had changed my mind about campaign work, and I wanted to do everything I could to elect a Democratic president. I traveled all around the country, and my favorite event was a huge rally at Crissy Field in San Francisco, with a view of the Golden Gate Bridge as the backdrop. Preparing a large event with a crowd of thousands of people was fun. I loved working with the production crews, walking on the temporary stages and press risers, testing the microphones and speakers, setting up barricades, and negotiating with the Secret Service on the buffer line between the stage and the first row of people. Watching the crowds pour into the shell of an event site before the candidate arrived was also deeply satisfying. Event production was a great job for me.

On that campaign, I continued to add people to my group, my new family. Then I worked the event in Boston for election night, when Dukakis lost to George H. W. Bush. It was hugely demoralizing, as we all feared how Bush would lead our country. I was also nervous, again, because I no longer had a job, but my campaign buddies quickly convinced me that I would have a job by January. Someone would hire me, and in the meantime, I should take a much-needed vacation in November and December. It sounded perfect.

By then, Toohey and I were more serious. We had found ways to meet up in different states across the country, which actually made the relationship more exciting than seeing each other every day in DC. During my downtime, we went to Isla Mujeres, an island off the coast of Cancún, for almost a month. We lived on twenty-five dollars a day in a shabby hotel that had been damaged by a hurricane. We read books, swam, fished for barracuda, and enjoyed not working for weeks. It was like a dream.

By the time I returned from our vacation, I needed a job and was recruited by a friend of the famous campaign operative Carl Wagner. I would be the scheduler for Ron Brown, a candidate for chair of the DNC. Ron was a lawyer at Patton Boggs, and the campaign office was in the same building as his in Georgetown. He was also Black, and my experience with Reverend Jackson's campaign would serve me well.

The campaign showed some of the fears that continue in the Democratic Party to this day. He was labeled too liberal and controversial because he served as Jesse Jackson's convention director in 1988 and worked for Senator Ted Kennedy, a friend of the more progressive side of the party. Race was not mentioned—"liberal" was the adjective used—but we all knew what the critics really meant. Not everyone in the Democratic Party was ready for Ron's leadership. We were a small team, but my coworkers and I were determined to elect the first Black chair of the DNC. When Ron won, he took all of us from the campaign to the committee. I asked to work for the press shop. My roots in journalism prompted me to get out of scheduling and into the world of working with the media. I became the assistant press secretary and worked for Ginny Terzano, the press secretary, and Mike McCurry, the communications director.

Ron created a great atmosphere at work. He was determined to elect a Democratic president and instilled in us the importance of everyone's right and access to vote. We often spent many long nights preparing for a training or some other deadline, and Ron was famous for cranking the music and leading us all in the electric slide.

In 1989, when the world was betting on whether the Berlin Wall would come down, Ron was asked by East German activists to meet with them. Another DNC staffer and I spoke fluent German and were sent ahead to organize his trip to both East and West Berlin. By the time he arrived, the wall had come down, and the feeling of elation in East Berlin was infectious. The people's desire to have free and fair elections was the top issue on everyone's minds, and I kept thinking that many Americans take our right to vote for granted and don't even bother to register. I could tell in East Berlin that everyone was going to vote once they had the chance. Ron received the rock-star treatment when he arrived. Everyone thought he could be the next US president because he was head of the party and in most European countries, a party leader becomes the prime minister. We even met with the daughters and sons of German women and Black US servicemen who felt a kinship with the energy and leadership Ron conveyed.

Coming back from that trip, I was even more committed to advocating for democracy, but my past came knocking on my door to distract me. One day, while I was in my basement office at the DNC, I received a call from a lawyer who asked if I wanted to join a class action suit against John McLaughlin. Several women were joining forces against him and suing him for sexual harassment. I told the lawyer I had to think about it. I hung up the phone and felt physically ill.

Senator Bob Packwood of Oregon had previously been accused by one of his staff of sexual harassment, and she had been vilified. Even all the feminist icons had stood by him because he was prochoice. The message I digested at that time was that young women had no power over influential men, so I decided not to join the lawsuit for fear that I would be blacklisted and lose my job. A lawyer friend of mine, Doug Rediker, offered to be my legal counsel pro bono, and he told me that if anyone involved in the suit ever called me, I should refer them to him.

Doug later told me what McLaughlin's lawyer said to him when the lawyer inquired whether I was joining the suit: "I hear Robin is very fuckable."

At the time, I was relieved to not be part of something so personal and base, but years later I regretted not having more courage. Anita Hill, in her testimony against Clarence Thomas, showed all of us that we should speak the truth, and I wished then that I had joined the suit. McLaughlin hadn't been the first man to harass or assault me, and unfortunately, he wasn't the last. But at the time I was too fragile.

Although I had a great work family at the DNC, the pay was dismal. I wanted to make more money to pay off my college debt and start saving. I also wanted to move up in the press office, but I could tell that wasn't going to happen anytime soon. When I was recruited to join a public relations firm in DC, where the pay would be triple what I was making at the DNC, I was sad to leave but jumped at the chance to be in a more stable and lucrative atmosphere.

At the same time, my relationship with Toohey was souring; I could not understand how someone so smart could be unemployed. We shared a great apartment in Capitol Hill with our cat, Sid Vicious, but we fought and weren't always faithful to each other. Still, I couldn't extricate myself from him. His intelligence and charm lured me in every time. He also convinced me that because I didn't drink, I had a warped perception of what it meant to do so. I believed him, and I loved him, so we continued in our dysfunction. It was hard for me at the time to digest that John had a drinking problem.

PART 4

ENDURING LOSS

THE ACCIDENTAL MADAM

1991

Serving as a media specialist in public affairs paid better than working for the DNC—but it wasn't as exciting. I mainly worked for telecommunications companies and trade associations, although I did get to work for the countries of Colombia and the Philippines. The hours were long but nothing like working on a campaign, when I was on call twenty-four hours a day, seven days a week.

One day, I was sitting at my computer typing a media report when the phone rang. I expected to hear the voice of one of my clients. Instead, an unfamiliar female voice with a strong New York accent started speaking to me as if I knew her.

"Robin, it's you. I'm so glad your grandmother gave me your direct line. I hate talking to those receptionists; they're so snooty," she said.

I had no idea who it was. I remained quiet and switched the receiver to my other ear, listening for possible clues. I went to visit my grandmother in New York every few months, but our relationship was not as tight as it had been when I was a child, so I was at a loss as to why this person was calling.

As she went on, I could hear the clicking sound of gum being chewed. Finally, she asked whether I knew who she was. I shook my head no, as if she could see me. This was long before videoconferencing came along.

"If you saw me, it would all come back to you. It's Connie. You know, the tall redhead that works in your grandmother's studio?"

Picturing Nana's girls, I remembered her now. When I was younger, they all looked like actresses and were beautiful. In the last few years, I noticed the girls seemed less educated and refined and definitely more raw. Like Connie. I asked how I might be able to help her.

"You talk real good; your grandma always said you were the smart one in the family. I am calling because your grandma is real sick, and I know how close you both are. She won't let any of us see her, but we talk to her every day when she calls to ask how many patients we had that day. She sounds so weak. We can hardly hear her on the phone, but yesterday she was very clear when she said I had to call you today. In fact, she said, 'Call Robin. She can run things while I'm sick.'"

My stomach tensed. I stood up and closed the door to my office. I felt a tightness in my neck. *No, no, no, she can't mean run her business. I am not even supposed to know what her business is.*

I breathed in, creating a pause as I thought about how to respond. I knew the breast cancer had come back; I had just seen her at Christmas when she looked weak and not her usual 140 pounds. It was now early January, and she obviously had deteriorated quickly.

"Has she been to the doctor? Why isn't she in the hospital if she is so sick?"

As I was talking to Connie, my assistant pointed to her watch, reminding me I had a meeting with our firm's managing director.

"Robin, honey, she won't let us take her to the doctor or the hospital. Can you come up and take care of her? You are the only one she trusts. I don't think she has deposited any of the money we have sent to her hotel, and she won't let us deposit anything because she thinks we'll steal from her bank account."

Now I realized that my grandmother must be very weak. She always deposited the money right away.

I searched for the folders for my next meeting. "Connie, I have to go to a meeting, and I have three proposals due next week." My heart pounded so loudly that I feared she could hear it through the phone. "I'll figure out a way to get there. I'll call you tomorrow and give you an update."

I rushed into my boss's office and, before he had a chance to say anything, told him what was going on.

"My grandmother's cancer is getting worse. I need to go to New

York to take care of her for a few weeks. I'll work out of the New York office, OK?"

What I didn't tell him was that in taking care of my grandmother, I would not only be spoon-feeding her oatmeal and carrying her to the bathroom but also managing her "studio."

RESCUING NANA

1991

After a four-hour train ride from DC, I arrived at Penn Station and was reminded of the city's aura: metallic car exhaust, hot dogs mixed with sauerkraut and grilled onions, and stale urine. It was not aromatic, but it smelled like home. I put on my game face. *Don't mess with me. I am NOT a tourist.*

I took a taxi to the old hotel where Nana was staying. The lobby was decorated with gold floral-patterned couches, ornate lamps, and a large red-and-blue Persian rug. The front desk was made of dark wood that had lost its shine, and the windows needed washing. I wondered why the hell Nana came here. She surely wasn't entertaining clients anymore. *Why isn't she in her apartment?*

I immediately felt the desk clerk's eyes on me. He showed his yellowed teeth as he smiled.

"May I help you?"

I said I was Greta Schepper's granddaughter and was there to see her.

"Normally, I don't give out room numbers, but for you, sweetie, I will. Your eyes look like hers." His breath was bad, and I backed up. "She is always going on about her smart, beautiful granddaughter. I thought she was exaggerating." He kept examining me as if I were a car he was interested in buying. "Are you in the business?"

He probably had no idea what my role in the business might become. Instead of engaging in conversation with him, I persisted in requesting Nana's room number.

He sighed. "All right. It's 312. The elevator is down the hall on your right."

I could feel his eyes on me while I walked down the hall.

When I got to Nana's floor, I inhaled deeply before knocking.

"Nana, *hier bin ich!* Here I am!" I spoke through her door and then heard the creaking of box springs, feet shuffling on the floor, and the top lock unlatching.

The woman who greeted me looked so small. I immediately wrapped my arms around her to hug her and could feel her ribs between my fingers. I pulled back, fighting tears.

"Mein Engelein," she said. "You came. Come in, sit down."

"Yes, I'm here."

I could not believe this was the same woman who usually lifted me off the floor every time she greeted me. She had shrunk so quickly since the second round of cancer and chemotherapy. Once she was five feet four and 140 pounds, with fine blond hair; a voluptuous body; strong, lean legs; and cleavage I envied. Now, at almost eighty, her weight matched her age. I tried to process the fact that a long white cotton nightgown with a ruffled collar had replaced her signature leopard-print dress with a plunging neckline and beige pumps. She also now wore her gray hair in a crew cut, as if she were in the military; she apparently no longer bothered with any of her many blond wigs. Her vanity had vanished.

Nana sat on the bed and patted the mattress for me to sit down beside her. I looked away to keep myself from crying.

"Engelein, I know I look terrible. I don't think any man is going to marry me now." She tried to laugh but started coughing and brought a carefully ironed handkerchief to her mouth.

I stroked her arm. "Do you need some water?"

She clasped my hand and looked deeply into my eyes. Hers looked empty.

"I need to die." She paused and took a long breath. "The pain is too much, Engelein. And what good am I anyway? I am no longer beautiful. I will never get married again." She gazed at her left hand sadly, searching for a wedding band.

"Please help me die," she pleaded. "You will know what to do. You are so much smarter than your mother." She gripped my hand with as much strength as she had.

My heart ached. I could not imagine a world without my grandmother. She had loved me unconditionally my whole life. I also knew
what she was asking.

Trying not to cry, I turned on my practical business expression
and placed my hand on top of hers.

"The first thing is we have to get you out of this place." I surveyed
the room, searching for a suitcase. "I don't understand why you came
here. Let me take you to the hospital."

"No, no hospital." Nana shook her head like a toddler. "Those doctors cut me up." I saw the anger in her eyes now and her body stiffen. "I
came here because I trust the manager to take care of me. And I can't
trust the girls." She took both my hands in hers and told me to take her
to her apartment. With that, all of her energy seemed to drain from
her body. Her shoulders sagged. Her gaze dropped to the floor. Her
hands flopped down between her legs.

I kissed the top of her head and stood up, scanning the room.

"Tell me where your suitcase is. I'll pack for you." Her eyes followed
me as I gathered her clothes, her glasses, her German magazines, her
brush, and her toothbrush. I couldn't find her purse.

"I hid it," she said. "I didn't want anyone to steal my money." She
motioned her hand toward the small couch and started coughing
again. I knelt on the cushions to look behind it and discovered a huge
brown-leather bag wedged between the back of the couch and the wall.
Inside were wads of cash peeking out of manila envelopes.

I tried to calculate how much money was there. *OK, six hundred
plus two hundred is eight hundred plus two hundred is one thousand
plus maybe two thousand.*

"Nana, shouldn't we put it in the bank?"

Nana smiled a little. "Yes, the bank, good idea." She grasped
the edge of the bed. "The girls bring the money here because I don't
trust them to deposit it." Her voice was hoarse. "You can do that for
me." She paused now, needing to catch her breath between every few
words. I said I'd make the deposit after getting her settled in her apartment. She reminded me to pick up the money from yesterday and deposit that too. I marveled that she was still a businesswoman, keeping
careful track.

I helped her put on her coat and buttoned it up to her chin. Then, after surveying the room one last time, hefting her orange duffel bag onto my shoulder, and draping her pocketbook over my other arm, I took hold of Nana and escorted her out.

The front desk clerk said she owed him two thousand dollars. I asked him if he was crazy and to see the ledger.

"Look at the books," he said. "She's been here for ten days. I usually charge twenty-five dollars an hour for a room, which would be six hundred dollars a day." Leering at me, he offered her a break of two hundred dollars a day, claiming it was a good discount. "I know the girls bring her money every day. She's lucky no one broke into her room and took it. I've kept her safe."

"Didn't you tell me that you've known my grandmother a long time?"

"Yeah, about twenty years. Not always at this hotel; I've managed others."

"So, I assume she brought the hotels business, right?" I felt my face growing red.

"Sure, she and her girls have been steady patrons for years." As he leaned across the desk toward me, I tried to block his foul odor.

"How about I give you eight hundred cash right now and we will be square?" I said.

"How about eight hundred with a kiss from you?"

I straightened up, filled with disgust. "I'll give you nine hundred, no kiss, and you get us a cab." I opened Nana's pocketbook and fished out two envelopes, one marked "$600" and the other "$300," and handed them to him.

After a short taxi ride to her apartment, I gingerly removed her coat and ushered her into her bedroom. Instead of lying down right away, she propped herself up and demanded that I join her on the bed.

"Engelein, give me your feet." She patted her hands on her lap and I obediently set my feet there. "Remember when I would massage your feet when you were little?"

I remembered, and then I asked her to tell me the story of when she got her massage license, even though I knew it well. She had graduated from nursing school in 1940, when my mom was five years old, and she had earned her massage license in 1962 after my grandfather died and she needed to make more money.

"I should have been a doctor. And you should be a lawyer. You are smart and beautiful. Better yet, be a lawyer *and* marry a smart man with good teeth that owns a house."

She had been telling me the same thing for years.

"Nana, you should take a rest. I will go shopping and get some food. I also need to check in with my office." I leaned over and put the spare blanket over her, kissed her forehead, and grabbed my shoes.

"OK, OK." Nana scooched her body down the bed and placed her head on the pillow. I softly closed the door.

On my way out, I spotted my favorite black-and-white picture depicting Nana and my mom on the deck of the RMS *Queen Mary*, probably coming back from one of their trips to Germany. Mom wore a pencil skirt, a shirt of raw silk with half sleeves, and very tall high-heel pumps. Nana was in a dark pencil-skirt suit with three-quarter sleeves and a choker of pearls around her neck. If only the picture could talk to me. I wished I knew what they thought of each other back then, because at this juncture, my mom didn't care at all that Nana was dying. At Christmas, she'd shown no empathy. She had tolerated Christmas Eve dinner with Nana because I had threatened her, saying that unless we all had Christmas Eve dinner together like a family, I would not spend any more holidays with her and Lars.

ONE LAST BIRTHDAY

1991

I decided that I'd try to get Nana into the hospital or hospice and would ask my mom to come up from DC to help me take care of her, even if their relationship was fraught. I needed to work, and Nana could not be alone while I did.

I slept on Nana's couch in the living room for the next several weeks, which wasn't that bad. She had extra feather beds in her closet, which I used to create a cocoon for myself, and I managed to get into a good routine. But then, one weekend morning, I headed to the kitchen sink and poured myself some water; the hot air from the radiators under the windows dried my throat, mouth, and lips.

I then padded into my grandmother's bedroom and saw her lying in her twin bed with her mouth open. Her skin was sallow, her cheeks hollowed out. She had lost so much weight since the cancer returned.

Glancing at her side table, I saw one of her German magazines, her eyeglasses, and the glass of water for her dentures. I also noticed a blue box with silver wrapping coming out of it, and as I inched closer, I saw that it was a laxative. For the past three weeks, Nana had been asking me to find sleeping pills she could take to not wake up. She wanted to end her life. The daily routine of having to be helped with getting up, eating her oatmeal and soup, and drinking her coffee had made her depressed.

I had explained that I could not help her die by suicide and that if I did, I would be arrested for assisting in a murder. I had tried to get her into a hospice, but the waiting lists were long, and I knew she would probably be dead by the time they called us. So the laxative was her solution. As a former nurse, she knew that people could die from dehydration. Since she couldn't get the sleeping pills, she would kill herself this way.

I pretended not to see the box and sat down softly on the side of her bed, placing my hand on her arm.

"Nana, it's time to get up. It's your birthday today."

Since I had come back to New York to take care of her, we spoke only German. A doctor had told me that if you learn a language after the age of ten or eleven, it is stored in a different part of the brain and is easier to lose. Since she had not learned English until she was sixteen, her English had been faltering.

She slowly opened her sky-blue eyes, revealing the same hint of curiosity that she'd shown for so many years.

"Engelein, it is you."

Nana slowly tried to rise, shifting her weight to one arm to push herself up. I tried to help her, but she insisted on doing it by herself. I pulled her nightgown off and saw her one sagging breast and the scar from the surgery so many years ago. The doctors hadn't thought she would live past seventy, but here she was ten years later.

After dressing her in a lovely blue dress I'd found in the closet, I offered to feed her, but she refused. She slowly placed little spoonfuls of oatmeal in her mouth.

"You know," she said, "the business is worth something. Connie wants it. Sell it to her for twenty thousand dollars. She can take over the lease, and you can give her all the furniture and my client list. I have nothing there I want you to have. All that is valuable is either here or in Jersey."

"Nana, we don't have to talk about this." Tears swelled in my eyes.

"Engelein, it won't be long now. You will know what to do." She had confidence in me, but all this responsibility was overwhelming. I was still in my twenties, running her business, going to work, and taking care of her at night. Now I had to also talk to her lawyer about how to liquidate her assets when she died. I needed help.

By now, my mom had come to New York to help me. At first, she had refused. Then she asked me to pay for her train ticket, which I reluctantly did. She stayed with her friend Gloria and relieved me during the weekdays. I'm not sure what she did with Nana, but she organized the apartment, folding clothes and sifting through the stuff that my grandmother had collected. On the weekend, it was all up to me. I felt very alone in this task of watching my grandmother die.

But on this day, we were here to celebrate.

"Happy eightieth birthday, Nana," I said, as I settled her at the dining room table and planted a kiss on her cheek. "Today is a big day! I am going to bake you a cake, and some people are coming over to celebrate with you."

Nana looked at me with her beautiful eyes. "Oh, Robin, you don't have to do that. I am not sure I have the strength to see people." She sighed.

I assured her that no one would stay too long. I offered to bring her cards, but she didn't want them.

"How about I turn on the TV and find something for you to watch while I clean up and get the cake ready?" I surfed the channels and landed on some Tom and Jerry cartoons. That was the channel she wanted.

In the kitchen, I dialed the number for Gloria's apartment to talk to my mom.

I tried to be upbeat when she got on the phone. I was so frustrated with her, but I needed her help and thought she should be with her own mother today. "When can you come over to celebrate her birthday?" I asked.

"I am so tired, Schatzi. I think you can handle the celebration yourself."

Anger flushed my cheeks. "No, damn it. It's her eightieth birthday, and she's not going to have another one. She'll probably be dead by next week. I *need* you to come over and celebrate your mother's birthday with me. And it would be great if you would bring Dad too so we can celebrate like a real family." I never gave up on my desire for a close-knit family.

"Did you forget what your beloved grandmother did to me and Dad? It is unforgivable. Why should I come over? I have been helping you every day when you go to work. I am tired. She doesn't deserve my love."

"I don't care," I said. "She's your mother. I know she did awful things. She is a little crazy, but if you took the time to find out what happened to her as a young woman, you would know why she is this way. So have a little compassion. If you won't do it for her, do it for me. Pretend."

"Fine. I will come over, but I am not bringing Dad. I will not subject him to her." I imagined the stern look on her face.

I told her to get there by noon and look happy. I was so tired of her wallowing in her grievances instead of having compassion for her mother. She wouldn't have existed without Nana.

I lied to my grandmother about the phone call and said it was my boyfriend. She asked me to tell her more about him.

"I know you always want me to find a man with a house. And, no, he doesn't have a house. He lives with me, and we rent an apartment together. He likes poetry and politics, like me. He's also a voracious reader and knows so much history. We have long conversations about the Kennedys, the Revolutionary War, and music."

"Politics, what does that mean?" Nana asked. "Are you going to run for president? You are so smart and beautiful; you could do it!"

I laughed. "No, Nana, we work behind the scenes trying to help other people get elected. He's a good man. Don't worry. He is kind, passionate, and funny. You would like him." In reality, my relationship with Toohey was not great, but I was not going to tell her that.

"I want to know you have someone good before I die. I know your mother has her man, finally. You must have a man in your life; otherwise, you might have to do some uncomfortable things to get by. Look at me. I regret I never got married again. Promise me you will get married and have children?"

"Yes, Nana, I will," I said.

She told me I was a good girl and reminded me that my astrological chart said I would have been a good lawyer. Then she said she was getting tired and asked me to bring her back to bed. I eased her onto the mattress and helped her lie down, and then she pulled me down close to her face.

"Engelein, the pain—the pain is too much. Can't you give me something so I can sleep and not get up? I have seen my eightieth birthday, but enough is enough," she pleaded.

"Oh, Nana," I said, fighting back tears. "I wish I could give you something, but I can't. I would get arrested. I promise it won't be long. Just sleep and get your energy so you can eat the birthday cake I am making for you, and I will figure something out."

"*Danke*, Engel," she said. "You know what to do. Your mother could not do it."

"Sh, sh, go to sleep now," I said before leaving her bedroom.

Tears streamed down my face in the kitchen, and I wished I at least had some sinsemilla marijuana from Santa Cruz to ease her pain. I had begun to mix the ingredients for chocolate cake when my friend Valerie arrived with flowers. She helped me make the living room more festive with candles for mood lighting and a paper Happy Birthday sign on the wall. My mom arrived soon after.

In the late afternoon, we woke up Nana and placed her in the comfortable chair in the living room. We cracked open a bottle of champagne, made a few toasts, and sang "Happy Birthday."

By the next morning, Nana felt worse. Mom came over to help me get her down the stairs. I hailed a taxi, and Mom and I gently positioned her in the cab while the cars behind our taxi were honking because we were taking too long. Lenox Hill didn't accept terminal patients, but I told the emergency room staff she was dehydrated and hallucinating. They helped her into a wheelchair. Nana knew I had a train to catch the same day; I was helping with a pitch to a new client and needed to get back to DC. Mom said she would stay in the hospital with Nana.

I crouched down to look up into my Nana's eyes. She took my hand and whispered.

"I love you, Engelein. You will always be my special child."

I choked back tears and gave her a hug.

"Go now; do your job in DC." I blew her another kiss and looked at my mom for direction.

"Go," my mom said. "I'll take care of things."

I hailed a cab outside to go directly to Penn Station. I sobbed, my stomach ached, and I found it hard to breathe. I knew I would never see my grandmother alive again. It felt like one of the connections I had to earth was evaporating, and I would be even more alone than I already was.

FRAGMENTS OF GOLD

1991

Nana died the next night in the hospital, alone. Mom said she came back the next day and her bed was empty. The hospital hadn't even bothered to call her. Nothing. Mom decided to cremate her, even though Nana was Catholic. I was so angry, and I asked why.

"Well, that's what I want for me."

I had to explain to her that Nana would not be able to be buried next to Grandpa because Catholic cemeteries don't accept ashes. I then called Dad and told him he needed to use his diplomatic skills to fix this. I told him that I had taken care of Nana's bills, run her business, and nursed her, and I wanted her buried next to my grandpa. I didn't care how they did it, but I wanted his gravestone to also have her name engraved on it, and I wanted to bury her ashes there, next to him. I was tired of doing everything. I made it clear that this was the one thing they had to take care of for my grandmother and me.

Mom, Dad, Valerie, Toohey, and I had a family breakfast at Gloria's house, where we all told stories about my grandma. Valerie wrote a poem commemorating her free spirit and desire to live life to the fullest.

> *She sang*
> *I love Paris in the Springtime*
> *I love Paris in the Fall*
> *She said*
> *I do not understand you*

But I love you, after all
She did
What she wanted to do,
Whether or not
It interested you.
As anyone who saw those eyes
Must now be changed,
By one so full of life, surprise.

Mom, Dad, and I took a cab to the cemetery in Queens. Dad had worked out the logistical problem, and we buried her ashes under my grandpa's headstone. In later weeks, Dad had the gravestone engraved with Nana's name. I was happy that she was back with her husband.

Working with Nana's lawyer, I sold the Studio to Connie. I paid all Nana's bills, gave notice on her apartment, got everything out of there, and then went to New Jersey to pack up her stuff. Mom came out and helped me. I sold the mobile home and the car, gave Mom the mink coats, and donated most of Nana's other clothes to charity. I saved her nursing diploma, photos, and old passports, as well as the few pieces of jewelry that reminded me of her: her wedding ring, which was too large for me; her onyx pinky ring; and her gold Tiffany charm bracelet. She had worn the bracelet to my eighth-grade graduation and had to take it off at one point because the charms made so much noise in church. Now I felt I could channel her when I wore it around my wrist.

There was no one else like her. I have my image of her cemented in my mind: her gray hair, dyed blond like her original, natural light-blond color; her big smile; her coral-orange lipstick; and the matching orange headband with false hair attached with bobby pins. Her black dress with the leopard push-up bra, which could just barely be seen. Her strong ankles and low-heeled black shoes. Her huge purse, open with dollar bills stuffed in the pockets. Her clip-on gold earrings. I still see her standing on Seventy-Ninth Street waiting for me as I run toward her with the biggest smile. I still feel how she smothered me with her arms and picked me up in her bear hug. She was so strong, and that is how I want to remember her, not as the shrunken eighty-pound woman on her deathbed. I always felt the love she had for me. No one has ever loved me like that. I missed her then and always will.

NEXT STEPS

1991–1992

Losing my grandmother left me untethered. Her unconditional love grounded me, and suddenly it was gone. It didn't help that my relationship with Toohey was growing more unsustainable. I needed to find a new path.

My first step was to move to a housing development of postwar apartments in Shirlington, Virginia, and I didn't ask Toohey to come with me, although I did bring Sid, whom I had adopted as a kitten when I worked at the DNC. He was the cutest gray cat, with white markings. Now that I was no longer sleeping with Toohey every night, Sid became my bed partner.

My second step was to apply for graduate school. With references from Chairman Ron Brown and an advisor to Dick Gephardt, I was accepted to the Johns Hopkins School of Advanced International Studies. They had a two-year program that would allow me to spend one year studying in DC and the other anywhere in the world. I wanted to go back to Eastern Europe and study how brown-coal plants could be converted to produce cleaner energy to help improve the health of citizens and decrease air pollution.

When the financial aid office informed me that because I worked at a PR firm, I was not a candidate for any loans or grants through them, I panicked. The tuition alone was forty thousand dollars, and I would have needed money for living expenses. I could have taken out loans from traditional banks, but having that much debt in my twenties overwhelmed me. It is still one of my greatest regrets that I didn't take the chance and go to graduate school. As I got older, I missed so many great opportunities because I didn't have that credential. Luckily, my life experience and ability to take risks still gave me many options.

My third step was to join Al-Anon, the program for the loved ones of alcoholics. I was mad at myself for being so weak in the face of Toohey's relationship with alcohol, not understanding how much it drained me, and I kept wondering, *If I'd had a father in my life, would he have guided me? Or better yet, if I had grown up with a mother and a father, would I have seen what relationships are supposed to look like?* I felt so alone, and the Al-Anon meetings saved me. I learned how substance abusers make you feel like you're crazy. They taught me I was not alone; relationships can fall into an unhealthy pattern, and I could get out.

In January 1992—one year after Nana died—I was asked to help a nonprofit group that wanted to have an impact at the Earth Summit in Brazil. Robin Smith and I traveled to Rio de Janeiro and visited the favelas—the poor districts—helping spread the message about the connections between poverty, pollution, and environmental degradation. Often, waste dumps and water treatment plants were located near poor neighborhoods because they had no political power. It was great to travel again and gain perspective.

When I returned after three weeks, Toohey showed up at my house and asked me to marry him. He knew I wanted to get married and start a family of my own, but going to Al-Anon and leaving the country had given me greater perspective. I said no.

A few days later, a Gephardt colleague asked if I would come to Little Rock, Arkansas, to help train young people that wanted to do advance work for Governor Bill Clinton, who was running for president. I said yes, and once I boarded the plane to Atlanta, I already felt different. A weight had been lifted now that my destructive relationship was over. I closed my eyes and envisioned the type of man I wanted in my life: tall, blue eyes, strong, healthy, smart, funny, dedicated to a cause or mission, well traveled, and bilingual. And not a businessman. And then, as I waited for all the passengers to take their seats, the most handsome man, with sandy-blond hair, blue eyes, a denim shirt, and a leather bracelet, sat next to me. It was like my vision had been realized in a few seconds. Nana had always told me I had the "sight," but this was unbelievable.

I don't remember how we started talking, but we didn't stop until we landed in Atlanta. He asked how long I had before my flight to Little Rock, and I said two hours. He was also on a layover bound for Los Angeles, so we found a restaurant at the airport and kept talking. He was a wildlife biologist with a specialty in the mating patterns of lions, and he spent most of his time in Africa but was going home to California to see his family. We exchanged numbers, and he told me he would be in DC on Valentine's Day. He asked if he could take me out on a date. I said yes.

Little Rock was small and very southern, and our advance training was like a college reunion. All the people I saw were campaign veterans with whom I'd worked in 1988. Now, Clinton had just won the New Hampshire primary, and his team needed more advance people on the road. A team of us taught the basics of advance work to a new crop of young political staff: about airport arrivals and departures, hotel overnights, crowd building, stage backdrops, what types of vendors you needed to establish relationships with, how to run phone banks in the press filing room, the political protocol for speaker lineups, how to hold countdown meetings, and how to work with the Secret Service. I loved having a skill that could be transferred to others.

I knew almost all the trainers, except for one guy. John Hoyt was handsome and, just like the lion-biology expert on the plane, I was drawn to him. Originally from Buffalo, New York, Hoyt now lived in Seattle. His dad was a state representative, and Hoyt had worked for Mondale in 1984 and Dukakis in 1988. We had an inexplicable connection. He made me feel grounded. I was shocked at how quickly we bonded, and when we left Little Rock, I knew I had to see him again.

The lion-biology guy came to DC for our Valentine's Day date, and we had a lovely dinner, but by that time, I had fallen for John. I told the biologist I had met someone from my political family and the timing was all wrong. He understood and gave me the greatest compliment when he was leaving.

"I know we didn't work out, but you give me hope that there is another woman who is smart, beautiful, and compassionate about the planet waiting for me." Years later, I often wondered what my life would have been like if I had picked him.

Hoyt and I were both searching for a connection. His father had just died of a heart attack, and I was still grieving about Nana. The emptiness we felt was filled with a new romance. We talked on the phone every night, even with the three-hour time difference between Seattle and DC. We made plans to see each other, and I even got him hired at my new job, where I was the vice president at Chlopak and Associates. He would help me write a grassroots training manual for the Ancient Forest Alliance, a coalition of environmental groups trying to save the ancient forests in the northwest to protect the spotted owl.

We bonded over our love of trees, fish, and making the world a better place. I visited his beautiful home in Seattle and heard my grandmother's voice in my mind. *Good girl. He has a house.* Hoyt and I had so many friends in common that we wondered how we had never met each other before. I kept getting more calls to work full time for the campaign in Little Rock, and my friend Dee Dee Myers wanted to send me out as a state press secretary. I kept turning everything down, still concerned about money and paying rent.

After the convention in late August, it was time for the general election season. I quit my job at Chlopak and went on the road to do advance work for Clinton's presidential campaign throughout all of September and October and up to election day in November. Around the same time, Hoyt had asked me to come live with him, so I moved everything to Seattle. We planned to go on a long trip to Asia after the campaign was over.

Like so many of our friends, we watched the election night returns on TV and popped a bottle of champagne when it was clear that Clinton had won. All the hard work on the campaign trail had finally come to fruition to elect a Democratic president. As soon as the election was over, some of our friends went straight to work on the transition team to help fill the political jobs in the new administration. Most of my friends sent their resumes to the Presidential Personnel Office. I really didn't understand that process, and no one explained it to me. I came to find out later that there was a publication called the "Plum

Book" that listed all the political appointee jobs at the White House and different administrative agencies.

But at that time, my career mattered less to me. I was in love and wanted to make a life in Seattle with Hoyt. I didn't want to be in DC any longer. I wanted to get married and break the cycle of family dysfunction.

Later in November, Hoyt and I did go to Asia, starting first in Bangkok and then taking a train to southern Thailand, to the Krabi province. We went to the beach every day, swam, snorkeled, and found a hotel that was a dollar a night, where we took showers in the afternoon when the water tanks had been warmed by the sun. It was glorious to read, laugh, and have no obligations. From there, we took a two-week trip to Nepal, where we climbed the Annapurna Circuit, and then went north to the Golden Triangle in Thailand. We'd loved Krabi so much that we returned to spend our last week there before leaving to go back to Seattle.

By Christmas Eve, I had fallen deeper in love. Hoyt took me to a little island where we were all alone. He had arranged with our hotel a picnic basket of food and provisions for the night. As we sat on our blanket on the beach, he handed me a coconut wrapped in grass string and told me it was my present. I opened it and found a little blue box nestled in bougainvillea petals. As I took out the box, Hoyt got on one knee and asked me to marry him.

I sprang into his arms and said yes. He placed the emerald-cut diamond engagement ring on my finger and explained that it had belonged to his maternal grandmother.

Once we got back to the mainland, we called his mom and my mom and told them we were getting married. I was finally getting my wish.

But there were a few surprises. One night after Christmas, I was lying in bed and felt a sudden sting in the base of my palm. I was convinced I had been stung by a snake and could feel the venom traveling up my arm. The last thing I remember is crying out to Hoyt, "I got bit by a snake."

Then I fell unconscious.

I don't know how long I was out, but when I woke up, Hoyt was sitting on me and holding both my arms down on the bed asking me questions. "What's your mother's name? Where were you born? Who won the '92 election?"

I answered correctly.

"Oh my God, you're back," he said.

Luckily, our hostel neighbors were Swiss doctors and figured out I had had an epileptic seizure. They suspected it was caused by the malaria medicine I was taking, Lariam. The European Union had issued many warnings about the drug, but we both had been given it as a precaution before we left Seattle. When I saw the concern on Hoyt's face, I was so happy I finally had a man who would take care of me and share the burden of life with me. But I also noticed he was developing a black eye.

"You punched me," he said.

He had been trying to hold me down during my seizure, and apparently, I didn't like that. Later in our relationship, I wanted to give him another black eye based on his behavior, but I never did.

SEIZURES, A WEDDING,
AND A PYRAMID

1992–1997

When we got back to Seattle, Hoyt was determined to find out what was wrong with me. We went to a neurologist and other specialists, but every time I went to another doctor, I had to fill out another health-history medical form, which reminded me of the hole in my heart. I would draw a diagonal line and write "NA" on one side of the paper—Not Applicable—because I knew nothing about my biological father.

I tried to forget about the seizures because I wanted to look forward and focus on getting married, but my anger about my missing medical history escalated. I wished my mom had told me more. Perhaps my father had epilepsy, perhaps another disease. I needed to keep myself healthy; I was getting married, and I desperately wanted children. *But what if something terrible is lurking in my DNA and I don't know?*

My dependence on Hoyt increased because I felt so alone. I took test after test, and one day, when there still had been no conclusive evidence, he proposed another possible solution.

"We have to contact your biological father."

I had told him about my previous attempt to get in touch with Ray Hulz, and Hoyt said that one of his high school classmates was a private detective.

"I'll call her. She can find him."

It was amazing what she found in thirty-six hours using credit card data. Ray Hulz was still living in Valencia, California. After she got us the address, I sent a letter to him asking only for his medical history and enclosed a picture of Hoyt and me. The detective suggested we send the letter via registered mail so we could be sure it would get to him.

While we waited to hear back, we planned our wedding in Buffalo. Since I had no family left in New York, we thought it would be fun to have the wedding in John's hometown, where he had a large family. We invited our friends and his extended family and wrote our own vows. We even designed an incredible invitation based on postcards I had collected—one from New York, one from Buffalo, and a third from Seattle. I bought my wedding dress at a secondhand store, and we booked a fantastic band for the party. Both my mom and stepdad walked me down the aisle. It was another time that not knowing my biological father stung. *Wouldn't he want to be at my wedding? Meet my husband?* I had to push it all away.

We built our life in Seattle. I loved the city and the beauty I could see every day, including the view of Mount Rainier when it wasn't too cloudy, and the multiple islands in the water as I looked west. Plus, everyone was active all the time—biking, hiking, kayaking, snowshoeing, skiing. Seattle had a lifestyle that matched my interests.

Hoyt and I started a public affairs firm, which we named Pyramid Communications. We hired young people who we could train and who didn't need high salaries, and we didn't pay ourselves for months as we grew the business. We wanted to prove that we could create a firm centered on helping foundations, nonprofits, environmental groups, Alaskan Native corporations, and eclectic causes—like vetting funding proposals for the members of the band Pearl Jam, who were very civic minded and with whom Hoyt had worked closely before. It was fun to be in the middle of so many progressive projects. I relished the idea of a mission-driven for-profit firm, unlike the PR firms I had worked with back in DC. We could make a difference in the world, make money, and work with our friends all at the same time. It was a perfect combination for me.

Unfortunately, as we built the business, I had more seizures. I normally had them when I was asleep, usually around 2:00 or 3:00 a.m. If Hoyt wasn't there, I would wake up to find Sid on my chest, purring loudly to make sure I would wake up. One time, I had a seizure on a plane from DC to Seattle, and they had to divert to Minneapolis. I could feel it coming on: the stinging in my hand, once again working its way up my arm. I knew I had about thirty seconds before I would become unconscious, so I told the woman sitting next to me that I was about to have a seizure. Everything went black seconds later. It was a relief to wake up in a hospital, despite feeling exhausted.

I dreaded every seizure, and whenever I began to lose consciousness, I always wondered if I would ever wake up or if this was going to be the seizure that killed me. It was always a fear lurking in my life. The doctors still had no answer as to the cause, but they did tell me that it would be prudent if I never got pregnant. In fact, there was a law in Washington State saying epileptics should not get pregnant. If I had a seizure while pregnant, the baby could lose access to oxygen and have brain damage. And the stress of childbirth could force me to have a seizure during delivery. There was no way to enforce that law, but the whole situation crushed me. In addition, I was on a very strong drug called Dilantin, and the neurologists advised me to be strict about birth control because it could cause birth defects.

Hoyt came from a family of four kids. I saw how close they all were, and I'd been wanting what he had for so many years now. I loved his brother and sisters, and we met up every year for an adventure. I wanted the same for my own children too. But my vision of a husband and two or three kids was falling apart. John said it didn't matter and that he really didn't want kids. But we had talked about kids before, and he knew I wanted to be a mom. I think he said that so I wouldn't feel pressured or bad if I couldn't carry a pregnancy.

However, I was successful in creating more family around me in a different way. When I got engaged, I had reached out and found my stepbrother, Little Lars, whom by now I just called Lars. We had not spoken in years, probably since our family trip after high school, but I was thrilled to learn he was living in Brooklyn with his girlfriend, Nan. Hoyt and I went to see them one time when we were back visiting, and he told us that he and Nan, who were also engaged to be married, would be moving to Seattle soon. My heart soared, imagining how he and I would be in the same city after so many years of not being in touch.

When we received our invitation to their wedding in Seattle, I immediately called my mom with the good news and asked when she and Dad were coming. They told me that they weren't coming to the wedding because Lars's ex-wife, Jeannette, would be there. I was livid. *How can my stepdad not go to his own son's wedding?* In my mind, it was childish and ridiculous to worry about his ex-wife. Lots of people get divorced and figure out a way to both be there for their children. But my parents could not deal with conflict or put the needs of their children ahead of their own. They asked me to "represent" the family. I refused and said Hoyt and I would be representing ourselves and no one else.

Lars was crushed but not surprised. He hardly had a relationship with his father, and I decided to focus on rebuilding my relationship with him and developing a newfound friendship with Nan, who became a true sister. We spent many weekends at their fabulous home on Bainbridge Island. Despite my seizures, I felt content that I had married the love of my life and that I had a stepbrother and sister-in-law close by. Life was good.

In 1996, I was approached by the local Rotary in Seattle to participate in the Rotary Business Exchange, a program where four business owners from Seattle would spend a month visiting other businesses and Rotary groups in the Dominican Republic as a cultural exchange, and four Dominicans would come to Seattle to do the same. I leaped at the chance to improve my Spanish and leave our firm for a little while.

Hoyt and I had been fighting about how to grow the business. He wanted more clients, which meant hiring more people, and I argued that we could make just as much money with the staff we already had and fewer clients. At the same time, my epilepsy drug was affecting me. It was like being on an antidepressant; my mood and personality became flat, with no ups and downs, and I lost my sense of humor. I also had to take liver-count blood tests every month, which each time reminded me that I was unhealthy.

I fretted about leaving Hoyt for a full month, but he told me not to worry and have fun. My group was an interesting mix of businesspeople, and the Dominican Rotarians took care of us and took us all over the country. Of course, we also had to dance the merengue after every Rotary meeting. I don't think they expected women on the trip.

On April 3, 1996, two days before my birthday, my old boss Carl

Wagner called me in the Dominican Republic. I don't know how he found me at my hotel; John must have helped him. When the hotel told me I had a phone call, I knew something was wrong. I took the phone and placed it to my ear.

"Robin, it's Carl Wagner," he said.

I asked why he was calling me in the middle of nowhere.

"I have some very bad news. There was a plane crash in Croatia, and Ron died along with many others."

Tears welled up in my eyes. My throat constricted. I couldn't speak. While I struggled for words, Carl said that Ron Brown, as secretary of commerce, had gone to Croatia with other government officials and business executives to identify investment opportunities in the war-torn area that was formerly part of Yugoslavia. I remembered how his staffer Bill Morton—whom I had known on the Jackson campaign— had always asked me to come do advance work overseas for Ron. I kept telling him that one day I would. Now, I never would. Ron was dead. And I was devastated.

Carl told me about the funeral, but I ended up not going, feeling obligated to finish the Rotary program. In hindsight, I wished I had left the Dominican Republic, gone to the funeral, and returned early to Seattle, because finishing the Rotary program ignited the destruction of my marriage.

When I returned, I sensed something was different with Hoyt, but I couldn't place it. He welcomed me home, but he seemed secretive and spent more time at work. We had been together for four years by then and married for three. Our marriage had been full of adventure, travel, art, building a business and a fabulous home, and lots of sports: skiing, hiking, and kayaking. I'd thought I had the perfect marriage, but I was wrong.

Once a year, our Pyramid office had a fun event. In 1996, we decided to have a picnic on the beach. After we all ate barbecue, Hoyt announced that he had some gifts for each of the staffers. As he handed them out, another young staffer named Lisa commented on how they had bought the gifts together. It was at that moment I knew they were having an affair. I had been the one who initially convinced Hoyt to hire her, to build the ranks of smart women in our firm, and now I found myself running to the public bathroom, sobbing. Later, as we drove back home, I confronted him.

"Are you having an affair with Lisa?"

He denied it. After that, life at home became very tense, and I was suspicious of every move. He had a client he visited in Alaska, and he took Lisa with him. I sank deeper into depression, realizing that he no longer loved me, although I was still in love with him and the life we had built together.

I knew I had to leave our firm, and thankfully it was time for another presidential election season. While my marriage was falling apart, I became the Washington State director for the Clinton-Gore reelection team, a job lasting from late August to November. The campaign sent two young men to work with me, and we created a kick-ass team despite my sadness. Even though Hoyt and I still lived together, my long hours at work gave him ample opportunity to continue his affair without me knowing the details. I poured my energy into work and ignored my personal life. I knew I no longer had control.

I decided to attempt to keep my marriage together one more time. After the successful presidential election in November, Hoyt and I went on holiday to Hawaii. We stayed in a beautiful home on Kauai and did what we normally did on vacations: we swam, went biking, explored, played tennis, and slept together. I tried to show him how much we had in common and what a good team we were. But he wasn't convinced. I even forgave him for his infidelity, but he had made up his mind. He did not want to be married to me anymore.

When we returned to Seattle in early December, we slept in different rooms. Hoyt's sister Cary was getting married in Buffalo, so we agreed to keep the dissolution of our marriage quiet until after the wedding. When I arrived in Buffalo to help prepare for the wedding, my sadness must have seeped out of my skin. I was staying at Hoyt's stepmother's home; Susan knew instantly that something was amiss and then proceeded to tell me how his father had cheated on her, how Hoyt's uncle had been unfaithful to his wife, and how his brother also had a wandering eye. It was a Hoyt tradition. We went through the motions of the wedding while my heart broke.

By January 1997, I had become a madwoman, looking for evidence in phone bills and pants pockets to confirm his affair with Lisa. I was unsuccessful, but it was still clear we had to go our separate ways. We agreed that he would move out for a month, and then

I would move out for a month, to give each of us time to figure out a long-term plan.

Once he left, I hardly showered. I cried and used so many tissues that empty Kleenex boxes littered the floor. The next month, I moved in with some friends who were very kind to me. Another friend, Teresa, called me every day and asked me how I was and if I had gotten out of my pajamas.

The loss was monumental, and yet again I was worried about my future. Not only was I losing my husband, but I was losing my source of income and my home because Hoyt said I could no longer work at Pyramid. In addition, I lost my sisters-in-law and brother-in-law, as well as my mother-in-law, who also lived in Seattle. Hoyt had told his friends and family that they were either for him or me but not both, further compounding my isolation.

HEADS OF STATE

1997

I left Seattle and dragged myself to Denver for the next three months. I also hired my dear friend Robin Smith to be my deputy there and live with me. We would be preparing for seven heads of state to meet with President Clinton; the pace was fast and the intensity was great. But the work was familiar. Ever since President Clinton had been elected, I had been on overseas trips advancing the president about twice a year while I worked at Pyramid.

And being in Denver with my professional colleagues and friends was comforting. I channeled all my pain and energy into my work and was even able to be fun and entertaining when the Italian, English, French, German, Canadian, Japanese, and Russian delegations came to town for site walk-throughs and negotiations.

My favorite moment was when Robin Smith, our colleague Eileen Parise, and I decided we needed to add some female energy to the summit, right before the heads of state were about to meet.

We entered the newly constructed beige-and-redbrick Denver Public Library in silence, nodding hello to the Secret Service agents posted at the entry. It was already 9:00 p.m., and most staff had left the building. The agents took a glance at the special pins affixed to our jackets, which meant we were cleared to advance into the building. With eight heads of state, including President Clinton, expected at the building in less than twelve hours, the entirety of the library had been inspected for bombs, hidden weapons, and any other type of threat. The magnetometers were already set up to screen all the staff and press that would arrive the next morning.

I recognized an agent near the magnetometer and addressed him.

"Hey, Charlie, everything all set for tomorrow?"

"Of course; now, we are depending on you to keep all the press under control," he retorted.

My title at the summit was director of media operations. We had already credentialed about one thousand print, radio, and TV journalists from Canada, France, Germany, Italy, Japan, the United Kingdom, the United States, and the newly invited guest, Russia. My team had set up press operations—including press risers, electric power, telephone lines, and long tables to file stories—at all the locations where we planned to have events. Even though the summit was only for three days, I had been working with the entire team in Denver since February, ensuring that everything was set up properly and that we would be gracious and well-prepared hosts for the representatives of the seven visiting nations.

I set my walkie-talkie on the security conveyor belt to be scanned, along with my pager and cell phone.

"Charlie, you know I can handle the media. You've seen me do it so many times before."

He nodded and then asked why we were there so late. I assured him we just wanted to make sure the room was all set so the press could do their photo ops before the meeting started. The three of us then sauntered down the hall, our heels clicking in a loud echo.

We found another set of agents at the door to the central room that would host the meeting for the heads of state in the morning.

"Good evening, gentlemen. We're just here to check on a few things in the room. We won't be long," I said. They opened the doors for us.

We stepped slowly into the room and absorbed the history that was going to be made the next day. Steel nameplates were already placed on the round birchwood-inlaid table, which had been specially designed and built for this meeting. The walls were painted white, with wood columns every four feet. From the ceiling, a large remote camera from the Reuters News Agency dangled below a glass atrium framed in bronze-colored metal.

Smith walked around the table, calling out the names of the leaders while I plugged in the boom box.

"President Bill Clinton," she yelled out to us. She had already taken off her high-heeled shoes. "Prime Minister Tony Blair."

"President Jacques Chirac," Parise said in a singsong French accent.

We all circled the table and touched the wood lightly, ensuring we would not make any smudges or leave fingerprints.

Not to be outdone, Smith turned on her French accent and announced Prime Minister Jean Chrétien of Canada, and I used my exaggerated German inflection to announce Herr Chancellor Helmut Kohl. Together, we named Prime Minister Romano Prodi and Prime Minister Ryutaro Hashimoto.

"And who can forget the latest addition?" I said. "Making it a summit of eight: President Boris Yeltsin!"

We all laughed, and then Parise and I slipped off our high-heeled pumps as Smith had done.

"Well, ladies, what do we think is missing at this table?" I grinned, waiting for their answer.

"Female energy and power!" they declared in unison.

I pushed the play button on the boom box. We heard the familiar guitar riff. Meredith Brooks.

"Ready?" I asked. We climbed onto the special tabletop and planted our feet, ready to play air guitar to the refrain of our anthem, "Bitch."

I knew every word to that song, having played it every day in our Denver office, the "Summit of the Eight" headquarters. It had been set up in a converted and condemned department of motor vehicles building, and at the end of every day, around seven or eight, the women from the summit team would come into my office and declare it was time for some female energy. I would press play and lead a conga line, holding the boom box, as we formed a human train and danced into the other offices to invite the other women to join us in our daily ritual. I had started the ritual to relieve the tension from our twelve-to-fourteen-hour days and from my painful separation from my husband. But it became a women-bonding ritual in the sea of powerful men we were representing. We wanted to be seen, even if we weren't represented at the very high levels of government.

Our boss, Harold Ickes, would always shake his head and laugh as we passed him in the hallway. He was a tough boss and expected excellence, but he supported us and was willing to promote women. If we needed to dance to let off steam after a long day of good work, that was fine with him.

Now, we belted out the lyrics in the library about all our roles and just wanting to be accepted for who we were.

I felt an enormous sense of kinship with Smith and Parise as the song played. Women had come a long way since the days when my mom and her friends had to entertain heads of state; at least now we were more integrally involved in arrangements made for visiting dignitaries. But I had a hopeful longing that one day in my lifetime, our role would be much more evolved, and the heads of state at a G8 would actually be primarily women. If that were the case, the leaders would focus on education, jobs, health care, and the economy—and, hopefully, not constant war.

When the song ended, we held each other's hands to climb down to the floor. I noticed a smudge mark on one section of the table, which I buffed with my sleeve.

As we left, the Secret Service agents smiled at us, shaking their heads.

"Good night, Charlie," I said as we passed the magnetometer. "See you tomorrow."

Poor Charlie never knew about our clandestine activities, carried out right behind the backs of the agents that were supposed to be watching for secrets.

Once the successful summit was over in June, and we knew President Clinton was happy, a group of us rented a red Sebring convertible and headed for the Pacific Northwest. Our drive took us through Steamboat Springs, Jackson Hole, and Yellowstone National Park, around Flathead Lake, and past Sun Valley en route to Seattle. We spent our nights cooking amazing Italian meals and conducting readings of Rilke and *The Art of War*. But as we neared Seattle, I secretly began to hope that Hoyt missed me so much while I was gone that he would want to get back together.

I was wrong. He went so far as to tell me that I couldn't live in the house—the house that we had bought together and decorated inside and out. I told him that I had nowhere else to go and I would stay in the guest bedroom. He insisted I leave, but I stayed. I was too desperate and exhausted to look for another place to live, and I felt that the house was rightfully mine too. I was worried that if I left, he would just take it and not give me my fair share of it.

A pile of mail awaited me, and one letter stood out from the rest. It was an airmail letter with black writing in a European hand. I knew it was a death notice because my grandmother and mom had received similar letters from Germany when I was young. But the return address wasn't from Germany. It was from Valencia, California. I ripped open the envelope.

> *Dear Robin,*
>
> *I wanted to let you know that Ray passed in May from prostate cancer. I know you thought he was your father, and I don't know if that is true or not, but if you want to come visit and talk, I would welcome you into my home.*
>
> *All the best,*
> *Beate*

I immediately booked a flight to LA.

STILL SEARCHING
FOR THE TRUTH

1997

Beate's house was on a quiet street in a middle-class suburb of Los Angeles filled with orange trees. I walked up the path past her well-manicured garden, inhaled a large breath, and knocked on the large green wooden door.

An older woman, immaculately dressed in khaki trousers cinched with a pink leather belt, a pale-blue Izod collared shirt, and a stylish scarf around her neck, answered the door. She held out her hand to me.

"Welcome, Robin. I am Beate. Please come in."

"Nice to meet you," I said, crossing the threshold.

Then she said something so strange. "You grew up to be such a beautiful young woman."

"You mean you have met me before?"

"Oh yes. You were about two years old, and your grandmother had sued my husband for child support. You were at the hearing."

I told her I didn't remember any of that as thoughts swirled in my mind. *This is typical—another event that my mom and grandmother fail to tell me about. Or another reason that my mom is probably angry at my grandmother for meddling in her life.*

She ushered me into the kitchen, and having noticed her accent, I asked her where she was from.

"Austria," she replied.

From that moment on, we spoke in German for the next five hours about all sorts of things and, of course, about whether or not Ray was my father. She apologized for telling me all those years ago that he wasn't.

"I had two teenagers at the time, and Ray insisted he wasn't your dad because we had done research on our own."

"What do you mean?"

"When your grandmother sued, we arranged for a blood test, and you didn't have the same type of blood as him, which is how they tested for genetic correlation back in 1965. Later, I asked Ray again if he was your father, and he said no. But he was a lying cad. He was very good-looking—tall, blond, blue eyes. He was originally from Nuremberg, Germany, and very charming. He ran off with my neighbor a year ago. So it is possible he had an affair with your mother all those years ago. He actually lived about fifty miles from you in Seattle when he died."

We kept talking and talking; she offered me coffee and *Apfel Strudel*, and the visit reminded me of being with my grandmother. She showed me pictures of Ray and her children; we all had the same color eyes and hair, but I couldn't see any other resemblance. I asked about his health history, and there was no epilepsy that Beate knew of. I wished I could have confirmed whether or not he was my dad, but there was no way to do that in 1997. Consumer DNA testing simply didn't exist.

I was looking for an explanation for my seizures, but I was also desperate for a family connection since my marriage had fallen apart. My anchor to the earth, Hoyt, had been ripped away, and I longed to replace it with my biological father's family. But I couldn't be sure. Something inside me said Ray might not be my dad. I left and never talked to Beate again. I also never told my mom that I met her.

CLOSING THE DOORS
TO THE PAST

1997

Hoyt and I worked with a mediator to divide our property before the tax year ended in 1997. He refused to acknowledge I had any role in building our public affairs firm and even denied that we had used joint money to invest in Microsoft and Starbucks stocks. I had a good lawyer, but I didn't have the energy to fight him. He kept the house in Capitol Hill overlooking Lake Union and gave me a small portion of its value, as well as a small portion of the value of the business. In hindsight, I should have fought harder for my share, but I was so sad and deflated; I just wanted it to be over.

A friend told me that a small one-bedroom apartment downstairs from hers was available. It was right on the water, and I could watch the ferries as they shuttled passengers between Seattle and the nearby islands. It was a downgrade from my beautiful craftsman house, but I didn't have the money for anything more. Her proximity was exactly the tonic I needed to heal. She was funny and had a great dog, Lucky, that got along with Sid. I cooked many dinners for her, and she watched Sid when I traveled. That Christmas we took Lucky and drove for ten days from Seattle to Santa Cruz, laughing all the time.

Traveling also helped me heal. At the beginning of 1998, I ended up back in DC for a temporary assignment working for the Organization of American States on their fiftieth anniversary. Soon after, I was in Uganda to organize a presidential visit for Clinton. I came back to

Seattle briefly before I went to Berlin to serve as lead advance for the anniversary of the Berlin airlift, which was where Clinton was going to meet Chancellor Kohl. My German language came in handy, and it was fun to be back in Europe. After the trip ended, I went to see my parents, who were back living in Vienna, and my dear friend Evi.

When I got back to Seattle, the city now felt too small. And there were too many reminders of Hoyt. I dated, but only men from my past. One man I was very passionate about was from the Gephardt campaign. We had always danced around each other, but it had never worked out. Now that we were both divorced, we met up in Seattle, Berlin, and DC and hit it off once again. Although the passion was incredible, the relationship wasn't sustainable. He even put my poems to music, but I think I was too wounded and needy to be a good partner.

I also dated a dear friend from grammar school who had found out I'd gotten divorced. He and his brother came to visit me in Seattle, and our connection was deep and strong. It was easy to be with someone who had known me since kindergarten. But he lived in Buffalo, the city of my ex-in-laws. He didn't want to move, and I couldn't make a life in a town where my former brother-in-law was the state representative.

In June, I was offered a job in DC to work for the PR firm GMMB. Frank Greer, the "G," and his wife, Stephanie, lived in Seattle and had previously consoled me when Hoyt and I broke up. One of their senior people was going on maternity leave, and they asked me to fill in for her. I jumped at the chance, and once again, I convinced Smith to go with me.

Before I left Seattle, my mom called from Vienna and asked me to do something for her.

"Robin, Dad really wants to formally adopt you."

Seriously? Why now?

"We thought, since you have so much experience with lawyers from your divorce, you could do the paperwork. We'll pay for it."

I was angry, but being the dutiful daughter, I complied. When I told my lawyer, she told me it was the strangest request she had ever gotten. Usually, it's the parents that contact the lawyer, not the other way around.

When we got closer to the court date when I would be formally adopted, my lawyer cautioned me to get my original birth certificate, because once I was adopted, my birth certificate would be changed, and Lars Lofas would be listed as my father. I would never have access to the original birth certificate again.

I was livid when I learned this and even more so that I had agreed to the process. Lars adopting me would have no effect on my life, and my mom would finally have her wish, erasing her past and putting his name on my birth certificate. I was also angry that adoption laws seemed to favor the adoptive parents and didn't recognize the rights of children to know the truth. I screamed out loud, wondering how many fathers' names on birth certificates were wrong. I asked my lawyer if "adopted father" could be written on my birth certificate, and she said no. Not wanting a confrontation with Mom, I stood by my word and completed the process. But when the judge declared I was formally adopted, I felt empty, as though my past had been erased and would never be found. I placed both birth certificates in a special binder to remind me that I did everything I could to protect the truth.

PART 5

STARTING A FAMILY

SURPRISING DEVELOPMENTS

1998–2000

I had already packed up my place, and the movers had come for all my stuff. I said goodbye to my friend and her dog and loaded Sid into a crate in my car. A drive back east was my way of saying goodbye to the Seattle chapter of my life. It would give me time to process and offer a distraction. I also loaded the car with cassettes of female vocalists like Alanis Morissette and Alana Davis to keep me company, and I set a route on Interstate 90 that would take me through Wisconsin, where I could visit Denise, and on to Buffalo to see my old school friend and former mother-in-law.

Once I made it to DC, I found a craftsman bungalow that reminded me of my former home in Seattle. It was on the canal, and in good weather I was able to bike to work in Georgetown. I reconnected with a variety of political colleagues, including friends from the G8 summit, and went to lots of Italian Embassy parties until three in the morning. I also developed a Latin/French circle of friends. This time in DC was different, in a good way.

But after about a year and a half at GMMB, I grew frustrated with not being the boss and not being compensated when I brought in new business. To the rescue came my old campaign colleague Laura Quinn, who had been working for Senator Rockefeller; she asked me if I wanted to take over the Senate Democratic Technology Committee, which was essentially the TV and radio studio for the Senate Democrats. I jumped at the chance to interview with the chiefs of staff for Rockefeller and Daschle, and when I got the job, I inherited a great staff of TV, radio, and internet experts. Our job was to get out the Democratic message every week and help senators get on local TV back in their states. We had a studio with the Capitol as the backdrop and satellite time almost every day. The staff were smart and dedicated, and they gave me the chance to manage and lead. I felt like the job matched my skills, although my wardrobe didn't fit the typical Senate attire. I wore a lot more leather.

One day, Senator Daschle's office manager, Kelly, came into my office. I was at my desk, pushing my swivel chair back and forth.

"The legislative director thinks you're cute."

"So, what am I supposed to do with that? What are we, in high school?"

"Well, I think you should meet him. His name is Eric."

I had no intention of trying to meet this person. He worked in Daschle's personal office in the Hart Building on the fifth floor, and I worked on the sixth. It would be weird for me to just show up.

Sometime in January 2000, all the Democratic Senate staff directors were asked to come to the Capitol to get a briefing on the Clinton administration's budget. I went downstairs to take the Capitol subway from the Hart Building to the Capitol, and whom do I see in my car but Eric. I had figured out who he was after Kelly had told me about him, so now I walked up to him and introduced myself.

He shook my hand and turned beet red. When we got to the Capitol, he rushed to the escalator and disappeared ahead of me. We ended up in the same briefing room, but he sat as far away from me as possible.

That afternoon, Kelly showed up in my office and gushed. "I heard you met Eric."

"Yes, I did, and he was totally scared of me," I replied.

"Well, what did you think?"

"Obviously, he's shy, and he seems a little young and too straitlaced for me. I'm not used to these Capitol Hill types. Give me a guy in a ponytail any day." Ever since visiting clubs in New York in the 1970s, I was always drawn to the guys who dressed and looked edgy. My time in Seattle sealed the deal.

Months passed, and I didn't see him. I was busy with work along with all my extracurricular activities. Smith and I had tango lessons on Tuesdays and salsa on Thursdays. I practiced soccer on Monday and Wednesday nights. I played games on Saturdays. Plus, we were in a boot camp every morning. I had done the AIDS bike ride from North Carolina to DC the year before, and I was determined to stay in shape.

Then, in early March, one of the agriculture legislative assistants invited me to Daschle's personal office for a birthday party. As I walked toward the inner office, I could hear Eric joking with colleagues.

"Why are they teasing you?" I asked him as I walked past his cubicle, just outside the senator's office.

"I'm the environmental guy, and the ag guys don't always agree with me," he said.

I stopped and noticed a beautiful picture of a mountain. "Where's that from?"

"Denali in Alaska, also known as Mount McKinley. I'm training to climb it in May." He looked down at his shoes, obviously avoiding eye contact with me.

After an awkward lull, I suggested we go in to the party. I noticed that Eric was smiling and easily talking to our Senate colleagues, which made him now more intriguing. He laughed heartily. He was clearly intelligent. What I had just learned about his mountain climbing and interest in the environment also made him attractive. As soon as I got back to my office, I sent him an email suggesting we have lunch at Union Station sometime. He agreed and we set a date.

Soon after our first date, we went biking on the canal, and he made me dinner at his house. We went out at least two nights a week, and my favorite game was to race him to my house from the Senate garage— my Volkswagen Golf against his BMW. I often won. He later told me how sexy he thought it was that I loved to drive fast.

In May, he went to Alaska to climb Denali as planned, and when he returned three weeks later, I discovered I was pregnant. I was in shock. So much of my life had centered on my professional career, and I worried about how this would impact that. I had also been longing for a family for so long, but I was worried about what Eric might say or do. I wasn't even sure how I felt about him, and I processed my inner turmoil in my journal.

The thing I have wanted more than anything, for so many years, has finally happened. Now at thirty-seven,

*with a three-month-long relationship, I am pregnant.
The challenge is I don't really know Eric. I know he
will accept me, he may eventually understand me, he
is a good egg, and he is kind and cares about me. But
are we guaranteeing a disaster for our relationship?
Developing a healthy relationship is hard enough, so
how do we do it with a child in our life?*

I thought about abortion as an option. But when I had one at eighteen, I'd told myself that if I ever got pregnant again, I would do whatever it took to raise the child.

*I own a house, I have a job, and I have great friends. I
am sure Smith would help me. I cannot imagine my life
without a child. I am nervous to tell Eric, but I have no
choice.*

I feared that I might be repeating what my mom had done—getting pregnant without being married or in love—but I was determined to have this baby. I was also scared that it could kill me. I had not had a seizure since my divorce, but the fear of seizures still loomed large in my life. When I finally told Eric, he didn't run away. He said we would figure everything out and he would help support the baby. He was kind and thoughtful, and I knew that even if I didn't marry him or have an ongoing relationship with him, he would be a good father. He would be there for the child, unlike my biological father.

MY BODY DOESN'T WORK

2000

One morning, while driving to the Senate, I suddenly felt wet and sticky between my legs. I looked down. My blue pants were stained with blood.

Instead of continuing to the Hart Building, I made a turn and headed toward my gynecologist's office. I grabbed the blue-plaid blanket my mom told me to always keep in my car, wrapped it around my waist, and hurried inside. The woman at the front desk, seeing my distress, brought me straight into an examining room. A nurse took my vitals and gave me a gown to change into as well as some towels to clean up with.

"I'll tell the doctor to give you some extra time before he comes in," she said.

Once she left, I slowly took off my pants and underwear and saw all the blood, dark red with clots. I imagined it was my baby, although there was nothing visible to confirm my suspicion. I cried as I washed out my clothing in the sink.

When the doctor came in, he said we'd do an ultrasound to see what was happening. He motioned for me to lie down on the table. After a few minutes, he pointed to the screen.

"I am so sorry, Robin. I can see that there was an enlarged sac, but nothing is in there anymore."

Tears trickled down my face as I wondered if God was punishing me for my abortion at age eighteen.

"How many weeks old do you think it was?" I asked.

"I can't say for sure. When was your last period?"

We talked more and estimated I was about eleven weeks along. He told me that the next time I became pregnant, I should come to him right away so he could discuss with me how to take care of my body since I was in my late thirties and any pregnancy would be risky for me.

I told Eric he no longer had to worry about being a dad.

I wasn't sure how to feel. *Am I sad, relieved, or heartbroken?* Probably all three, but I focused my attention back on work. That was the only way I knew to get through it.

RINSE AND REPEAT

2000

It was another presidential year, and Vice President Al Gore was the Democratic nominee against President George Bush's eldest son, George W. Bush. I still worked for the Senate, but Senator Daschle asked me to also set up a duplicate video, radio, and internet studio at the Democratic Convention in Los Angeles. For over four months, I worked part time for the Senate in DC and part time for the convention, ensuring that none of my campaign work conflicted with my work at the federal building.

I relished the distraction from my miscarriage. When I was in Los Angeles, I ran what was called the Democratic News Service (DNS), which had also existed at previous conventions. It offered an opportunity for elected officials and for candidates—presidential, Senate, House, and gubernatorial—to do satellite interviews from wherever the convention was located. But this year was different; it was the first time that we would have an internet studio and use the World Wide Web to promote our Democratic message at the convention.

I was accustomed to long hours and deadlines, but now that I was the director of the DNS, any glitch would be blamed on me, so the stress was heightened. I prided myself on being a good manager of people, but the team grew from my usual staff of eleven to about two hundred. Then there was the budget to abide by and the overall requirement that all the senators, congressional members, governors, candidates, and the Gore-Lieberman campaign were happy with our services. The convention lasted only a few days, but every day felt like a week of work. I was exhausted before it even started.

One night, when a colleague and I were walking back to our shared room at the nearby Holiday Inn, one of the security guards asked whether I was a salaried employee.

"Yes. Why?"

"Well, I saw you leave at 3:00 a.m. yesterday and come back at 6:00 a.m. today, so I know you aren't getting overtime."

And that summed up our workload at the convention.

While in Los Angeles, I was still dating Eric. He came to visit me once, and we had a fun time inline skating in Santa Monica, but he didn't seem to understand the pressure and rhythm of campaigns. When I asked him to join me on a vacation to kayak in Maine after the convention, so I could recharge, he initially said yes. But later he said no. I was no longer sure we had the same values and priorities.

Starting over in my late thirties with another serious relationship was challenging. It had been a couple of years since the divorce, but I was still wounded and worried that my ability to pick the right guy was flawed. I had thought Hoyt was perfect for me: we were both political, had the same interests, and liked to travel and have fun. We had created a beautiful home and business together. But over time I realized we didn't have the same values. I'd thought marriage was forever, and if we had bumps along the way, we would talk, go to therapy, and work it out. But that did not happen. I had also tried with Claus, but the difference in the values of our countries kept us apart. I kept thinking that if I had a dad in the same house growing up, I would be better at picking suitable men.

While Eric and I kept dating, I had long chats with my girlfriends about the qualities of a lover versus the qualities of a husband and father. I interviewed friends who had been married for a long time and asked them what they thought was the key to a great marriage. Not everyone said the same thing, but if there was a consistent message, it was about having respect for the other person and a good underlying friendship. Passion would fluctuate, but friendship lasted forever.

With this advice, I started evaluating Eric as husband material. I wanted someone who would be loyal, kind, loving, and able to work through any challenges along the way. I wanted someone who would commit to a family and consider adoption since the risks of epilepsy still plagued my mind.

After the convention, I received an odd and exciting voicemail.

"Robin Schepper, you have won a free trip to Sydney, Australia." The message ended with a phone number to call.

I knew that voice. It was Mark Steitz, with whom I'd worked for Ron Brown and in 1997 on the bid for the Athens Summer Olympics. I was intrigued and called back. He didn't answer, so I left a message.

"I am not saying yes, but talk to me."

When we finally connected, he told me that the International Olympic Committee (IOC) had threatened to move the 2004 Summer Olympic Games because the Greek National Olympic Committee had done nothing in preparation during the three years since Athens had won the bid. I remembered how hard we had worked to secure Athens as the winner, and it came as no surprise that the men leading the bid committee were not as organized as my old boss, Gianna, had been. He also said that the IOC demanded that Gianna come back to lead the organizing committee, and she had said yes. She wanted the old team back together, which meant us. I jumped at the chance for an adventure.

Within two weeks of getting home from the convention, I quit my job in the Senate and took a twenty-four-hour flight to Sydney. Luckily, my housemate agreed to take care of my beautiful home and Sid.

The team from 1997 was there, and although our job was seemingly simple, we had our work cut out for us: staff Gianna's office, build relationships with the Olympic media, and learn as much from the Sydney Olympics as possible so we could replicate it in Athens.

I oversaw media relations, scheduling interviews for Gianna and strengthening the relationships with the Olympic press corps. Many of the reporters that had been at the G8 summit in Denver were in Sydney, and my previous relationships with them made it easier to build a network. The mornings were filled with clipping newspapers and arranging, and then staffing, interviews. The afternoons were spent soliciting advice from journalists at the main press center. We learned a lot, but I was tired, still not quite having recovered from the convention.

There was some time for fun, however. I was able to attend the

US-Norway women's soccer match as well as the closing ceremony on October 1. Since we had a week in between the Olympic Games and the Paralympic Games, I took a vacation in the Australian outback and climbed Uluru, otherwise known as Ayers Rock. I rode a camel in the desert and took a sunrise hot-air balloon ride.

After the Paralympic Games ended in mid-October, I returned to DC, certain Sid would have disowned me by then.

TYING ME DOWN

2000

I became part of the team at TSD, a strategic communications firm. As always, things were busy, and I kept working at a frenetic pace. It was still presidential election season, and I longed to do my part to get Al Gore elected. So in addition to everything else I had going on, I helped his campaign organize an event in Davenport, Iowa, which ended up with a front-page photo and headline above the fold of the *New York Times*. Not bad for someone who hadn't done domestic advance work since 1992.

From there, I headed straight to Nashville to work on election night. Again, I was on the media team, making sure the hundreds of reporters from all over the world had what they needed. The stage for the vice president was already set, and we built an incredible press riser—thirty-six feet high, fifty feet wide, and eight tiers for all the TV reporters.

As the returns came in that night, we heard on our walkie-talkies that Gore was going to give a speech. The large monitors on either side of the stage showed the election results on CNN. We stood in the rain waiting for the TV anchors to call the tally of electoral votes and whether we were victorious or not. It was close.

However, the results from Florida were in question. At one point, we thought Gore was coming onto the stage to concede, and then we heard that his speech was delayed. This happened over and over again; I can't even remember how many times we thought Gore was about to make a speech. Our team had worked election nights before, in 1988,

1992, and 1996. This was not the same. Our emotions whipped up and down every time we thought he was going to be declared the winner.

We all looked like drowned rats from standing in the rain when we finally left at 5:00 a.m., still not knowing the answer. Later, when the plan for a recount was announced, the campaign asked if I could go to Florida, but I declined. I already had plans to go to Athens, to prepare for an IOC visit, just two days after returning home from the election.

By the time I returned home from Athens, Eric and I hadn't seen much of each other for several months. We were sorely in need of some quality time together, so we flew off to Belize and Guatemala, where we decompressed by sitting on the beach, reading books, snorkeling and fishing, eating great food, petting stingrays, and watching dolphins, manatees, and nurse sharks. We also headed into the jungle to see Mayan ruins at Tikal and Caracol, and one night, while eating dinner at Francis Ford Coppola's lodge, Eric sort of popped the question.

"I think we should get married."

He didn't get down on one knee or even have a ring. It was a statement.

"Are you asking me?" I said as I carefully sipped my red wine.

"Yes, Robin, I am asking you. Will you marry me?"

I stood up from my side of the table to plant a kiss on his lips.

"Yes, I will marry you."

I was elated that I had a future with this smart and kind man.

SUNFLOWERS AND SNEAKERS

2001

Over the next several months, we planned the wedding. We wanted the ceremony to be simple, with around forty-five close friends and family—mostly from DC—and within our budget. I no longer had a connection to New York, and Eric had moved thirteen times before the age of eighteen, so he wasn't attached to any particular place. DC was too expensive, so we settled on South Dakota. He had worked for Senator Daschle for years and knew Governor Bill Janklow well. When the governor offered us his summer residence, Valhalla—situated in the picturesque Black Hills—as a venue, we accepted.

I relished organizing the wedding; it was as though I was doing advance work for myself. We found a caterer who would serve local game and fish and bake a simple angel food wedding cake, which was Eric's favorite. She even offered to pick sunflowers from a nearby field for my bouquet and arrangements. I bought my white backless gown in the prom section of Lord and Taylor in DC, and then, two days before the wedding, we all flew in to make sure everything was set up.

Early on Saturday morning, we hiked Harney Peak (now known as Black Elk Peak), the highest point in the United States east of the Rocky Mountains. After that, it was time to get into wedding mode, and I gathered my close girlfriends to help me with my makeup.

There was a knock on the door, and my friend Teresa went to open it. She came back to me with a message: my mom had forgotten her dress.

"She's all upset," Teresa said.

The nerves in my neck tightened immediately. I had purposefully asked my friends, and not my mom, to help me get ready because she and I were always on edge with one another. My friends looked at each other, and Denise said, "Just call us the fix-it girls."

Meanwhile, I tried to compose myself. *Why can't my mom just let one single day be about me?* I straightened out my dress and walked to the mirror. Maris rushed over and put more powder on my face to tone down the redness in my cheeks. Evi, who had known me and my mom the longest, walked up behind me and hugged my waist as she whispered in my ear in German.

"Focus on *you* now, OK?"

I took a deep breath and opened the door to walk downstairs to meet Eric. We had planned to take pictures before the wedding so we could be with our guests right away after the ceremony. I donned my light-blue Nike sneakers and hiked with him behind the cabin to take some romantic photos. As soon as we were done, the ceremony was ready to start.

I didn't believe in the symbolism of being given away at my wedding. My parents had given me away at my first marriage. They didn't own me, and at thirty-nine years old, it seemed silly to be given away. This time my partner and I were going down the aisle as equals. Besides, I had pretty much raised myself, and Eric and I preferred the idea of showing that we were two individuals coming together instead of a man accepting a woman from her father. So, hand in hand, we walked between rows of wooden benches, populated by our friends and our small family, to the arbor decorated with pine cones at the end of the grassy lane.

We had three officiants. One was John Cooper, the head of the South Dakota Game, Fish and Parks Department, who was one of Eric's good friends. The others were a Sioux tribal chairman and a Sioux shaman, who said they were honored to marry us after all the work Eric had done for the Lower Brule Sioux Tribe to get them better access to water.

Cooper said the official words to marry us, according to the laws of South Dakota. Altwin Grassrope, the shaman, anointed our heads with Black Hills earth and water. He bound our arms together with red felt, tied eagle feathers in our hair, and burned sage around us to unite our spirits forever. Mike Jandreau, the Sioux chairman, offered traditional blessings in his native language. Most of our guests had never seen a traditional Native American ceremony, and I felt truly blessed to share it with everyone.

Long tables, adorned with sunflowers in simple aluminum pots, formed our reception area. We served South Dakota specialties: grilled elk, pheasant, and venison with wild berries. Eric and I sat in the middle, flanked by our fathers. My stepfather, Lars, had also forgotten his suit, and unfortunately, we had no friends that had extra clothes that would fit his six-foot, 150-pound frame. He looked funny in his Hawaiian shirt and khaki pants, a stark contrast to my mom, who was dressed in a gray-silk suit borrowed from my friend Maris. Lars had a look of distress in his eyes, despite the smile plastered on his face, and my mom sat at stiff attention on his left. I couldn't help but sense the tension emanating from them, and at one point I asked him if there was a problem.

"What's wrong with Mom?"

He kept smiling but leaned close to my ear to whisper.

"She doesn't feel well. Her stomach is upset, and she threw up after the ceremony. Her nerves are shaken."

He folded his hands in his lap with a look on his face as if expecting me to say something, but then he went on.

"You know how fragile your mother is. She doesn't like crowds, and she's upset that so many people know the true story of her not being married when she had you, and me not being your biological father." He took a drink from his water glass, again waiting for my reaction.

I felt my blood boiling. I put my napkin to my lips to conceal my gritted teeth and asked if she needed some antacid. I wasn't going to comment on his last remark. I'd made so many comments over the years that I felt like I could rewind a tape and say the same thing to my mother: *I will not lie, and no one cares anymore; this is not 1963. I am proud that you kept me, I am proud that you were a single mother, but every time you lie about how I came into existence, you try to put your shame on me, and I will not take it anymore.* I started eating my elk and corn muffins. I couldn't talk to him anymore.

Eric sensed my tension and suddenly gave me a kiss on the back of my head and ran his fingers through my hair. I turned to face him and buried my head in his neck.

"Are you OK?"

I nodded and whispered in his ear. "I love you. Let's make sure we don't end up like our parents, OK?"

THE WORLD IS SHAKEN

2001

The first few months after we married and honeymooned in Greece tested us. I was spending half my time in Athens to work on the 2004 Olympics and half in DC, working for TSD and making sure the international media got the information they needed to write their stories. The Athens organizing committee was under constant pressure to build the Olympic venues, and Gianna wanted positive stories in the press. In one article, a Greek staffer wrote about a meeting in Turkey and referred to the capital using its Greek name, Constantinople, rather than its official name, Istanbul. This publication would go to the Turkish National Olympic Committee, and we couldn't offend them before the games even started. But there was only so much I could do.

And then, in the early afternoon on September 11, 2001, I was sitting at my desk when one of the Greek media staff members said that a plane had hit a building in New York. He motioned me over to the TV in the central area of the office. I thought what he said must have been a lost-in-translation moment, but when I reached the TV, we all saw the damage to the World Trade Center. The station didn't censor the footage, and we watched as people jumped out of the buildings. No one knew if this was an accident or a terrorist incident. Tears streamed down my face. When we saw the second plane hit the other tower, we knew that this was no mistake. We were under attack back home.

When news hit that a third plane was heading to the Capitol, I panicked. Eric went to work there every day as Senator Daschle's legislative director. I ran back to my desk and tried to call his office, but I got a busy signal. I tried our home, and no one answered. I paged him and got no call back.

It was hours before we spoke and I learned he was safe. By that time, the plane headed for the Capitol had crashed in Pennsylvania, but another plane had hit the Pentagon. I, like every American, was in shock. I watched the news nonstop and could not believe what was happening to the city where I had grown up. Gianna called me that night to make sure Eric was OK, and I thanked her for her kindness.

I went home for two weeks after September 11 and then back to Athens for my October trip. I had so many miles on Lufthansa that I was upgraded to first class from DC to Frankfurt. The security at every airport was tighter now, but that didn't mean we were necessarily safe. A few days later, Eric called me at my desk and asked if I was watching CNN.

"No."

"Turn it on and stay on the line."

I hurried to the TV near my desk and turned on CNN International. At first, there was nothing noteworthy.

"Schep," he said, "we got a letter today filled with anthrax. When the legislative correspondent opened it, I was the first one upstairs to see the white powder, and now the whole office is quarantined."

I didn't know what to say except to ask if he was all right. Then CNN showed the Daschle office in the Hart Building, and I could see the staffer, whom I knew, through the wide windows. I kept thinking about 9/11, and I was worried.

"Don't worry, we will be fine," Eric said.

We hung up, and I returned to my computer screen and started writing. Work was the best way I knew to keep my mind from wandering and worrying. Meanwhile, Eric was put on Cipro, like the rest of his office. The Pentagon regularly monitored the staff, drawing weekly blood samples. The Senate staff was the first case of a bioterror attack, and they wanted to study it.

As all this turmoil was unfolding, Eric also told me the funniest story about the day they found the anthrax. The Capitol Police told everyone to stay in their offices, but at some point, the staff got hungry and ordered pizza. When the pizza guy showed up, the police let him in to deliver the food and then allowed him to leave. Minutes later, everyone realized that with an airborne substance like anthrax, the delivery guy had been exposed too. Luckily, they reached him and put him on Cipro as well.

Unfortunately, the same couldn't be said about two mail carriers who had no idea they were exposed; they later died. Eventually, the main suspect, a scientist who allegedly wanted to warn the government about bioterrorism, died by suicide in 2008.

MOTHERHOOD

2003

There is something about death that propels you to want to create life. Ever since my miscarriage, Eric knew I wanted to be a mother, and with my epilepsy, he was open to adopting. I mourned the fact that I would never again be pregnant or pass on my DNA. But over time I realized I was more interested in becoming a mother than being pregnant. I also realized that with an unusual family such as mine, perhaps it was better not to pass on my DNA. What I really wanted to pass on were my values and beliefs. I had already seen that DNA did not guarantee a happy family.

Adopting is not an easy process. Step one was the home study, where we worked with a social worker to prove that we were fit parents. We had to do an FBI background check, attend three interviews with a social worker evaluating us, and show paperwork to illustrate that we were financially stable. All that took three months.

While we were waiting for approval, we explored different avenues to find a child. It wasn't easy. The State Department had a spreadsheet online that showed which countries Americans could adopt from, the typical age of the children, how long the process took, and any restrictions on the parents. For example, you had to be Catholic to adopt from Poland. One parent had to be Indian if you wanted to adopt a child from India. And China only had girls available for adoption. We knew we wanted a child as young as possible in the quickest amount of time, which led us to Kazakhstan.

Four months into the undertaking, we received a video of our son

Marat. He was lying in his playpen, propped up on his hands, with curious eyes. I cried when I saw him for the first time, and I watched the video every day. I was already in love with him. When we were finally approved to go to Kazakhstan, I could not contain my excitement.

We arrived in Saint Petersburg on January 5. Although we were adopting from Kazakhstan, we thought a few days in Russia would be an opportunity for a short vacation before we became parents. After passing customs control, our first introduction to this global city was the cold air inside the airport. It was not heated, and as we waited for our luggage, we could see our breath. The airport vendors selling coffee and souvenirs were wearing down-filled coats because it was ten degrees Fahrenheit inside and minus twenty degrees Fahrenheit outside. Luckily, when we stepped outside with our luggage, we found a taxi, but in those few minutes I felt my nostril hairs freeze.

After our arrival, our adoption coordinator told us that our dossier was held up in the Foreign Ministry, and it might take weeks for it to get approved. She suggested we return home and wait. I did *not* like that answer. Our son Marat was living in an orphanage, and every day we could not get to him was one more day he did not have a mother and I did not have my son. I was determined to get this adoption completed.

Using his connections in Senator Daschle's office to speed up the process, Eric called an energy lobbyist, Scott Segal, who had business in Kazakhstan; he called the vice president of Kazakhstan. Our dossier was released within three days, along with the dossiers from a family from Louisiana and a single mom from Maryland. I was so proud of Eric and what he had accomplished for us and the other families.

But there were more bureaucratic hurdles with the Ministry of Education and the Frank Foundation. We pushed to get a date set— January 23—which meant we would still have to wait two more weeks. Airplane tickets were expensive between Russia, Kazakhstan, and Washington, DC, and we did not want to spend those two weeks waiting in Saint Petersburg. We found a cheap flight to Vienna, Austria, where I had once lived. I showed Eric the city. We visited museums, ate *Apfel Strudel* and *Wiener Schnitzel*, and allowed ourselves to be taken care of by friends. We even got in a day of skiing in the beautiful Austrian mountains.

On January 23, we finally left for Kazakhstan. We landed first in Chelyabinsk, a city in west-central Russia close to the Ural Mountains and the place where we would catch the plane to transfer us into Kazakhstan. Since we were traveling to another country, we had to deplane, collect all our luggage, go through customs, and declare all our money. We were nervous writing *$7,000* on our declaration forms, and our anxiety worsened when the customs agent made us count our money in front of the whole line.

Finally, at four o'clock in the morning, we boarded our plane. I had hoped for a more modern Aeroflot plane, but ours was old. Later that morning, we walked the streets of Ust-Kamenogorsk, an industrial mining town near the borders of Mongolia, Russia, and China. It was extremely cold there too; our footsteps crunched on the snow, and icicles were suspended from tree branches hanging over the river.

I looked at Eric with anticipation. "Today is the day—the day we meet Marat," I said.

Our van pulled up to the orphanage, and we saw the signage in Russian on the concrete walls indicating that we were finally there! After we had waited so long, it seemed unreal. As we entered the building, we were grateful for a rush of heated forced air blasting us. We also saw the other families whose dossiers had been released, waiting expectantly for their children too.

The interpreters guided us to the director's office, and as we opened that door, three women greeted us, each with a baby wrapped in traditional Kazakh blankets in her arms. I yearned to determine which bundle was Marat. And then I saw the tuft of red hair. I had watched the video of him every day for four months, and I knew exactly what he looked like.

A short woman with black-and-gray hair and two gold front teeth held him. I walked toward her with mounting expectation, and she smiled and placed Marat in my arms. When I felt his warmth and the beating of his heart, I knew he would be connected to me forever. In my mind I told him that I would love him, raise him, protect him, and cherish him. His brown eyes looked up at me in wonder. All the years of searching for my father didn't matter anymore—at least not then. I had a son. Eric beamed beside me.

"Do you want to hold him?" I asked.

He shook his head. "I like watching you hold him. You look so happy."

After a few more moments, I handed our sacred bundle to Eric. "We are a family now."

After an hour and a half, we were told to return our baby to the caretaker. It was so hard to give Marat back, and this started a process that went on for the next eleven days. Every morning, we, along with the other adopting families, left for the orphanage after breakfast. Upon arrival, we were allowed to interact with our babies for about one and a half hours in the playroom. We each snuck in formula after we heard that once the babies were three months old, they were being fed horse's milk because formula was too expensive. After that, when the caretakers came in to take the babies away for their naps, we returned to our hotel for lunch, and then we went back to the orphanage for another ninety minutes to be with our children. Then it was back to the hotel for the night. It felt like the Bill Murray movie *Groundhog Day*, with each day an exact repeat of the preceding one.

We wanted to take our children home! As I watched Marat every day, I soon realized he was a curious, smart, and social child. He loved to be tickled and fly in the air on his papa's back and be held by me while we danced around the playroom.

One day we saw a group of two- and three-year-olds at the orphanage while we waited for our babies in the playroom. A little blond girl locked eyes with me as she went down a plastic slide. She smiled, and I smiled back. Eric noticed.

"We only have a visa for one child. We cannot bring anyone else home," he said.

He was right, but I had to investigate. I asked our interpreter to find out more about the little girl. The next day, she gave Eric and me some news.

"The little girl you saw is named Lila, but she is not up for adoption. The law in Kazakhstan states that if someone from the children's families comes to visit them at least once in six months, the children can't be adopted. Lila's grandmother visits every three months."

It broke my heart. I would have taken her back with us if we could, in keeping with my intention to build a big family with love.

After the delay in Saint Petersburg, where we'd spent a week, and our two weeks in Austria, Eric wasn't able to stay with me any longer. He had to get back home to start a new job as a partner in a law and lobbying firm.

So I stayed in Kazakhstan for the remaining two weeks and completed the process of going in front of a judge and filing paperwork with Marat's new name: Marat Peter Schepper Washburn. Once that was done, he was officially our son. The next day, I went to the orphanage with the other adopting families to pick up our children. It was very emotional. We put our babies in diapers for the first time and dressed them in the clothes we had brought from home; Marat was precious in a light-blue snowsuit. We handed the clothes they had been wearing back to the caretakers who, having raised these children since birth, and knowing they would never see them again, cried when we left.

While on the old Aeroflot airplane back to Moscow, I remembered the last conversation I'd had with the social worker in DC. She had asked if there was anything I was afraid of about adopting.

"Yes," I had said. "There is no handbook. I had a strange childhood, and I'm afraid I will mess it up."

"Robin, you will make mistakes. No parent is perfect. But the greatest gift you can give your child is to acknowledge your mistakes and say you are sorry."

It was great advice, although it pained me at the time because my mom had never said she was sorry to me for all the lies she told and the ones she made me tell. I vowed I would tell my child I was sorry whenever I made a mistake. I wanted him to learn how powerful the truth was.

It was a long flight home for a baby, and I had not anticipated all the complications of having a baby on your lap in business class, with mostly men as your fellow passengers who did not have the same affection for babies as most women. You cannot put down the tray table to drink or eat. You cannot gracefully use the restroom. Your arms will probably fall asleep, and your baby might not sleep at all.

Upon landing in DC, we breezed through passport control and the INS process, picked up our baggage, and exited through the arrival doors. Outside, I saw Eric waiting for us and deeply exhaled. I couldn't believe this little human was now a part of our family. It elated me. And it terrified me.

Upon my return, I arranged with TSD to work from DC for a year so that I wouldn't have to travel, promising to return to Athens before the 2004 games. I quickly settled into my new routine as a working mother. Marat settled into his own routine, which involved a lot of eating. When we officially adopted him at ten months old, he was only fourteen pounds, but once I brought him home, he sucked down formula all day and gained a pound a week for six weeks. His red hair glistened in the sun, and he always had a smile on his face. He loved our dogs, Winston and Lola, and they loved him.

I hated the fact that I knew nothing about his birth parents except his mother's name. I did not want him to go through what I had experienced. Pairing up with another mom from our trip to Kazakhstan, we hired a private detective to find out more about his family. A month later, we received a report and pictures of Marat's biological mother, Raisa, and her two boys and little girl. The investigator also forwarded a letter from her in which she described how poor she was and that she knew she could not support another child.

Years later, when I showed Marat the photos, his eyes focused on the little shed next to their small house on the farm.

"What is that?" he asked.

I explained that it was an outhouse and that his biological family had no indoor plumbing. They had to go to the bathroom outside. I will never forget the look on his face.

"Mom, I am soooo glad you adopted me."

When the spring of 2004 arrived, I moved to Greece with Marat to work the final months before the Summer Olympic Games in Athens. Eric stayed home. Evi offered to take care of Marat while I worked, and we agreed that she would take him to Vienna during the games in case there were any terrorist attacks in Greece.

Although we were always hearing bad media stories that the venues for the games would not be ready, Gianna demanded results and made sure all the buildings were built on time. The Greek contractors even hired Albanians to work the night shift, and construction went on twenty-four hours a day. Our small team, which had started work in the fall of 2000, had grown, and I was proud of the young Greeks that I'd trained. Some had become dear friends too. I had my political family, but now I also had a Greek family once again. I had commuted back and forth to Greece every two weeks for over two years, and we often had Sunday lunches of pasta and seafood that lasted for hours. Now that I was a mother, Marat joined me whenever I was with them, touring the Parthenon or dipping our toes into the Mediterranean Sea.

The games proceeded without a problem. I worked out of the Main Press Center with thousands of other reporters, fed stories to NBC's *Today Show*, and made sure all the other reporters got what they needed to cover the games. Occasionally, I ventured out to see an Olympic event at one of the venues: track and field, swimming, or my favorite summer competition, soccer. On August 26, the women's soccer gold-medal match was at Karaiskakis Stadium. It was the United States versus Brazil, and it was the first time I was able to be a spectator and not on the clock. I forgot all about my role at the games and screamed "USA!" whenever the Americans got possession of the ball. The United States won 2–1.

I was elated, and wanting to celebrate after the match, I joined some colleagues at a local bar. Although I had not yet eaten, I accepted the Limoncello shots being offered. I felt a buzz immediately, since I hardly ever drank alcohol. The whole bar was dancing, and I joined in, ending up on the bar at some point. I always loved dancing; it was my way to relax.

When I arrived at work at the media center the next morning, I was tired. I kept getting texts from all the young staffers asking me if I wanted to party again that night. I had no idea what was going on; usually I didn't get those kinds of invitations from the twenty-year-olds. Then I was shown footage from a story about tourists letting loose in Athens, and there I was, dancing between two guys on Greek national TV.

They had seen another side of me, not the stiff boss they called "Frau" at staff meetings.

After the closing ceremony, we all let out a collective exhale, congratulating ourselves on four years of hard work. I was proud of the team and the small country of Greece, which had delivered a spectac-ular event, despite all the negativity we had received right before the opening ceremony.

As with the end of a campaign, I needed a vacation. I flew to Vienna to meet up with Eric and pick up Marat from Evi's house. We went on a short vacation to Salzburg and Kitzbühel and went hiking, with Marat on Eric's shoulders. They returned to DC, and I returned to Athens for the Paralympic Games for another two weeks of work. When I finally got home in September 2004, I settled into my routine again and enjoyed every second of being a mother.

A BROTHER FOR MARAT

2006

I thought it was a given that we would adopt another child, but because we were older parents, Eric was fine having just one. Every time I asked him about it, he would say that "we just got this routine down; we don't need to start again."

Being a former campaign operative with great powers of persuasion, I tried every argument I could think of. One day I played the death card.

"Come on, Eric, we *are* older parents, which means that when we're dead, Marat will be alone."

He didn't budge. "He'll make friends like you have."

Another day I said, "You have two brothers. Marat should have at least one brother."

"I'm not that close to my brothers."

I could *not* figure out how to convince him. I needed to find what he cared about most and determine how I could tap into that value. I found it one day when Eric was mad at me.

"You are such an only child," he said. "You always want your way."

I saw my opportunity. "Well, I guess you want Marat to be just like me."

The next day, Eric found me at the kitchen table with Marat. "I have been thinking; we should adopt another child."

I smiled from ear to ear and went down to my office in the basement, returning with a white binder. I asked him to sign some paperwork. We were going to find a brother for Marat.

The adoption agency told me the process would be a little different this time. A couple in the United States had killed their adopted Russian child, so there were more bureaucratic hurdles to overcome, and we would need to go to Kazakhstan twice. We also probably would not know which baby we would be adopting, as we had with Marat, in advance. It would be a blind adoption.

We engaged the same social worker that had helped us adopt Marat. This time I had a different question for her. "How will I know how to raise a second child? What if they are really different? What do I do?"

"I know from your questionnaires that you're a gardener," she said. "Tell me, do you treat all your plants the same?"

"Of course not. I have perennials in the ground and annuals in pots, and I have some shade plants and some sun plants. They all need a little bit different care."

"Well, then, treat your kids like your plants. Each one has different needs, and you can adjust," she said. I filed that advice in my brain for future use.

When we traveled to Kazakhstan to adopt Shokhan, the surroundings were more comfortable. We rented a small apartment and were able to cook our meals. Between when we were there in January 2003 and when we returned in July 2006, the country had gained more wealth, and this time we were in the largest city, Almaty, instead of a small mining town. As before, we had an interpreter, but this time there were no other adoptive families with us.

We met with the director, and she asked what we were looking for. We showed her pictures of Marat and asked to adopt a baby that looked like him—so they would look like each other, since both of our children would not look like us. A nurse took us to a small room, where we waited with the interpreter. Fifteen minutes later, a caretaker entered holding a baby boy in her arms and motioned for me to hold him. For some reason, I did not have the same emotional reaction as I did when I first saw Marat on the videotape. I was happy to play with him, but something inside me said he wasn't the right brother for our son. When we returned to our apartment, I shared my feeling with Eric.

"Honey, I don't think we can adopt the baby we met today. I'm not feeling any attachment to him, like when we adopted Marat."

I could tell he was angry by the expression on his face. "We didn't come all this way to reject this child. We spent thousands of dollars on plane tickets, and this whole process, and now you want to say no? You were the one that wanted a second child." He paced, his sour mood in contrast to the rich red fabrics decorating the room.

"Well, maybe we can see if there is another child available?"

Eric picked up a magazine and started reading. The conversation was over.

When the interpreter arrived the next morning to take us to the orphanage, she told us that the baby we met the day before was no longer up for adoption. His mother was in a psychiatric ward and hadn't signed the necessary paperwork. I breathed a sigh of relief and squeezed Eric's hand. The universe had also been sure that that baby wasn't right for our family.

As soon as we sat down in the waiting room, the nurse presented us with a different baby, Shokhan, who had been named by the orphanage's pediatrician after a famous historical figure in Kazakhstan.

It was love at first sight, just as it had been when we first saw Marat. This eight-month-old baby was meant to be our son. I cradled him in my arms, and my heart filled with joy. Now my family was complete. I couldn't explain to Eric why this child felt right; I simply called it "mother's intuition."

We knew what to expect at the orphanage: visiting twice a day and waiting to hear when the paperwork would be accepted, which took longer and was more complicated than before.

Meanwhile, I missed Marat, who was at home with my dear friend Caroline, his godmother. Like before, Eric returned home to work, and I stayed for the remainder of the process, another two months. Finally, we headed back to DC. When four-year-old Marat greeted us at the front door, I lowered the blanket so he could see his new little brother's face.

"Mommy, he looks just like me."

My heart swelled, and I knew we had made the right decision.

THE HOME-AND-CAREER
JUGGLING ACT

2006–2013

Eric and I settled into life in DC with our two kids. We hired babysitters and then an au pair to give me some breaks. I wanted to be a fulltime mother, but I also knew that I still needed to work to keep my mind engaged. I had met some coaches and liked the idea of working with people to develop their visions for their futures, so I decided to become a certified life and executive coach. Once I finished the certification program, I started a small consulting business and offered coaching, facilitation, and strategic planning. It allowed me to work nine to three and still be able to get Marat from school every day.

I longed to provide my kids with the opportunities that I never had, some structured and some not. They both played sports, and Marat was excellent at soccer and baseball. For some reason, I was determined that they learn how to ski, so while Eric worked on weekends, I drove the kids to Whitetail, a small ski resort in western Pennsylvania.

They also both loved art. Shokhan was a master Lego builder and had the patience to sit for hours to work on a project. We all built forts in the living room and spent hours on the wooden floor with race cars and fire trucks.

Eric and I also developed friendships with the parents of our kids' friends, and in the summertime, we started a tradition of renting a house in France for two weeks with my friend Robin Smith and her family. That was less expensive than a house in Cape Cod or East

Hampton, and we'd travel the French countryside to see Dordogne, Ardèche, Brittany, Normandy, and Alpes-de-Haute-Provence. Our summers were filled with laughter, adventures, and lots of great food. One of my favorite memories from that time is having an "aperitif" every day with the kids: Robin's blackberry and lemon frozen drinks, served alongside popcorn. We'd then take turns rubbing each other's feet.

Back at home, I became very involved with the school. I even successfully applied for a federal grant called Safe Routes to School to get three miles of sidewalk built in our neighborhood. I started a walking school bus—a group of children who safely walk together to school—for local kids in order to help advocate for more stoplights in our neighborhood. We received the national Safe Routes to School Award in 2009.

I also teamed up with the local senior services coordinator and found out that seniors left their apartments only when the school crossing guards were out. In other words, they needed the same help as the elementary kids to cross the street.

One day, Eric asked me in jest how much money I was making with all my volunteer work. He already knew the answer and suggested I find a job that would pay me for the type of work I was doing as a volunteer. I told him I didn't think anyone was going to hire me to advocate for more sidewalks in their neighborhood.

However, I had learned during my life-coach training how to create a vision of what you want in your life and in your career. I knew I no longer wanted to work in communications and hoped to shift to more policy work to have a greater impact. As a mom in DC, I saw the number of kids that didn't have the same opportunities as my children, and I wondered how I could help them. My vision was bold.

It's 2010. I advocate for the health of schoolchildren.

I help create more sidewalks and bike paths in neighborhoods.

I pair movement with healthy eating and add fruits and vegetables to children's diets.

I meet with the Department of Transportation and the Department of Education to leverage existing programs.

I meet with Michelle Obama and leverage her new program, Let's Move!

Michelle Obama had just announced her program to address childhood obesity by promoting increased physical activity and healthy eating. Her message resonated with me, and I thought that by mentioning her program in my vision, others would understand the type of work I wanted to do.

Two weeks later, a friend from the 2000 Democratic National Convention, Jenny Baucus, called and asked if I would be interested in running Michelle Obama's new initiative, which had been announced but did not yet have an infrastructure. She asked for my resume.

I laughed because I had no resume. All my jobs had been referrals. I had never needed one.

I scrambled and put one together, and that same week, I was asked to come in for interviews. I met with Pete Rouse, my old boss in Senator Daschle's office and Obama's former chief of staff when he was a senator. I also met with the First Lady's chief of staff, Susan Scher, and after about three weeks, I was asked to come to the East Wing to meet Michelle Obama.

The timing was not great for an interview. A few days previously, I'd had a hysterectomy to address the endometriosis, painful cysts, and fibroids that had plagued me since 2002. Although the surgery was a laparoscopy and I still had my ovaries and cervix, my core was still sore. It was initially sad to give up my uterus, but once the surgery was over, I lost five pounds and the pinch in my neck ceased. The surgeon told me I had a fibroid the size of an orange adhered to a nerve in my spine. I had never felt better, but I was still recovering.

I warned the First Lady's staff that it was hard for me to get up from a sitting position. When I arrived at the East Wing, they told me to wait in her office, and I sat on the plush yellow couch. When Mrs. Obama entered the room, my inclination was to stand, but I couldn't use my stomach muscles. She motioned for me to keep sitting. She asked me why I wanted the job and what I had to offer. After a thoughtful conversation, she told me I was hired. I smiled, and she left her office before I boosted myself up from the couch.

It took a month for my paperwork and security clearance to be completed. I felt guilty leaving Marat and Shokhan, who were entering fourth grade and kindergarten, respectively, at the time, but luckily we had an awesome au pair from Bosnia who took great care of the kids.

I was named executive director of the Let's Move! initiative. It was a demanding job with an enormous workload.

At first, I had a small shared office in the East Wing, right outside the policy director's office. But I asked the First Lady for a bigger office because I needed more staff—and more room for them to work. My budget only included one salary—mine. But I was able to get two people detailed from different federal agencies. And I also hired some great interns.

With my team, I handled at least four hundred emails every day from people all over the country trying to help or asking for endorsements. I started a weekly newsletter to interested groups, identified opportunities for the First Lady, and often gave speeches in her place.

My overall goal was to facilitate the roles of every sector in society in improving the health of our children: Let's Move! Cities, Towns and Counties; Let's Move! Outside; Let's Move Faith and Communities; and Let's Move! Museums and Gardens. I discovered that I was a master at working with other federal agencies and cobranding their programs with Let's Move! to get more traction and publicity.

One of my proudest moments was working with the Bureau of Indian Affairs and the Bureau of Indian Education to create Let's Move! in Indian Country. My previous work in Washington State with the tribes had cemented my desire to highlight their cultures and traditions. Now I was in a position to convince the First Lady to plant a traditional Indian "three sisters" garden in the White House gardens. I also invited a number of Native American staff and their kids to the ceremony to inaugurate the garden. A week later, I went to Wisconsin to launch our effort in Indian Country and met several tribal chiefs who told me of the challenges of getting good nutrition on their reservations. They were honored we were highlighting the work they were doing to bring healthier food to their people.

I was driven by the desire to make a difference in people's lives, and I had come a long, long way from where I began. But the job was difficult with two kids at home. Marat was struggling in school—not getting good grades and acting up in the classroom. And I could tell that Shokhan really missed me. I knew I couldn't sustain the hours required to do the job well. I also had waited so long to be a mother, and I wanted to spend time with my young kids and not just at work.

Eric helped, but he wasn't the type of dad to be on the floor with the kids like I loved to be. He had also left the Senate and started his own consulting practice, so he was often preoccupied with his work, although he loved Marat and Shokhan fiercely.

I noticed that the mothers who worked at the White House fit into three categories. For some, their kids were already in college or older and not at home, so these mothers could work twelve to sixteen hours a day. Some were mothers who had husbands playing the primary-caregiver role at home. And the last category was women who had two shifts of nannies—one for the day and one for the evening—which gave them the freedom to work long hours into the evening.

None of those categories applied to me. I wanted to be home with my kids.

In 2011, I left the White House and started work at a think tank called the Bipartisan Policy Center. They had started their own nutrition and physical activity initiative with two former secretaries from the Department of Agriculture and two former secretaries from the Department of Health and Human Services. The hours were more conducive to being a mother, and I could still remain in policy and leverage the work of nonprofits, foundations, the private sector, and academia. We produced a report called *Lots to Lose: How America's Health and Obesity Crisis Threatens Our Economic Future.*

I took a special interest in the Department of Defense. My thought was that since military bases were like towns—with schools, childcare, grocery stores, convenience stores, hospitals, housing, restaurants, and dining halls—it would be fascinating to conduct a study using all the policy recommendations we had made in our report and measure whether the changes led to better health outcomes. Strangely enough, Lisel Loy, who ran the initiative, and I were approached by the Office of Military Community and Family Policy at the Pentagon to help implement their new project called the Healthy Base Initiative. I thrived using my brain and working on issues that mattered to me.

PART 6

FINDING PEACE

STOPPING THE CYCLE

2014

Since I had become a mother, my vision had been that Marat and Shokhan would know what it was like to have engaged grandparents, and I tried to foster a relationship between them and my parents. But I was not successful.

When Marat was two, I took him to visit my mom and dad in Laguna Beach, where they had retired after an initial stint in Vienna. I had brought toys for him, and he was an active kid who liked to make noise. One day, after going to a yoga class for an hour, I returned to learn that my dad had already contacted our airline and changed our tickets to leave the next day. I was livid that he had modified our itinerary without asking me.

It was rare for me to have a vacation; I was not going to cut it short. I called a dear White House friend who lived in San Diego, and she invited us to stay with her for a few days. When I told my parents this, they made it clear that they were still afraid, after all these years, that I would say something about the true relationship between me and my dad. The incident triggered my sense of loss. And after that trip, I decided I needed to set boundaries. If they didn't want a relationship with their grandchild, it was their loss.

A few years later, after we had adopted Shokhan and I had just started my coaching business, I sent them a copy of my marketing email newsletter. The theme for the newsletter was creating family; I described how Eric and I had created a family through adoption and how I had come from a blended family with a stepfather and stepbrother.

Then I got a call from my dad. He said Mom was very upset that I had "publicized to the internet and the world that I had a stepfather." He wanted me to apologize to her. But a newfound strength rose up inside me, and I said no. I told him that I had been the adult in the relationship between my mom and me for my whole life, and I had always been the one to take the first step and accommodate her tantrums. I was not doing it anymore. If she wanted to talk, she could reach out to me, but I was done with navigating the land mines of her shame and sensitivity. I had my own family to worry about.

She didn't talk to me for a year. My dad negotiated a truce, but I did not apologize. I couldn't apologize for creating a family out of love instead of DNA.

Years later, another chance arose to establish a relationship between them and my kids. In the intervening years, my parents had dutifully sent money for every birthday and Christmas, and after we moved to Colorado, I took the kids to visit my mom and dad in their new home in Arizona. Even so, we stayed at a hotel.

Meanwhile, all was not happy at home. Eric and I had fought frequently in DC, but by now we were in Steamboat, and I had hoped a move there would erase our tension. I wanted him to do more fun activities with the kids and me, but he was always tired. I think, from his perspective, he was a much more engaged father than his father had ever been, but I wanted even more. I got tired of going to family events alone with the kids.

With the help of a great therapist, I realized that with each passing year, we were both getting triggered: we were comparing what was happening in our kids' lives with whatever had been happening in our own lives at the same age. For me, this triggered memories of sadness and fear. For Eric, anger percolated with memories about his parents' divorce.

And then my mom excavated the ruins of her upbringing when she came for a visit. When she arrived, the kids were polite, and she tried to connect with them and make them laugh. She had always been good with little kids and animals. Marat was more eager, but Shokhan, my shy and reserved one, kept his distance and stretched his arms around my body for security. It pained me to see how little they all knew of each other.

One day, to give her a sense of our ski resort town, I drove her around to show her the different homes and neighborhoods, and she particularly relished our trip to the Saturday farmers market. When I took her to the stall to buy smoked salmon from the Austrian butcher, and dark sourdough rye bread from the German baker, she couldn't believe we were speaking German in the middle of the Rocky Mountains. She warmed to Steamboat at that point.

But then we went to a lovely café for lunch on the river, and my mom initiated a difficult conversation.

"I don't know why Nana hated me so much. She was mean to me. I remember she would egg my father on and tell him things that would make him mad, and then he would take off his belt and swat me with it on my rear end. She hated me."

"Mom, did you ever consider that Nana was traumatized in her youth? Do you remember when she was dating men with children after Grandpa died, and she always thought that they were all sleeping with their own daughters? Who thinks like that? You get thoughts like that when you have experienced child abuse."

"You can't know that for sure," she said.

"You're right, but she gave clues along the way. Why did Tante Trude and Nana leave the farm as soon as they could? Why did she hate Onkel Hermann and Onkel Otto so much? If she really was abused by them, it might make sense that she thought other men were abusive too. She might even have thought that her husband, your father, was sleeping with you."

Mom looked down at her plate and stabbed a piece of lettuce with her fork.

"You know, Robin, you may be right. I remember Tante Anna telling me that the three sisters would bathe together and help wash each other's hair, and at the end of each bath, their father would come and inspect them. They had to stand naked in the bathtub, and he would touch them and tell them whether or not they had done a good job washing."

"Well, Mom, I think you have your answer. Imagine what it was like for her. She was touched—and probably even had other things done to her—by her father. The man who was supposed to protect her. And Nana was the prettiest of all the sisters; that's probably why Oma hated her. I wouldn't be surprised if Oma thought her husband was giving Nana more attention than her. Nana's own mother was not kind. We both met her. She didn't treat Nana in a loving way. I feel sorry that she never accepted the idea of therapy and never got help. I often wonder if there was a relationship between her childhood abuse and her massage business. I think she would have treated you and Dad differently if she had tried to deal with the abuse in her family."

"I never thought of that," she said.

That conversation chipped away at the wall between us. Years later, when we needed to send Shokhan to a small private school because of bullying, my mom and dad were very generous and helped us pay for the tuition. Our relationship was not tight, but it wasn't fraught anymore, in part because I didn't have the energy to remain mad. My focus was on being a good mother, which meant putting a stop to the cycle of conditional love.

DNA AND ME

2017

When the boys were little and we still lived in DC, Eric and I watched a National Geographic documentary about Dr. Spencer Wells and his research tracing the migration routes of humans through DNA. He even traced a man in Kazakhstan to the Navajo Nation in Arizona, as he shared numerous DNA markers with several members. National Geographic was conducting a study in Kazakhstan, and intrigued, I submitted Marat and Shokhan's DNA, hoping that one day we could find out more about their biological relatives. Eric and I submitted our DNA as well just for fun.

After several weeks, we each received maps that showed where our ancestors thousands of years ago had traveled. As suspected, Marat and Shokhan both had Mongolian and Kazakh markers, but Shokhan was also related to the Saami people in northern Scandinavia, and Marat had significant Italian DNA. I shared the results with the boys, but the National Geographic reports were more about ancestral lineages and not about direct parents.

In 2017, Eric decided to take the 23andMe DNA test because it included health data along with ancestry information. I did the same for the boys and myself. In the years that had passed since our first DNA test, technology had advanced, and these new results showed specific percentages of different nationalities and ethnicities. The boys were fascinated, and Shokhan asked if this information would help us find his biological mother. I told him that although DNA tests were popular in the United States, they probably weren't in Kazakhstan. But perhaps, as he got older, more people would enter the DNA database, and we could find his biological mother then.

My curiosity was also piqued by my results. With the information my mom had told me about Ray Hulz, I was expecting to be 50 percent German from his side, since he was born in Bavaria; another 25 percent German or Polish from Nana; and 25 percent Austrian-Hungarian from Mom's father. But my profile was more diverse than that: 31.2 percent French and German, 27 percent British-Irish, 23.5 percent Eastern European, 7 percent Scandinavian, 7 percent Southern European, 0.5 African, and the rest broadly European.

As soon as I saw the British-Irish and the African percentages, I knew Ray, who was 100 percent German, couldn't be my father. It had to be someone else. The mix seemed to me to be typically American.

I convinced my parents to also take the 23andMe test. I was able to link my results to my mom's profile and see exactly which strands of DNA I'd inherited from her and, through a process of elimination, which were from my father. I stared at the half circle with its prompt to "connect father," but I couldn't do it. I didn't even know his name. I'd thought I had gotten over caring about who my father was, but once I realized it wasn't Ray, I cared again.

The testing brought me closer to my kids. They understood that I, like them, didn't know my biological dad. When Marat was younger, he'd asked whether I knew, and I told him I had no idea.

"I thought so; you are just like me," Marat had said.

For Mother's Day in 2017, I traveled to Arizona to visit my parents and spend a few days with them. Mom and I went to the pool; Dad stayed home. His body was getting older and frailer, but his mind was sharp and always curious. One evening, after a dinner of sardines, boiled potatoes, and sour cream, I took out my laptop to show them the results of their tests. I showed them the kids' DNA results as well.

Dad was as expected: 100 percent Scandinavian—Swedish and Norwegian. I told him that I'd shared the results with Lars and his children, Johan, Finn, and Ava. Mom's results weren't surprising either: 50 percent German from her mother and 50 percent Austrian, Hungarian, and Croatian from her father.

As we sat at the dining room table staring at the computer screen, I decided to show them my results. I pulled up my profile, and at first nothing registered with them until I pointed out the half circles that illustrated what DNA I got from each parent. On the side of my mom it said "Trudy Lofas" and showed the expected European lineage from my grandparents. Even though there was no name associated with my father, except a blue box that said "connect father," we all could see his DNA profile of British-Irish, French German, Southern European, and African.

Both my parents were quiet until my mom stood up from the table. Dad, who was always analytical, pointed to the father's side and looked up at my mom.

"Trudy, I thought Ray Hulz was German. How come there are all these other ethnicities?" He pushed his glasses farther back on the bridge of his nose.

I looked up to see what my mom would say.

"Oh, Ray was adopted, so he didn't know where he came from."

Dad quickly responded. "You never told me that."

Mom walked away toward the kitchen. Dad looked at the profile again, and I could see his lips moving as if he was memorizing the data.

I had to suppress my reaction. I knew Ray was born in 1930 in Germany because of what Beate had told me in 1997. I also knew it would have been impossible for a German family to adopt a British, Irish, Italian, or African child in 1930. My mom was lying, but I didn't want to start a fight, so I sat on my hands to control myself. Her lies— or "fibs," as she liked to say—sustained her, and I would gain nothing by confronting her.

But the possibility that one day I might find a DNA relative on my father's side rekindled my interest in my past. Then she could no longer hide from the truth. DNA doesn't lie.

HAUNTINGS

2018

Living in Steamboat sometimes felt like I was in a bubble isolated from the world. Most of the mothers I knew didn't scour the *New York Times* and the *Washington Post* like I did every morning. In 2018, I was still shell-shocked that Trump was the president of the United States, and I was also still angry that Senator McConnell had blocked President Obama from giving Merrick Garland a Senate hearing to become a Supreme Court Justice. Now President Trump's Supreme Court nominee, Brett Kavanaugh, was going to be confirmed by the Republican majority in the Senate.

I watched on CNN as Dr. Christine Blasey Ford prepared to testify at the Senate hearing, wondering if anything had changed since Anita Hill had testified against Clarence Thomas in 1991. I'd watched that hearing, where all those white male senators—Joe Biden, Ted Kennedy, and Arlen Specter—had disparaged her integrity and believability. I found out later there were other women that could have corroborated Hill's accusations, but they were never called to testify.

Now, in 2018, a well-respected doctor was testifying against Kavanaugh. This time, I noticed that some members of the Senate committee were more respectful in their questions, and the Republicans had even hired a female attorney to question Ford. She was very credible and calm. But those senators who found her testimony politically problematic attacked her, as happens so often with victims of sexual violence. Those attacks reflected their own political desires and insecurities, rather than her credibility. In the end, it was exactly the same playbook they used with Anita Hill—and the same playbook used in courtrooms across this country when attorneys attack witnesses who challenge authority. In Kavanaugh's case, the prevailing sentiment was that she was just plain wrong. On the political shows you could hear the Republican pundits say things like "She is credible, I don't doubt it happened, but she is mistaken; it was not Brett Kavanaugh."

Ford's testimony reached deep into my being. Thank goodness my children were at school because I couldn't stop sobbing. The pain of repressed sadness and anger poured out of my body, causing me to make noises I didn't even recognize. I was shaking, tapping my feet unconsciously, and feeling hollow inside.

By coincidence, I had scheduled a therapist's appointment for that day. I had been seeing someone to help me with Shokhan's anxiety and depression, but today it was me that needed help. As I sat in Will's chair, my tears kept streaming down my face and my body kept shaking. I hugged my right arm around my stomach, trying to settle myself.

My voice cracked when I told him I had been watching the hearing and some horrible memories came flooding back. He was gentle and patient with me.

"Tell me the story, Robin," he said.

I closed my eyes to try to remember what had happened almost forty years ago and how my desire to play sports in ninth grade caused a series of events that blindsided me. I wanted to play so badly that I didn't think twice when my coach offered to drive me home one day after school. He said he wanted to talk about my defensive playing skills.

Instead of taking me the twenty blocks to my apartment, we ended up at a diner in Queens. I had a vanilla milkshake and french fries. We might have talked about the New York Knicks. Or maybe we talked about my life without a dad. Certain details from that day are completely blocked out.

In her testimony, Ford talked about the bedspread on the bed where she was assaulted, and this awakened an old memory for me. Images of burnt-orange, brown, and white flowers came to mind. I was lying on a bed, on my back, still partially clothed. My coach told me how I looked so much older, and that no one would believe I was only fourteen. He said I was so mature and had a presence that most twenty-year-olds didn't have.

He knelt on the bed beside me and began to rub himself. Averting my eyes, I could see the door to the white bathroom and the rabbit-ear antenna on the TV. And then he ejaculated onto my bare stomach. Back then, I had no idea how a man's body worked or what had just happened. He took a towel and rubbed the semen off my skin. I don't remember if he ever actually touched my body, or what clothing I still had on. But I knew one thing for sure: I felt dirty.

He took me to my apartment before my mom returned home from work. I was numb. That day, the next day, and the day after, I went through my daily rituals of taking my dog for a walk, cooking dinner, and eating with my mom.

"I should have known better," I said. "I'm a New Yorker. No one fucks with me. But he obviously did, and I let him. He didn't have a gun or a knife. He didn't force me. It was all my fault. I could have stopped it." I was holding my stomach instinctively and sobbing again.

Will spoke to me in a soft voice. "It was *not* your fault. He was in his forties, and you were fourteen. He was a predator. He probably knew that you didn't have a dad and that you were a scholarship kid. That is what predators do. They look for children in vulnerable situations and exploit them."

I tried to process what he said. "You're sure it's not my fault?"

He explained that I was a sexual assault survivor and that all my feelings of guilt and the loss of power were normal. He pointed out how I was holding my stomach. He noted that when the incident happened, there was no one to comfort me, and now I was soothing myself, as I had learned to do.

Now angry, I told him how my coach had offered me a job helping with his bookkeeping. I surmised that it was his way of keeping me quiet.

Will probed to see if I remembered my coach touching me ever again, and I told him I didn't think so. But often a part of the brain, the hippocampus, protects you from trauma and represses memories. So, if the coach had touched me or repeated his behavior, my brain might have been protecting me from an event too hard to digest.

I explained that the trauma came not only from my feelings of guilt but also from the fact that I never reported him. I could still feel the shame living in my stomach. Will and I discussed how my coach must have targeted other girls before and after me. A predator is a predator. I'd always had a haunting sense that I should have protected other girls, as irrational as that may be. I should have at least told the school, but I was afraid no one would believe me, and I would have lost my scholarship and my dignity. The best I could do was help other girls avoid getting pregnant.

I left Will's office feeling better now that I had talked about it with someone, but also feeling weak. The images of being raped in DC when I was eighteen also flooded my brain. I could not turn them off. I was so ashamed that I had been violated and so angry that I hadn't been able to stop it. I wanted to tell my boys what happened, but Eric discouraged me. When he suggested that would be too much for them to understand, I became furious. *Another white man telling me what I can and cannot say?* I cooked dinner that night and left it for the boys, as I could not stay in the house. I drove around town for two hours, crying and yelling in the car. Anyone who saw me must have wondered what was wrong with that wild woman.

My boys were worried, and I decided I had to tell them. I asked them to sit down. At this point, they were in eleventh and seventh grade, and looking at their young faces made me angry and sad because I had been abused at a similar age.

"I am sorry I left the house in such a hurry. I am very upset about what is happening in DC right now. It reminds me of my past. I was abused by my coach, and it still hurts. I could never say anything back then and felt like I had no voice in ninth grade. But I do now. I'm telling you this because you need to know, and as I've said before, if anyone in authority ever tries to touch you on your private parts—a coach, a teacher, a parent—you tell me. You say no, you scream, you run away. I don't want you ever to experience what I went through. Never."

I hugged them while I cried. I don't know if they grasped what I said, but they hugged me back and then went upstairs to bed.

Over the following days, I watched the Kavanaugh hearings with disgust. I saw another similarity to the 1991 playbook: Kavanaugh played the victim and accused the Clintons of having something to do with the "smear campaign" against him. Like with Anita Hill, there were other people who could have corroborated Ford's claims, but the FBI was never allowed to interview them and share the information with the senators. It was a sham. He was confirmed.

My renewed anger inspired me to do something. I wrote an email to the new headmistress at my former school about what had happened so many years before. I was nervous to click "send," but if Ford could stand up in front of a bunch of senators and tell her story, then I could send an email to my old school.

When I heard back from the headmistress, she was kind. She apologized that the school had not protected me. We had more than one follow-up conversation, and as time passed, she let me know that there was going to be an investigation and asked if I would be willing to talk to the firm they had hired.

I said yes.

When the school's New York lawyer arrived in Steamboat, she looked out of place in her suit and heels. We met in a conference room at a local hotel. Her demeanor was professional and warm, and she told me that she believed me and my accusation, but she needed to ask me several questions to be thorough.

I sat at the other end of the large conference table, sipping from my water bottle. I wasn't nervous, but I didn't know what to expect. Her questions were detailed: How did you get to the hotel? Did you take off your clothes, or did he? Did he penetrate you with his fingers, his penis, or anything else? How did you get home? What did you talk about? What did you have for dinner? Did you tell anyone else?

I have to say, the process was awful. Going into such detail made me relive the event slowly and methodically. It made me wonder if something else happened that I couldn't recall. I thought maybe I should go to a hypnotist and try to unravel my memories. *But why would I want to know more? What good will it do me?*

She told me that they had found the coach. He was still alive, and they would approach him. I asked that they not use my name. I didn't want to talk to him.

She told me they were going to send a letter to the alumna of the school and see if anyone else would come forward. I said if anyone else did come forward, I would be happy to talk to them, to be supportive.

I stressed again that I was not going to sue the school. The school had changed the trajectory of my life, and I was grateful. I just wanted them to know about the predator that had been present.

In June, I received the letter that the school sent out about the accusation. It included an 800 number and email address for anyone who wanted to come forward with other allegations. In sending this letter, our school joined many other private schools that had gone through this process.

Months passed. The investigator called again and said they were going to close the case unless I wanted to go to the next step and have them contact my former classmates. The risk would be that they, or the coach, might figure out that it was me. I thought about it for twenty-four hours and then called her back.

"Go ahead. Contact them."

"Are you sure? Your name might come out."

"Somebody has to say something, and if it's not me, then who will it be?" I could not believe that he had only targeted me.

The crampy feeling in my stomach returned.

I decided to call Genevieve, the young girl I had taken care of when I was in the eleventh and twelfth grades. She now lived in Maine. After catching up about life, kids, and work, I told her about my coach in ninth grade, how I had contacted the new headmistress, and that there was an investigation. I asked her if she remembered me saying anything when we were girls. I doubted that I had because I could only remember the incident in ninth grade—two years before I nannied for Genevieve—and also because I had always been very protective of her. She was like my little sister.

After a slight pause, she said she remembered something from when I was in eleventh grade.

"We were sitting on the bed in my mom's room, and you told me that something had happened that day at school. You were agitated and said that the coach had asked for a blow job behind the copier in the office. And you gave him one. You seemed upset, but you also tried to brush it off like it was no big deal. You were probably trying to shield me from your emotions."

I didn't remember that at all; I didn't even find him attractive. By eleventh grade I was seriously in love with Jean-Marc.

Genevieve said she also remembered seeing the coach in the halls, watching me. "I think he was in love with you," she said.

I needed to ask one last question. "Do you remember me working in the bursar's office? I thought I'd done some bookkeeping work for him, but when the investigator contacted him, he denied all the allegations and said he'd never hired anyone to work for him. I worry they don't believe me."

"Yes, I remember you worked there," Genevieve said. "You needed the money. I don't think my mom paid you much."

"Twenty-five dollars per week plus food and boarding," I replied.

Genevieve said how sorry she was that this had happened to me. "He was in a position of power, and I am sure you felt like you had to do what he asked because you needed the job."

I asked if she'd be willing to talk to the investigator and tell her what she'd told me. She said she would.

The realization that something else had happened with my coach hit me hard, rendering me paralyzed and powerless for a long while. I tried to reach back into my brain to recall the incident behind the copier, and I could remember the office, but not much more. *What else happened? Is that why I have always had problematic relationships with men? Is that what drives me to make sure women are heard?* It was all so confusing. I became a strong woman, and I also liked men and sex and touching, but there was a big difference between being with someone you desired and being forced, even psychologically, to be with someone because they had power over you.

There are days I still feel paralyzed. I like to think that all this is over, but it isn't. I hate the word "victim." I even dislike the word "survivor." I know abuse is part of my story, and I like to think about it as a book on my shelf instead of trauma in my body. But when my chest constricts, the tears build, and I can't breathe, I know it is not over.

One day, I was helping a young woman in Steamboat with her college essay, and I learned that she had been raped. I was so proud of her that she wrote about her attack for her college application, but I also wanted to erase the event for her, to wave a magic wand and make it disappear. I felt so helpless, and I just hope that more women are believed, and more institutions will do a better job keeping predators away from the most vulnerable and precious gifts we have in this world—our children.

DNA DOESN'T LIE

2019

After a fantastic family trip in April 2019, where we trekked to Everest's South Base Camp in Nepal, reaching over seventeen thousand feet, I decided to catch up on email. Ancestry.com regularly sent emails telling me that I had third and fifth cousins. Now I had received a notification that I had a message; this was different.

It was from another subscriber instead of the platform. Given the email's date, I had already been tardy in responding, but when you are in small teahouses at high altitudes in Nepal, email is not on your mind.

The message changed my life forever.

> *Hi Robin—I just did my DNA and you popped up as a potential first or second cousin. That's interesting because to my knowledge—I had no first cousins. My dad was an only child and my mother only had one brother—who had no children as far as we know.*

The sender, a sixty-eight-year-old Nebraska woman named Susan, had little experience with genealogy and asked if I would be interested in "finding our connection." Surnames in her family included Kerr, Lynch, White, and Lentz. Her mother had passed away in 2016 at ninety-two years of age, and her grandparents were also in their nineties when they died. She hoped she had inherited the longevity gene.

I wrote back, thanked her for reaching out, and told her I had been trying to find out about my family history because I didn't know my biological father. I also told her a little about my lineage, including that I'd learned that my biological father was English, Irish, German, maybe French, and broadly northwestern European. I didn't know any of the surnames she mentioned or who they could be, unless perhaps one of her male relatives had had a clandestine relationship with my mom in 1962. I confirmed that I wanted to find out more about what had been a hole in my life for decades.

She wrote back the very next day.

> *Hi Robin—I'm so glad to hear from you. . . . My eldest daughter and I have concluded, correctly I assume, that my dashingly handsome uncle Jack is probably your father. I'm sorry to say that he passed away about a year ago. He was ninety years old.*
>
> *To my knowledge, Jack was married three times and had no children. He adopted two children belonging to his first wife—the daughter died in her early twenties, and the son was a mess. . . . I think, if you are his child, you were conceived around the time that Jack and his first wife divorced.*
>
> *Let me just say this—Jack was a wonderful man. He was handsome, smart, somewhat of a playboy, and also a risk-taker. He loved living well—and worked hard to be able to do that.*

She went on to say that, in the end, he had a wonderful life with lots of good friends.

Jack's last name was Lentz. She attached his obituary, which indicated he was born in 1928 in southern Illinois to Art and Chloe Lentz. He had one sister, Peggy, and two nieces. Susan was the one who contacted me, and the other niece was Patricia.

After serving in the US Army during World War II, Jack attended the University of Illinois and graduated from the Los Angeles Arts Center. He worked in advertising, public relations, and publishing. He also earned a law degree.

Jack enjoyed the sea and sailing. When he retired, he kept busy by helping friends with their businesses and founded PostalAnnex+ to combine all the services he was offering under one roof.

He often used the word "family" to describe the atmosphere of the home office's staff as well as his franchisees and their families. Jack was also generous in his support of charitable organizations and served on several nonprofit and trade association boards. His gift was making connections and bringing people together to fill the needs of those less fortunate, both here in the United States and in Mexico.

The obituary, published in the *San Diego Union-Tribune* on July 8, 2018, ended with abundant praise:

> *His generous, kind, and ambitious spirit made Jack Lentz a true man's man: chivalrous, patient, an engaged listener, resolved, trailblazing, resourceful, loyal, risk-taking, and more. In a world of "speak first, consider later," Jack displayed the opposite with his listening skills and high Emotional IQ. He understood people, what motivated them, and how to work with them. The world will be a better place the more we are able to emulate his spirit.*

When I absorbed the obituary, my heart sank. I had been searching for my biological father for over fifty years, but by the time I finally found him, he was already dead—and only for one year. I had always said that I just wanted to know who he was, but I realized now that hadn't been enough. I wanted to meet him, but I would never get that chance.

I read his obituary over and over, trying to remember every detail. He was a successful businessman. He started a nonprofit in Mexico to help kids. He was married three times, his third lasting for thirty-five years. He adopted the two children of his first wife. He gave to the Epilepsy Foundation. I thought that might have been a clue that he had the condition too, but I found out later it was his adopted daughter who had epilepsy, not him.

In the description, he sounded like me, and I finally felt like I belonged to someone. *Do personality traits and behavior get passed on?* Of my two adopted children, one son is more like me and the other more like my husband, so DNA isn't everything. This has been the debate forever: nature versus nurture.

Still, the more I found out, the more I realized I was like Jack. All my life I had been wondering why I was so different from my mom and thus decided that it was just my different upbringing. I had been determined to succeed because it seemed like everyone was counting me out; I was a child out of wedlock. Or because I was a woman. Or because pretty girls can't also be smart.

I googled him and read about his business. I wanted to know more. Susan was very kind and emailed stories that she had about him, and I came to believe I'd inherited Jack's drive and generosity.

At first, I couldn't see any physical resemblance, except for blue eyes, because the obituary photo was taken when he was ninety years old. And then, a few days later, she sent me his senior-year high school picture. I immediately recognized the face: those eyes, those lips. I scoured my digital photo library and found a picture of myself at a similar age. I thought I might be imagining it, wanting us to look alike, but whenever I showed our two photos side by side to my husband and friends, the first response I got was always consistent.

"Wow!"

The second response was a question. "Are you going to tell your mother?"

I wasn't sure.

After our recent visit, when I had shown her my DNA results and she had said Ray was adopted, I was sad for her. After fifty years, she still carried the shame of being a single mother and couldn't let it go, rather than accept the truth that she didn't know who my birth father was. I also wondered if she couldn't tell the truth because she had created a certain image of herself with Lars. Maybe she feared that if he knew she had slept with more than one man around the time I was conceived, he would think less of her. I tried to understand how someone could hold this shame and burden for so many years and the toll it must have taken on her mind and body. I had decided a long time ago that I could not lie about my past anymore; it wasn't worth the pain physically and emotionally. It was just part of my story.

That meant I couldn't withhold this information from her. But I also couldn't just call her and tell her over the phone. It needed to be in person. Luckily, she and I had planned a trip to Norway for a cruise to see the fjords. I was bursting with excitement that I finally knew who my father was, and I was eager to ask her if she remembered him. But I also decided I would only tell her what I had learned at the very end of our trip—or not at all.

The challenge would be keeping this to myself for ten days, until the cruise ended, and simply enjoying the voyage with my mom. I would keep the conversations focused on her and her life, and on enjoying the present moment. If I started talking about myself and my feelings, or even going in depth about my kids, I'd blurt everything out.

We saw spectacular scenery in Norway. One day we went up the Geirangerfjord, a World Heritage Site. We watched waterfalls and took pictures of the little red, yellow, and white houses with grass rooftops. We strolled through small towns and took an excursion to the Lofoten Islands, where we visited a traditional Saami family that raised reindeer and lived in houses made of reindeer leather, very much like teepees, during the summer.

In the evenings, we watched romantic comedies that I had downloaded on my iPad, including one of Mom's favorites, *Mamma Mia!*, about a young woman who was raised on a Greek island by her American single mother. The young woman, about to be married, reads her mother's diaries and discerns the identity of the three men her mother "dated" in the summer she was conceived. She invites them all to her wedding.

There were so many lines in the film that pierced my heart. It's hard for others to understand what it feels like to not know a parent, but there are constant reminders. Every time another ABBA song came on, my mom started dancing in our small cabin. I tried very hard not to cry. Did she see the irony that *Mamma Mia!* was also about her? Maybe she did, but I felt her focus was always on how *she* felt and never what it was like to be in *my* shoes or how hard it was for me to go through life without a father. It was all about her shame, with no room for my sadness. Like the mother character in the movie, my mom did not think about the true identity of my father anymore, and therefore neither should I. She could rewrite history and shut out the past. But when it involved my identity, I could not.

On the last day of the cruise, we spent two hours looking at my laptop. I decided to start by telling her more about what I'd learned about the Schepper family. Through Ancestry.com and 23andMe, I learned that we had cousins from her father's side. He had an older sister who had come to the United States before him and sponsored him to immigrate to New York when he was sixteen. Her name was Maria Schepper, and she married a man with the last name Sporn—a name my mom remembered. They had five children together, and through these online platforms, I had found a bunch of Maria's grandchildren—cousins to me. My mom was intrigued, and I realized that if I showed her the connections on the Schepper side of her family first, then perhaps I could explain how I found my biological father. I also wanted to know why my mom never knew her aunt. It was strange, as though secrecy was part of my DNA even before I was born.

I shared with her the information I had also discovered about an Austrian club in Passaic, New Jersey, called the Burgenlander Club, and she vaguely remembered going there as a child with her father. We looked for a cousin by marriage, Seppl, that she had known and re-membered to be kind. We found him and saw he had died in the 1990s.

She was happy to learn about the connections, and I felt closer to her as we talked about the shared history of our family of immigrants. But I still kept the information about Jack Lentz to myself. I didn't want to ruin the trip for her.

We spent our last night in an Oslo hotel downtown after disem-barking from the ship. This was my last chance to talk to her about my discovery. My instinct told me that I would never feel this close to her again, that I would never spend this much time with her again, and that this was the moment to share my news.

We sat in our pajamas, leaning against the pillows on the head-board. I sat up and faced her.

"Mom, remember the scene in the movie *Mamma Mia!* where the young woman is about to be married and all three dads want to walk her down the aisle?"

She nodded.

"And remember when the daughter said, 'I don't care if you slept with one hundred men, you're my mom and I will always love you'?" I blurted it out, watching her reaction.

"Yes, I remember," she said, looking at me more intensely.

I searched for the words and then, suddenly, they came naturally. "Mom, I love you, and I am so glad you had me. I know you always thought Ray was my biological father, but he wasn't. I found out who my father really was."

Her eyes widened, and she sat up straight. "What? How do you know that?"

I explained to her that my first cousin had found me and that we shared 20 percent of our DNA. And how, through a process of elimination, we concluded that her uncle Jack was my father.

My mom didn't want to believe me. She wasn't mad, but rather curious. "What's his name?"

"Jack Lentz," I said.

She shook her head and smoothed the wrinkles out of her pajamas. "I don't know a Jack Lentz." Then she smiled. "Can't it just be the Holy Ghost, and I was like Mary with the Immaculate Conception?"

I laughed, and my nerves subsided. She was taking this better than I had expected.

"Tell me about him," she said. "I don't remember the name, but maybe if you share some of his history, it will trigger a memory."

Her eyes were gentle, and I could see she was trying to digest it all. I had been afraid she would think I was trying to hurt her, but it seemed that she understood my curiosity and that I wasn't judging her. I read from his obituary, and she listened. When I got to the part about him being a commodore at a yacht club in San Diego, she interrupted me.

"Did he have a sailboat?"

"Yes! In fact, he lived on his sailboat in 1962 when he was getting divorced from his first wife."

I stood up to stretch my legs and give her space to think without me looking at her. I could see her mind processing all this as her hand stroked the duvet.

"Well . . . there was a guy when I lived in Sausalito who taught me to sail."

I looked at her more closely, and she grinned.

"He would call me up in the morning. 'Trudy, meet me at the dock in thirty minutes.' And then he would sail to where I lived and pick me up. We would sail together the whole day." She lowered her voice to a whisper. "But I don't think we did anything else. I don't remember that."

"Mom you were twenty-six, beautiful, and very charming. He was handsome, had a boat, and obviously liked you. Perhaps there was some alcohol involved. And it *was* the 1960s, after all."

She laughed. "I still like the Holy Ghost version."

We didn't talk about it anymore. I was exhausted and relieved. I crawled into bed beside her. I gave her a kiss on the forehead.

"I love you, Mom."

"I love you too." Then she chuckled. "You and your research. You always find something."

I turned off the light, and we went to sleep.

The next morning, we ate breakfast downstairs and reminisced about our time in Norway. We took a cab to the train station and then the express train to the airport. Once we were in our seats on the plane, my mom took my hand. I fell asleep on takeoff, and when I awoke she started talking. She had read the obituary again.

"Jack seemed like a very nice man, and successful too." She added that she wished she had known it was him. "He could have helped us."

At that moment, I felt a stab in my heart, remembering how hard it had been for her to raise a child as a single mother in the 1960s. I'd really wanted a dad, and she'd really needed a husband. We held hands for much of the flight.

When we landed in Denver, I had a surprise waiting for her. She had not seen her grandson Marat in years. He was there when we got out of customs and gave us both a big hug. She was genuinely happy to see him.

I made sure she had a snack and ordered her a wheelchair escort to take her to the gate for her flight to Phoenix, which departed in a few hours. As we hugged goodbye, my years of resentment about her lying to me melted away. I finally understood that she never knew the answer to who my father was for all those years. I bet she didn't even know she was pregnant until she was a few months along.

When I think about it now, I realize she was probably too embarrassed to say she didn't know who my father was. She didn't want to be judged. I know it was hard for her, and I hope that knowing his identity was a relief not only for me but for her as well.

FILLING THE VOID

2019

After years of belonging to a family where my bloodlines ran only to my mom (an only child) and my grandmother (who had left her family in Germany), I suddenly had cousins. I was dying to meet them.

Susan suggested we all travel to Jack's hometown of San Diego to meet people who had known him. She said she would set up the entire trip after we found a mutual date that worked for all of us. Joy, her oldest daughter who tracked the family roots, would join us.

In the meantime, Susan found more pictures. Jack on his sailboat. Jack the photographer. Jack in his fifties, the age I was when I found him.

If I had been shocked when I saw the high school pictures, I was dumbfounded when I studied the others. It was like looking in the mirror. My whole body sighed while questions surfaced in my mind. *Am I a photographer because he was? Did I take to sailing because he loved it? Was I conceived on a boat? What was the name of his boat? Would he have taught me how to sail?* I meditated on all of this, holding his image in my mind. Imagining we were on a boat together, I wrote a poem in honor of my father:

> *Your confidence makes my fear fall away*
> *I place my feet on top of yours yearning to be taller*
> *You laugh, you place my small hands on the steer-*
>   *ing wheel*
> *I look up at you and you tell me to look straight ahead*

You show me how I can tell the direction of the
wind from the little flag on the mast
You explain how the steering wheel is attached to
the rudder
I soak it all in, eager to have you as my teacher
You place your hands on top of mine
We feel the vibration of the hull on the water
together
I giggle
Salt sprays on our faces and I dart my tongue to
taste it
You guide my steering while you switch the direc-
tion of the sails, and we tack
You place a kiss on my head and tell me how
proud you are that I am your daughter
We stay frozen in place, two beings melded as one,
our hearts touching

Susan organized everything for the trip. She and Joy met up with me in San Diego, and we spent the weekend at a bungalow owned by one of Jack's friends. Over dinner on the first night, Susan sketched out the schedule for the next two days and explained whom I would meet and how they were related to Jack.

After we ate, I asked if they were up for going to the beach. I couldn't come all the way out to California and not put my feet in the sand and the water. We drove along the ocean, found an entrance to the beach, and parked the car. The sun was lowering in the sky, and surfers were sitting on their boards waiting for a wave while families played on the beach. Susan sat down on a low concrete railing that wrapped around the lifeguard station, while Joy and I took off our sandals and walked to the ocean. My feet were happy wiggling into the sand, and the cold rush of the tide lapping at my toes was invigorating after my long day of traveling. I couldn't help but smile. I always feel a special connection to California.

And even though I had just met both of them, I already felt a special kinship with Susan and Joy after our numerous emails and calls. I wondered if we had any family resemblance, but I couldn't see it. They were both tall—at least five feet nine. They had brown hair and brown eyes. But even if we didn't resemble each other, we were family.

Susan had planned a full agenda for us the next day. Our first stop was St. Paul's Cathedral in downtown San Diego, where my father had been on the board of the church. He must have touched the same door I touched, maybe even sat in the same pew. I wished so much I could go back in time. *How many times have I visited San Diego and not known he was there?* My last visit had been in 2013 when the kids and I drove from San Diego to San Francisco on Route 1. Jack could have met his grandkids then.

At the cathedral, we met up with Angela, a dear friend of Jack and his third wife, Marty. She showed us the plaque on the wall that honored them and held their ashes. I touched it, wondering if the energy from my hand could reach him somehow. It made me wonder about an afterlife. *Is his soul watching me now? Does he finally know he has a daughter?*

We sat in the last pew, and Angela told us how she met them. Her husband, Gus, was a doctor and had been treating Marty for larynx cancer. Somehow, they all ended up having dinner together, and a new friendship was born. She said Gus and Jack became best friends, and it was Gus who had convinced Jack to check out the new body-scan machine at the Sharp Rees-Stealy Hospital, where they discovered he had kidney cancer.

We then drove a few blocks to the Sharp Rees-Stealy Hospital. A sign outside reads "Marty and Jack Lentz Medical Center." Inside, a picture shows the two of them on a plaque engraved with their names. Jack had donated two million dollars to the hospital to be received upon his death, and Angela commented that it was a shrewd move because he got excellent care for his kidney and bladder cancer right up until he died.

In Jack's honor, we all had lunch at one of his favorite restaurants. King's Fish House was near his business, and we ordered his favorites: sand dabs with flash-fried brussels sprouts and Arnold Palmers. Over lunch, Angela prepped us for our next meeting.

Patrick was the current president of Annex Brands, the mailing-supplies company that Jack and Marty built together. The company had numerous brands under it, each for different types of products you might want to ship. I found out they even shipped helicopters. Patrick and his colleague Mary Anne met us at the front door and led us into a conference room where we talked about how Jack and Marty started the franchise. They never acknowledged that I was Jack's daughter and directed their comments and questions to Susan. I asked what kind of person Jack had been, and they both said he was a man of action, and not a big talker. When Patrick finally did look at me, he said that Jack was conservative.

"In fact, we are all conservative. If you went to his house, he would have Fox News blaring on the TV."

I smiled and said nothing, but now I understood. *Oh, you don't want to recognize me as Jack's daughter because you researched me and found out I'm a Democrat. And you want to make sure I know I'm not like Jack.* Having worked in politics for decades, I was well versed in how to behave in hostile territory. I was polite and smiled. I didn't ask more questions.

Patrick left the room and returned with boxes of photographs for Susan. She was Jack's closest living relative, with Marty and his step-daughter having died years before and him not being close to his step-son. We waded through several of the boxes, finding photos of Jack and his sister Peggy, who was Susan's mother, and an envelope containing Jack's report cards from his childhood, his law degree diploma, and other awards. There were photos from the 1930s, 1940s, and early 1950s, and then later from the 1980s, but nothing in between. Nothing from the 1960s when he would have known my mom. Since Jack had been a photographer, I kept hoping a photo of my mom would surface, but no. Patrick and Susan both suggested that Marty had probably disposed of everything that was a reminder of other women.

The next day, we went to the Southwestern Yacht Club where Jack had been a commodore. I saw his picture on the wall of the club next to all the other commodores that had come before and after. We were set up to have lunch at the club with his close friends and neighbors in Mexico, Steve and Barbara. I ordered an Arnold Palmer and fish, and for dessert I requested a cup of vanilla ice cream. Everyone stopped talking after I placed my order.

"Vanilla ice cream was Jack's favorite too, along with Arnold Palmers," one of them said. It was weird to find out that, like me, he didn't drink coffee and loved vanilla ice cream. *What else did he pass on to me?*

The conversation was easy, and they told me about Jack's efforts to start a kite-surfing competition and his desire to ensure that young Mexicans also learned how to teach kite surfing to earn an income. I guess he was always a businessman.

I felt welcomed. All the while, Steve and Barbara kept staring at me.

"Your eyes, your jawline—you look like him," they said. And then, as we were leaving, Steve made my day.

"He would have been thrilled if he had known about you."

After lunch, we toured Jack's home in the hills of San Diego, and when it was finally time to separate, I worked hard to steel my emotions and refrain from crying. I was afraid that if one tear emerged, I would never stop. I held it together until I stepped into my car at the Denver airport, and at that point the floodgates opened. I was so sad I never got to meet my biological father, and I felt robbed of a lifetime of love—love that I had so needed. I wondered what he would have thought of me, and now I would never know.

WHAT DO SECRETS BRING?

2020

After finding my father and telling my mom about him, I felt like the wall between us crumbled. I also thought there were no surprises left to be uncovered. But I was wrong.

During the COVID-19 pandemic, I was recruited by our local county commissioners to help with communications about the virus and other public health announcements. They didn't have an information officer, so I built up an infrastructure to inform the public and the media. One of the mechanisms for disseminating information was the county's Facebook page, which I managed, and at the same time, I also kept my personal page current.

One morning, when the pandemic was well underway, I checked my private messages and came across a name I didn't recognize. The message had been sent on December 14, 2020.

> *Hello Robin. My name is Mark Robert Auren. I'm trying to locate one of my sisters. My father had four children with three different mothers. By any chance is your birth name Robin Francisca Auren Schepper? I would be delighted to find her.*

I was absolutely astounded. And I responded immediately.

> *Yes, that is my birth name, BUT my mom put a name*

on my birth certificate that was not my birth father's.
Where did your dad live?

Mark wrote back the same day. He said he believed I would know best who my birth father was, but that his understanding was that his father, Robert Franklin Auren, had an affair with my mom when he was the district manager of Air India.

> *He told me he had gone two times to Tahiti with your*
> *mom. He lived in Sausalito, California, and his office*
> *was in the San Francisco area. I just thought it was my*
> *obligation to find out the details and the possibility of*
> *us being related. I have another half-sister that lives on*
> *Nantucket. I am just trying to tie up his life and not*
> *lose contact with a possible sister. I live in Mallorca, an*
> *island off the coast of Spain.*

I wrote back and told him that I didn't think my mom went to Tahiti. At the time of my conception, 1962, she would have been a stewardess with Pan Am, and she was based in San Francisco, where I was born. I also assured him that I did a DNA test and found my true biological father last year. I wished him luck with his quest but reiterated we weren't related, although I would have loved to have had a half-brother.

Mark wasn't quite done.

> *My mother and other stewardesses confirmed the rela-*
> *tion my father had with your mother. He had great feel-*
> *ings for her. There is a reason she wrote his name down*
> *on the birth certificate. Trudy must have been the apple*
> *of his eyes.*

I laughed thinking about how he had been doing research to confirm facts about my mom while I was trying to find my father. My mom had definitely told me she was in love with Robert Auren, and one last time, I wondered if they had married, would they have said—or even thought—I was his biological daughter? I would have never known that I didn't know my true biological father. Would I still have completed 23andMe? Would my path have been different growing up in California with two parents? Would I still have the same values and ethics? One thing was almost certain: I would have grown up without the stain of being a "bastard" child.

Reading the message, I realized how little I still knew about my mom's life. She told me some stories of her travels while she was a stewardess, but a part of me was almost envious that the son of her lover knew things about her that I didn't. Understanding that he might know more, I decided to write him back, and we exchanged more information.

Mark was also born in San Francisco in 1966, three years after me. He had a sister, Maica, who was born in 1965, and a half sister born in 1956. If Mark's father had been my biological father, I would have had three half siblings. Mark's mother was from Germany and had been the best friend of the wife of one of my mom's other lovers, Ray Hulz. I still couldn't believe that my mom managed to have relationships with two men in California whose wives had been best friends growing up in Europe.

Mark also revealed that his father had signed my birth certificate and that he knew my mom had four possible fathers for me. Of course, my mom had never said that to me. At this point, Robert, Ray, and Jack were the only possibilities I knew of. I wondered if she even remembered the possible fourth.

NO MORE SECRETS

2020

I also wondered if I should tell my mom about the conversation with Mark. Yet again, I decided I didn't want any more secrets. On our next weekly call, I relayed the whole story to her. She laughed.

"Robin, between the internet and the DNA testing, are there no more family secrets?"

I laughed. "No, Mom, no more secrets."

We both paused and laughed again. I was glad she was not upset and saw the absurdity of it all.

"Well, Robin, you can't say that either of us has had a boring life, can you?"

"No, Mom, not boring at all."

EPILOGUE

2022

When I walk the forested land of our property with my beloved rescue dogs, Molly and Rocky, I think about how far I have come. Unlike my walk from the East Wing to the West Wing, I am not in awe of my material surroundings or the powerful people around me but in awe of the peace that comes with fulfillment and happiness. The smell of pine and the decomposing downed trees infuse my breath with stillness and connectivity to the earth. As I touch the soil in the vast grove of aspen trees, all interconnected by roots and therefore considered one genetic individual, I think about how my journey has taken many routes to create who I am today.

My lifelong quest to learn the identity of my biological father is over. As much as I am relieved to finally know who he is, this knowledge cannot replace the years that I missed with him. I so wish I had met him as a child and had a relationship with him. I wish he could have helped my mom when she was struggling financially. But knowing who he is has broken down the invisible wall between my mom and me. We now have a good relationship. We laugh, we talk, and we care about each other. I admire her courage to be a single mom in the 1960s. And even though she may not accept it, I still consider her the first feminist that I ever knew, followed by my grandmother. These two women instilled the discipline, courage, and intellectual curiosity that continue to drive me every day. Although all three of us faced emotional and physical trauma, each of us refused to be a victim. My sexual trauma still gets triggered from time to time, but I focus my wounds on helping others struggling with the same issues. I also have come to let go of my anger toward my stepfather for not marrying my mom sooner. He did the best he could. I am eternally grateful that he has loved, respected, cherished, and provided a great life for my mom for many decades.

My journey to becoming a wife and mother was not a straight line either; nothing in the routes I took was in one direction. I fell in love more than once and moved to cities and countries to chase love or to escape from grief. But I landed where I wanted to be. I often wish I was younger than thirty-nine when I first became a mom, but perhaps I needed the heartache, loss of love, and miscarriages to appreciate what I have now. I am married to a man who supports me in every endeavor, doesn't try to change me, and allows me to be whole. He is my friend and partner, and he is the father of my most precious treasures, Marat and Shokhan. I love my boys with every fiber of my being, and we don't even share one strand of DNA. But maybe that's the point: leading with love is more important. Love is my North Star. Instead of my DNA, I hope I pass on the importance of leading with love to my children. I also imagine that my children may have the same questions I did about their biological parents, and if I can answer them, I will. I hope they know that there are many ways to create a family. Both of my children have "aunties" and "uncles" that would do anything for them. My stepbrother is still present in their lives, and my community of friends has grown from those I met when I was nineteen to others on campaigns and in newly adopted towns like Steamboat Springs. I know they will always have my back.

I still have political ambition, but it has taken a different turn. When I give trainings or lead retreats, I often say my career was an accident. I share that even though your career may not be a straight line, it's important to know your values and to find work that reflects your passion, because then it doesn't feel like work. In high school, I wanted to be a photojournalist, but I didn't have the road map or the social capital to attend an elite college or get the coveted internships. I didn't even know a road map existed. Instead, like my grandmother, I took risks and said yes, often, to every opportunity, from that first radio sound booth in Vienna, to events in Los Angeles for men wearing long white and red robes (the papal trip), to the farmlands in Iowa with presidential candidates. I learned about politics along the way, but more importantly, I learned about people.

My political ambition is now focused on democracy. How can I help every state copy the mail-in voting example of Colorado, where we have over 70 percent participation? How can I help more prochoice Democrats get elected? And how do we enshrine basic human rights like contraception, abortion, and gay marriage into every state constitution? If I could wave a magic wand, DC would be its own state with two senators and a representative in Congress.

With my children leaving home for their own journeys, a new chapter of my life is now unfolding, with my number one priority being the desire to age gracefully and spend time with the people I cherish. I don't know what awaits me, but I do know I will live with honesty, love, and the courage to face all the opportunities that come my way.

ACKNOWLEDGMENTS

I never thought that my short story assignments for Elizabeth Ayres at the Center for Creative Writing would lead to a book. Her exercises in *Writing the Wave* inspired me to reflect on the many moments of my childhood that would be worth sharing with a broader audience. Thank you, Elizabeth, and thank you, Helena Clare Pittman, another teacher at the center, who helped me find my voice.

You would not be reading this memoir without the heroic efforts of my editor Shannon O'Neill. She pieced together my short stories into a compelling narrative and identified the themes in the book I did not even understand existed. My publishing editor, Gail Kretchmer, refined the manuscript and showed me the importance of cutting lines and stories that distract from the storyline. Thank you.

I also want to thank the entire publishing team at Girl Friday Books. Their enthusiasm and professionalism have turned my dream of publishing my memoir into a reality.

This memoir would not be possible without the support of my husband and friend, Eric Washburn. His trust, guidance, and enthusiasm helped me in every step. Even though my sons, Marat and Shokhan, did not understand the difficulty of writing about my past trauma, I was inspired by their belief in me to write even on the hard days. I am forever grateful. And I have to include my many pets, Gin Gin, Sidney, Winston, Zoe, Rocky, and Molly, who always listened and comforted me when I did not want to show my tears to any human beings.

Writing this book helped me appreciate my mom even more. The sacrifices she made to have me and raise me as best she could will never be forgotten, and I am so happy that she found the love of her life, Lars Lofas, who has been at her side for decades and who has loved me as well. I also need to thank my stepbrother, Lars, who helped me unravel our shared childhood memories.

I have been so lucky to have a group of friends who encouraged me to write my truth. Thank you for supporting and challenging me to get it finished: Valerie Marks, Genevieve Anderson Morgan, Ned Claflin, Evi Wareka, Robin Smith, Denise Gaumer Hutchison, Maris Segal, Kiki McLean, Mary Meagher, Abby Spring, Teresa Vilmain, Cathy St. Denis, Jill Alper, Kelly McBride, Miguel Silva, Bianca DeLille, Richard Hoppe, Liz Barrett-Brown, Caroline Cunningham, Ann Liston, Jenny Baucus, Emmy Marcoglou, Tara Gedeon, Melinda Sherman, and Julie Tourigny.

For all the others who have been part of my journey, thank you for teaching me to love, to accept, to be resilient, and to always be hopeful about the future.

ABOUT THE AUTHOR

© Beau Bella Photography

For more than thirty years, Robin F. Schepper served at the highest levels of American politics and government. She worked on four presidential campaigns and in the Clinton White House, was staff director for the Senate Democratic Technology and Communications Committee under Sen. Tom Daschle, and served in the Obama White House as the first executive director of Michelle Obama's anti-obesity initiative, Let's Move! She's advised numerous nonprofits and helped draft policy reports for the Bipartisan Policy Center. She lives in Steamboat Springs, Colorado, with her husband and two sons.